HUMAN DEVELOPMENT POLICY IN THE GLOBAL ERA: A PROPOSAL FROM AN EDUCATIONAL VIEW

Aki Yonehara

University Education Press

To Tsugumasa, Honoka and the future world
in which they and their fellows will enjoy *constitutive freedom*.

Preface

"Why do you, a Japanese person, study about Tanzanian education at an American university?" I was asked when I was a graduate student in the United States. At that time, I was not able to answer to this question very well. It was partly because my English was not good enough to explain my thoughts; also partly because I had too much thoughts on this question to explain them in a few sentences. However, now, I know how to answer to this question in only two words: "Why not?"

The term *globalization* is not new at all, but at our *real* life level, how *real* is the term to us? I had a Brazilian coffee with a mug made in China this morning. We could call such a situation "a globalized life" or *material globalization*. However, how *real* do we *feel* it beyond the material facts? Having Brazilian coffee with a Chinese mug, a kind of *material globalization*, would no longer be questionable to us today, but still, some people may feel unnatural to see a Japanese person studying in the United States about Tanzanian education. On the other hand, very few would feel strange if a Japanese living in Osaka studies about educational issues in Tokyo. It implies that one can naturally feel *reality* to his or her national identity but not straightly to *global* identity. In this sense, I believe that *real globalization*, not *material globalization*, is a phenomenon in which everyone can naturally feel reality to his or her identity as human beings, no matter what part of the earth he or she happens to live.

Although I do not have enough space here to discuss this fact, we live, as a fact, "in a world with remarkable deprivation, destitution and oppression" (Sen, 2000, p.xi) and we also live in a world which contains an extremely poor part as many statistical data show. Since we cannot get out of the web of *material globalization* today, it would be not very fair to ignore these facts. When having Brazilian coffee in a Chinese mug, how many people's faces do we really *feel* behind it? Do we feel real sense of responsibility as human beings to the fact of global inequality, regardless of our nationalities?

So, why not does a Japanese person in the United States think of an issue of Tanzania in this global era? From a perspective of *real globalization*, following Rawls' sense (1993, 1999a, 1999b), it is an issue of social justice in this global era. The expression "social justice" might sound too serious or too formal, but in *real globalization* that I assume, it should be one of the most natural principles which lead our global identity and our daily action beyond our differences of nationality, gender, culture, and any other differentiations of our identities.

The answer "why not?" may be the shortest answer possible to the question stated at the beginning of this short preface. It may be simple and easy, but may not be enough to illustrate whole my thoughts. The most precise - and maybe the longest possible - answer is here, whole this volume. It would be my pleasure if this volume can provide enough reason why the idea of human development is a matter in the global era. It would also be my pleasure if this volume can show a possible direction how human development policy contributes to *real globalization*.

Aki Yonehara
October 25, 2009

Acknowledgments

This volume is based on the dissertation completed in 2006 at Indiana University. I would like to send the first appreciation to my advisors of the dissertation committee: Dr. Margaret Sutton, Dr. Barry Bull, Dr. Ginette Delandshere, and Dr. Maurice Garnier. This volume would not be here without their support and advice. I also would like to appreciate the long-lasting support from my former advisors in Kyoto University: Professor Yutaka Shiraishi, Professor Shigeru Takami, Professor Takekazu Ehara, and Professor Hitoshi Sugimoto. Their instructions constructed my foundation as a researcher, which had been indispensable to completing this arduous work. Professor Hiromitsu Muta is another person whom I cannot help appreciating. His insightful advice always stimulates my postdoctoral study and encouraged me to pablish this volume. I also received millions of help, advice, support, cooperation, encouragement, stimulation and good energy from friends all over the world. I sincerely hope that my thankfulness will reach to each of them across the world. My grateful appreciation should go to the Fulbright program too. This scholarship program broadened the possibility of my research as well as my world view itself. I am also thankful to the Japan Society for the Promotion of Science (JSPS). Their financial support enabled to publish this volume as a book. Finally, the special appreciation goes to my family: Yasuhiro, Tsugumasa and Honoka. They always make me alive and keep me contented. I am gratefully thankful for their unchanging respect and acceptance to me for what I am.

It is unfortunate that there is not enough space here to list all the names that I should inscribe, but in a substantive sense, this volume should be called a collaborative work with all of them.

This work was supported by JSPS-KAKENHI
(*Grant-in-Aid for Publication of Scientific Research Results*: No. 215194).

Table of Contents

Preface i
Acknowledgments iii
Table of Contents v
List of Tables and Figures viii

Introduction: Why human development? *1*
    Problem statement   *1*
    Research questions and preview of the study   *3*
    Approach to the analysis of human development policy   *5*

Part I. Theoretical framework of human development *9*

Chapter 1
History of "development":
    In the context of international development *10*
    1.1 History of international development: An economic perspective *10*
    1.2 The power structure of the world?: A sociological perspective *18*
    1.3 Conclusion of the chapter: The need for a new perspective *25*

Chapter 2
The need for "human development":
    Beyond a classical meaning of development *34*
    2.1 The new generation of international development *35*
    2.2 Responding to the defects of Sen's theory *55*
    2.3 Conclusion of the chapter: Human development in the global era *62*

Chapter 3
A modified human development theory in the global era:
    Two claims *71*
    3.1 Claim one: A universal value of human development is consistent with cultural diversity and social particularity under Kantian liberalism *72*

3.2 Claim two: The right to basic education is a central instrumental freedom to promote human capability for one's constitutive freedom ··· *88*

Part II. Empirical analysis of human development ··· *103*

Chapter 4
Case study: Tanzania ··· *104*
4.1 History of Tanzania's educational and social policies ··· *105*
4.2 Tanzanian education and society today: Reality in the 1990s ··· *124*
4.3 Conclusion of the chapter: Significance of needs assessment for human development policy ··· *133*

Chapter 5
Modeling a modified human development theory ··· *139*
5.1 Preparation for modeling ··· *141*
5.2 HGLM: Technical introduction and model building ··· *157*

Chapter 6
Translating HGLM findings into policy recommendations ··· *187*
6.1 Interpretation of the models: Needs assessment and policy recommendation for literacy development ··· *187*
6.2 Limitations of quantitative modeling ··· *202*
6.3 Conclusion of the chapter: A comprehensive perspective on human development in Tanzania ··· *206*

Chapter 7
Conclusion: Toward human development ··· *210*
Summary: How much do we know about human development? ··· *210*
Recommendation for Tanzanian human development ··· *216*
Recommendation for human development research ··· *218*
The need for further research ··· *220*
Contribution of this study to human development policy ··· *223*

Appendices ·· *227*
   Appendix A: Nussbaum's list of human capabilities ································ *227*
   Appendix B: Histograms ·· *228*
   Appendix C: Wald test outputs ··· *230*

Reference ·· *231*

Index ··· *245*

List of Tables and Figures

Tables

Table 4.1 Additional teachers and classrooms needed for UPE 119
Table 4.2 Teacher training system in Tanzania 120
Table 4.3 Questions on literacy and numeracy 130
Table 4.4 Means of water-related variables 131
Table 4.5 Questions on material possessions 132
Table 5.1 Description of variables 147
Table 5.2 Correlations among writing, reading, and arithmetic: Rural 148
Table 5.3 Correlations among writing, reading, and arithmetic: Urban 148
Table 5.4 Frequency of reading and writing conditions 148
Table 5.5 Chi-square test and Phi coefficient: Rural 151
Table 5.6 Chi-square test and Phi coefficient: Urban 151
Table 5.7 Chi-square test for writing: Rural 152
Table 5.8 Chi-square test for writing: Urban 152
Table 5.9 District level variables: Rural 153
Table 5.10 District level variables: Urban 153
Table 5.11 Pearson correlation coefficients: Rural 155
Table 5.12 Pearson correlation coefficients: Urban 156
Table 5.13 Frequency and Chi-square test: Rural 168
Table 5.14 Frequency and Chi-square test: Urban 169
Table 5.15 Rural data 169
Table 5.16 Urban data 170
Table 5.17 Null model 173
Table 5.18 Level-one only model 176
Table 5.19 Full model (Unconstrained model) 180
Table 5.20 Final model (Constrained model) 182
Table 6.1 Characteristics of probability and odds 189
Table 6.2 Comparison of odds, probability, and odds ratio 191
Table 6.3 District means: Health services 194
Table 6.4 District means: Educational services 196

List of Tables and Figures   ix

Figures

Figure 1.1 Alternative responses to the impact of the West 23
Figure 1.2 The regression model of history of development economics ... 26
Figure 1.3 The blueprint of a new perspective on development 27
Figure 3.1 Hierarchy of human capability 89
Figure 3.2 Hierarchy of human capability factors 90
Figure 3.3 Hierarchy of human development 91
Figure 3.4 The conceptual relation between the individual and district levels ... 99
Figure 4.1 Enrolment in African schools, 1926-1956 109
Figure 4.2 Number of pupils enrolled in Tanzania, 1967-1975 118
Figure 4.3 Rural children's age 128
Figure 4.4 Urban children's age 128
Figure 4.5 Children's gender 129
Figure 4.6 Source of drinking water (Rural) 131
Figure 4.7 Source of drinking water (Urban) 131
Figure 5.1 The theoretical & empirical model of human development 142
Figure 5.2 Concept of the hierarchical model 158
Figure 5.3 Dichotomous outcome 164
Figure 5.4 Continuous outcome 164

Introduction
Why human development?

Problem statement

For more than half a century after World War II, tremendous efforts have been made for international development, both financially and intellectually. "The first generation" (Meier, 2000, pp.13-17) of development economists believed that national economic growth would contribute to solving the problems of poverty in developing countries (Baur, 1971; Chenery, 1979; Esho, 1999; Gershenkron, 1966; Hasegawa & Takagi, 1998; Hirschuman, 1958; Ie, 2000; Kageyama, 1997; Kusano, 1997; McKinnon, 1964; Nishigaki & Shimomura, 1993; Nurkse, 1953; Rostow, 1960; Takagi, 1996; Yamamoto, 1994). On the other hand, "the second generation" (Meier, 2000, pp.17-23) of development economists believed that improving the productivity of human resources was the critical source of economic growth. For example, human capital theory, which arose out of the second generation, has been used to justify educational development as a tool of economic growth (Adelman, 2000; Becker, 1967, 1993; Becker & Murphy, 1990; Esho, 1999; Hara, 1999; Hasegawa & Takagi, 1998; Ie, 2000; Kusano, 1997; Nakamura, 1998; Schultz, 1971; Streeten, 1981; Yamamoto, 1994).

Sen (1981, 1987, 1992, 1994, 1997a, 1997b, 1999a, 1999b, 1999c, 2000, 2002a, 2002b) questions concepts of development that have focused exclusively on economic growth, and he proposes human development theory, which focuses on individual "human capability." Influenced by Sen's theory, more and more attention began to be paid to the idea of human development (cf. UNDP, 1990-2005). This study will focus on developmental policy from a perspective of human development theory.

Human development theory aims at "expanding the real freedoms that people enjoy" (Sen, 2000, p.3). Sen (1992, 2000) defines two kinds of freedoms: instrumental freedom and constitutive freedom. Human life is composed of a series of choices that realize what each individual wants to be or to do, and instrumental freedoms, such as the freedom to become educated and freedom from poverty, help individuals realize their wants; in other words, instrumental freedom helps expand one's choices. Constitutive freedom, which has "the *intrinsic* importance of human freedom as the preeminent objective of development" (Sen, 2000, p.37), is achieved by using adequate instrumental freedoms. From this perspective on freedom, Sen considers that poverty, tyranny, neglect of public facilities, and intolerance of repressive states make people "unfreedom" (2000, p.3), and he assumes that developing "human capability" promotes one's freedom (1992, 1999b, 2002b). Human capability is defined as an aggregation of choices that an individual actually can enjoy, and the human capability approach focuses on a question of what he or she can *be* or *do* (an issue of freedom), rather than a question of what he or she can *have* (an issue of commodities) (Sen, 1999b). Human development theory has been developed largely by using the capability approach.

The concept of human development is also a significant idea in educational developmental policies. As noted, educational development has been justified as a tool of economic development by human capital theory (Becker, 1967, 1993; Becker & Murphy, 1990; Schultz, 1971), while the concept of human development considers education to be a promoter of human capability (Nussbaum, 1992; 2000a) or of children's future "freedom" in Sen's sense (Saito, 2003). Based on Sen's human capability approach, Nussbaum (2000a) created the list of "central functional human capabilities," which includes ten items as "a threshold level of these human capabilities" (p.75 & pp.78-80; also see Appendix A), and she includes education as one of the items of the list. Saito (2003) conducted an interview with Sen and cites his words: "The main argument for compulsory education is that it will give the child when grown up much more freedom" (p.27).

Many would agree on the significance of human development and the importance of education for human development. However, it seems still unclear what "human development" means in reality.

> The development debate appears to be, at last, coasting toward a consensus: developing nations must not focus their energies on the growth rates of their GDP, NNP, GNP, and the like but should instead try to achieve "human development" or "comprehensive development." A remarkable feature of these new goals is that everyone seems to be supporting them, although few know what the terms mean (Basu, 2000, p.61).

Even though the idea seems attractive, it is not readily transformed into practical policy. There is an imperative need to construct a bridge between the concept of human development and practical policies to foster human development.

Research questions and preview of the study

The goal of this study is to construct a bridge between human development theory and practical policy for human development. In other words, it is to translate the theoretical idea of human development into a quantitative model of human development policy.

What does "human development" really mean? What role does educational development have in human development? How is it possible to embody this abstract concept as a policy? To answer these questions, this study sets three main aims: (I) to clarify the meaning of human development; (II) to propose a theoretical model of human development to specify a role for education in human development policy; and (III) to test the theoretical model empirically by using existing data from Tanzania. The empirical model will attempt to assess the needs for human development policy in Tanzania.

To achieve goal (I), I will ask: what has the concept of *development* meant through out the history of international development after World War II? Chapter one provides a historical overview of development economics and sociology to understand: how the concept of development was created, how it has tackled the issues of international development, why development has become so significant today, and what kind of limitations the existing concept of development has. Responding to the limitations of the past approaches to development, Chapter two introduces Sen's theory of *human development* as a guiding principle for a new perspective on development.

To achieve goal (II), I will ask: what role should education have in the concept of human development and how can it be modeled theoretically? Chapter three proposes a modified human development theory, which argues that basic education is an essential promoter of human capability for one's constitutive freedom. This Chapter also develops the theoretical model of human development policy that is empirically examined in the subsequent chapters.

To achieve goal (III), I will ask: how is it possible to use the theoretical model of human development to assess the need for human development policy? I will focus on the case of Tanzania because of the historical uniqueness of its educational and social development policies. Chapter four provides an overview of the history of Tanzania's educational and social policies and describes the data included *in the Tanzania Human Resource Development Survey* (THRDS) (The World Bank, 1993, 1997; The World Bank & University of Dar es Salaam, 1993; Ferreira & Griffin, 1996). Chapter five introduces a modeling method called Hierarchical Generalized Linear Modeling (HGLM) and applies HGLM to the THRDS data. Chapter six discusses the interpretation of quantitative models to propose policy recommendations for human development in Tanzania.

This study will make a significant contribution to educational and social development policies not only for Tanzania but also for other developing countries and donor organizations in two senses: (1) in a theoretical sense, the study will develop a new theory of development, namely a modified human development theory, that goes beyond the classical meaning of development; (2) in a practical sense, it will propose an empirical quantitative model for assessing the needs for human development policy using a case study of Tanzania.

Approach to the analysis of human development policy

Here, I would like to clarify the approach taken throughout this study. This study can be considered as a policy study emphasizing *problem finding*. Policy studies can have two purposes: to propose an appropriate way to solve problems (*problem solving*); and to clarify a problem to be solved (*problem finding*). Although policy studies may include both, policy circumstances may make one more appropriate than the other.

Regarding the first purpose, Lindblom (1959; 1979) proposes an incrementalism perspective for problem solving in policy studies. Incrementalists establish immediate objectives rather than general goals. According to Lindblom (1979), "an aspiration to synopsis does not help an analyst choose manageable tasks, while an aspiration to develop improved strategies does" (p.518), and he proposes "strategic analyses," in which feasibility of policy is given the higher priority. The most important question for this approach is "how" : how is it possible to achieve an immediate policy objective?

On the other hand, regarding the second purpose of policy analysis, finding a problem to be solved, Wildavsky (1979) insists that "policy analysis creates and crafts problems worth solving" (p.386). According to Wildavsky, "problem solving for the policy analyst is as much a matter of creating a problem (1) worth solving from a social perspective and (2) capable of being solved with the resources at hand" (p.388), and he proposes three types of solutions: solutions as programs, solutions as hypotheses, and solutions as social artifacts.

In solutions as programs, a policy analyst "translates" the conflictive choices among different wants of different people into possible choices among programs. Therefore, "programs as embodiments of compromises are often imprecise, arbitrary, and imperfect" (Wildavsky, 1979, p.391), but they could make a better match between possible resources and objectives. In solutions as hypotheses, a policy analyst proposes a hypothesis to explain the existing situation, because "without recognition, to be sure, there is unlikely to be correction... to be readily recognized, error should be conspicuous and clear" (Wildavsky, 1979, p.394). Finally, solutions as social artifacts consider the solutions created by policy analysts as comprehensive diagnoses of a society, which include "not only a mix of resources and objectives, not only an implicit causal model of a segment of reality, but also a structure of social relationships" (Wildavsky, 1979, p.395). Therefore, policy analysts are ineluctably involved with society and culture beyond strategic matters such as resource allocation.

The most important question for this approach is "what" rather than "how" : what is the problem worth solving for people in the society? Although a strategic perspective is also significant to propose alternative programs, the role of policy analysts in Wildavsky's sense goes beyond that. Policy analysts are involved with society and culture, and "by proposing new programs, the policy analyst suggests new hypotheses, and hence new values that codify social relations" (Wildavsky, 1979, p.395). In this sense, policy analysts are craftsmen who create diagnoses or programs to improve the condition of the society.

These two purposes of policy studies reflected in the two approaches of Lindblom and Wildavsky depict different questions in policy studies: a *how*-question (*problem solving*) and a *what*-question (*problem finding*). This study will focus on *what*-questions, rather than *how*-questions. In other words, this study takes a problem-finding approach, rather than a problem-solving approach.

However, this study does not devalue a problem-solving approach. This study will conclude in policy recommendations for problem solving. Nevertheless, a policy solution formulated at a beginning stage of analysis should be modified or appropriated in the actual process of problem solving, as Kerr (1976) points out the iterative nature of policy development, and as Sutton and Levinson (2001) point out the dynamics of policy practice. Moreover, "Policy-making rarely looks like the textbook discussions of the policy cycle. Sometimes a solution goes looking for a problem" (Goodin & Klingemann, 1996, p.568). This study rests on the assumption that policy analysis includes the dynamics of problem finding.

Ackoff (1974) says that "successful problem solving requires finding the right solution to the right problem. We fail more often because we solve the wrong problem than because we get the wrong solution to the right problem." This study aims at finding problems worth solving for human development, and as such it may provide a model for developing human development policy. After more than half a century of development theory, it is the time to reconstruct the problem worth being taken into a serious consideration. Clarifying the problem of human development in an international context should be one step toward realizing social justice in all human societies in this global era. The ultimate goal of this study is to find and describe problems worth solving by providing theoretical analysis of human development and by developing needs assessment models for human development policy.

Part I
Theoretical framework of human development

History of "development": In the context of international development

Chapter 1

The concept of human development was born in the 1990s as a challenge to a dominant concept of economic development (Sen, 1981; 1987; 1992; 1994; 1997a; 1997b; 1999a; 1999b; 1999c; 2000; 2002a; 2002b; Haq, 1995; UNDP, 1990, 2003, 2004; 2005). Before stepping into the issue of *human* development, it is necessary to review the history of development and to clarify its meaning, in order to understand how the concept of human development has appeared and why it is important today. In this chapter, I will review the history of international development from a perspective of development economics (1.1) and introduce some grand theories of international development in sociology to compare and discuss their differences and limitations (1.2). In the last section of this chapter (1.3), I will clarify the challenges left for international development *today*.

1.1 History of international development: An economic perspective

The concept of international development as international assistance is said to have appeared after World War II (Kageyama, 1997; Kusano, 1997).[1] It is seen in such policy as *the Marshall Plan* in 1947-1951, which provided financial aid for reconstruction and development for the countries damaged during World War II. The meaning of international development at that moment was limited within a political strategy in the context of the Cold War [2] (Kusano, 1997, p.24, pp.100-102; Kageyama, 1997, p.4). However, after *the Colombo Plan for Cooperative Economic and Social Development in Asia and the Pacific* in 1950, the meaning of development has been expanded from the post-World War II political strategy to financial assistance for developing countries, and its focus shifted from the defeated European countries and Japan to the developing countries in Southeast and South Asia. According to this shift, the purpose of aid has also changed from political security against expansion of communism to economic development in those developing countries in Asia.

Two different meanings of international development can be seen in the post-World War II history of international relations: (1) the international development as the reconstruction aid from WWII for the defeated countries during the post-WW II period and (2) the international development as the economic developmental assistance for developing countries since the post-1950. In this study, I will use "international development" in terms of the post-1950 meaning. The following sections will examine two generations of development economics: the first generation during 1950-1975, which took a macroeconomic approach to development (1.1.1) and the second generation during 1975-2000, which shifted into a microeconomic approach (1.1.2).

1.1.1 The macro approach of the first generation: Post World War II

Meier (2000) categorizes the theoretical works of development economics over these 50 years into two generations: the first generation (1950-1975) and the second generation (1975-2000). According to Meier, the first generation can be characterized by their "grand models of development strategy" (pp.13-14); while the second generation "looked at the growth process in a more microeconomic fashion" (p.18). Development economists in the first generation took a macro approach to tackle the issues of international development as described below.

Nurkse (1953) describes "the vicious circle of poverty" by saying that "a country is poor because it is poor." According to his explanation, low-income produces low-saving caused by a large proportion of expenditure for necessities; low-saving by individuals produces low-capital accumulation by a society; low-capital accumulation produces low-labor productivity because of insufficient infrastructure improvement; and low-productivity sustains low-income (Nurkse, 1953; Takagi, 1996, pp.34-35; Esho, 1999, pp.14-15, pp.41-42). Nurkse insists on the importance of "balanced growth" under the control of a central government (Nurkse, 1953; Esho, 1999).[3] Rostow (1960) hypothesizes "the five stages of development," which assumes that a society should follow the hypothetical stages to achieve an economic "takeoff" to "the age of mass consumption." He insists that it is necessary for every society to overcome the first stage of "traditional society" since traditional cultures and systems neglect capital investment for economic development and prevent a society from achieving "takeoff" or being modernized (Rostow, 1960; Takagi, 1996, pp.39-41; Esho, 1999, pp.33-36).[4] Chenery (1979) proposes "the two gap approach," which considers two possible shortages of domestic savings and foreign currency to overcome the bottlenecks for economic development. According to this approach, when a developing country aims at a certain level of economic growth, it will find a gap between necessary investments and actual domestic savings to promote its industry. In addition to this gap, when this country needs to import the products from foreign countries to develop its industry, it will find another gap between necessary imports and actual exports. He insists that international assistance is inevitable for developing countries to overcome these two bottlenecks [5] (Chenery, 1979; Takagi, 1996, pp.171-173; Esho, 1999, pp.46-48).

These grand theorists in economics use the term "development" to mean "economic growth" and claim needs for capital accumulation and market control by the central government. Meier (2000) describes this tendency of the first generation by saying that "To many of the early development economists, a less-developed economy was characterized by pervasive market failures. To correct or avoid market failure, they advocated central coordination of the allocation of resources" (p.14); and Esho (1997; 1999) shows that these economic theories in the first generation shaped the ground of structuralism and the justification for governmental intervention.

Along with these grand models, it was widely believed in the early 1960s that the benefits of economic development would automatically "trickle down" (Hirschuman, 1958) to the field of social development (Kageyama, 1997, p.4; Nishigaki & Shimomura, 1993, p.56). Such an optimistic trust in economic growth led the United Nations to implement *The First United Nations Development Decade* in 1961, which set a goal of 5 percent economic growth for developing countries [6] (Kusano, 1997, pp.31-32; Yamamoto, 1994, pp.4-5).

However, by around the late 1960s and early 1970s, "deficiencies in industrial programming and comprehensive planning had become acute... Critics now pointed to the causes of government failure: deficiencies in the plans, inadequate information and resources, unanticipated dislocations of domestic economic activity..." (Meier, 2000, p.17). For example, *The Second United Nations Development Decade* adopted in September 1970 failed to achieve its goal of economic growth, and in addition, the North-South gap has increased more and more (Kusano, 1997, pp.32-35). Not only developing countries, but also developed countries experienced the Nixon Shock or the Dollar Shock in 1971 and the Oil Shock in 1973, which brought large perplexities into the international economy (Hasegawa & Takasugi, 1998; Ie, 2000). These perplexities led to a disappointment with international development called "aid fatigue" among donor nations (Kageyama, 1997; Yamamoto, 1994). This situation of "aid fatigue" in the early 1970s led to a search for a new perspective on development, which emerged as the second generation.

1.1.2 *The micro approach of the second generation: Since the 1960s*

Meier (2000) defines the post 1957 period as the second generation of development economics. He states that "If the first generation of development economics was visionary and dedicated to grand theories and general strategies, the second generation was almost moralistic, dedicated to a somber realism grounded on fundamental principles of neoclassical economics" (p.17). While the first generation is characterized by "grand models of development strategy" (Meier, 2000, pp.13-14), the second generation "looked at the growth process in a more microeconomic fashion" (Meier, 2000, p.18).

The second generation's standpoint can be represented by the approach of human capital theorists (Schultz, 1971; Becker, 1967, 1993; Becker et al., 1990).[7] Schultz's (1971) human capital theory emphasizes the significance of "residuals" of the production function, the contents of which was in a "black box" for a significant time period (Esho, 1999, p.64). The classical production function includes three factors: natural resources, labor power, and capital. These three factors are supposed to explain economic growth, but empirical studies showed that there is always a "residual" or a gap between the growth estimated by the production function and the actual growth. This residual had remained to be accounted for, but Schultz hypothesizes that the residual is due to the affect of human capital, depending on such things as education and health (Esho, 1999, pp.64-72; Schultz, 1971). According to Shultz, investment in human capital enhances laborers' knowledge and skill, which contributes to economic growth. Schultz (1971) says that human capital is composed of education, health, and other factors that improve the quality of labor. He also shows, based on a cost-benefit analysis of education, that educational expense should be considered not as consumption but rather as investment for a better income in the future.

Although human capital theory had already been proposed in the 1960s, it was around the 1970s that this theory was incorporated into strategies of international development, constituting the basic needs approach. The basic needs approach is a moralistic rejection of the failure of the macroeconomic growth models created by the first generation of development economics (Esho, 1999, pp.98-112; Kusano, 1997, pp.35-36; Streeten, 1981). In 1976, the International Labor Organization began to advocate officially the basic needs approach as a development strategy for the first time, and the World Bank followed by adopting the concept of basic needs into its developmental strategy in 1978 (Esho, 1999, pp.104-105). Due to the advocacy of major international organizations, the basic needs approach became one of the most widespread strategies of international development.[8]

Streeten (1981) clarifies what "basic needs" are by stating that "Basic needs is not primarily a welfare concept; improved education and health can make a major contribution to increased productivity" (p.3).[9] In the context of development policy, he specifies the constituents of basic needs and their indicators as: health (indicator: life expectancy at birth), education (literacy and primary school enrollment), food (calorie consumption per person), water supply (infant mortality per thousand births and percentage of the population with access to potable water), and sanitation (infant mortality and percentage of the population with access to sanitation facilities) (Streeten, 1981, p.93).

Regardless of the acknowledgement of the microeconomic approach, the reality in the 1980s was severe for the people on the ground. The world debt problem, mainly in African and Latin American countries, became worse,[10] and natural disasters, such as drought, made African development more difficult[11] (Kusano, 1997, p.36). Considering these difficulties, the IMF and the World Bank decided to apply a strategy involving structural adjustment on the part of recipient nations. Structural adjustment assumes that an essential problem of developing countries is an unbalanced structure of international payments; thus, in order to adjust the unbalanced structure, four conditions were imposed on recipient countries through Structural Adjustment Loans (SAL)[12] (World Bank, 1988; Esho, 1999, pp.89-95, pp.148-156).

The SAL conditions forced recipient nations to prioritize intensive investment in the economic sector over expenditure on the social service sector, which resulted in worsening indices of social development such as school enrollment (UNICEF, 1998a, p.13, Fig.5; Nakamura, 1998, p.10). The structural adjustment strategy is said to be opposed to the basic needs approach, with the result the 1980s have been called "the lost decade" because of its depression of social development indices (Hara, 1999, pp.190-191).[13]

Regardless of critiques from basic needs advocates, the structural adjustment strategy brought a certain extent of economic stability into international macroeconomics by the early 1990s (Yamamoto, 1994, p.6). However, another political event, the collapse of the Soviet Union, affected international development. Since international development strategies after World War II had often been motivated by the East-West political conflict, the collapse of the Soviet Union extinguished the political rationale for international development and demotivated Western donors (Ie, 2000, p.147).

However, it was not difficult for the Western donors and other industrialized nations to find alternative rationales for international development in the 1990s, since world-wide problems - such as environmental issues, human right issues, and equity issues in resource allocation - arose with intensity (Esho, 1999, pp.146-216; Hasegawa & Takasugi, 1998, pp.116-117). These issues inevitably require cooperation: cooperation that goes beyond boundaries of nations and academic disciplines. For example, human right issues occur across national boundaries, and the problems include ethical, educational, social, and political components not only economic components. The approach to international development that appeared in the 1990s has comprehensive and interdisciplinary characteristics, as Adelman (2000) points out below:

> The fundamental reason for the many sudden changes in the dominant paradigm in development economics has been the (inherently misguided) search for a single-cause, and hence a single-remedy, theory

of development... underdevelopment is due to constraint X; loosen X, and development will be the inevitable result... As a discipline, we seem unable to admit that the X-factor does not exist; that development policy requires a more complex understanding of social systems, combining economic, social, cultural, and political institutions and their changing interactions over time. (pp.104-105)

To provide an alternative perspective on the comprehensiveness of development, Amartya Sen (1981; 1987; 1992; 1994; 1997a; 1997b; 1999a; 1999b; 1999c; 2000; 2002a; 2002b) developed human development theory. In this theory, he centers the concept of development on "human beings," who are often ignored in theories of former generations,[14] and defines the meaning and objectives of development as below:

Development can be seen, it is argued here, as a process of expanding the real freedoms that people enjoy. Focusing on human freedoms contrasts with narrower views of development, such as identifying development with the growth of gross national products... Growth of GNP or of individual incomes can, of course, be very important as *means* to expanding the freedoms enjoyed by the members of the society. But freedoms depend also on other determinants, such as social and economic arrangements (for example, facilities for education and health care) as well as political and civil rights (for example, the liberty to participate in public discussion and scrutiny). (Sen, 2000, p.3)

Meier (2000) introduces Sen's theory as a starting point of the third generation by saying that "to the old generation, the objective of development was an increase in per capita real income... to be attained by growth of GDP. But it was increasingly realized that 'development' meant growth plus change and that change implied other objectives beyond simple GDP growth" (Meier, 2000, p.24). Meier recognizes the central characteristic of the new generation: comprehensiveness of development.

The details of Sen's human development theory, or human capability approach, will be introduced later in Chapter two with consideration of its applications and defects. Before moving to that stage, another perspective on development, a sociological perspective, will be reviewed in order to reconsider the meaning of development in the context of the world system.

1.2 The power structure of the world?: A sociological perspective

Not only economists, but also grand theorists in sociology are concerned about the subject of international development. As a challenge to a unilinear modernization theory of development, some critical theorists in sociology propose dependency theory to claim that the existence of the international power structure working in favor of developed countries creates a condition called "underdevelopment" (Amin, 1974, 1996; Chew, 1996; Frank, 1981, 1996; Gereffi & Fonda, 1992; Ogura, 1982, pp.35-43; Synder, 1980; Valenzuela & Valenzuela, 1979).

In this section, I will review dependency theory, in comparison to modernization theory, to clarify the effect of dependency theory on the concept of development: it has brought a normative perspective and a worldwide structure into the concept of development (1.2.1). I will also introduce Huntington's perspective on "the people of that society," which both dependency and modernization theories have overlooked, to claim that the idea of modernization is not always equivalent to westernization, and that modernization or social change can occur in cooperation with international development (1.2.2).

1.2.1 The claim from dependency theory:
A normative and global perspective on development

Dependency theory was developed from a primarily Marxist orientation to become holistic and interdisciplinary forms of social political economics (Synder, 1980, pp.736-744; Ogura, 1982, p.39). Synder (1980) describes dependency theory by saying that "dependency theorists thus recognize explicitly, as modernization theorists often did not, that definitions of development and underdevelopment are essentially normative and necessarily imply the exercise of moral and political choice" (p.744). It can be said that dependency theorists bring a normative perspective into the concept of development as a challenge to modernization theory (Gereffi & Fonda, 1992, p.424).[15]

Frank (1981; 1996), "the pioneer of what is known as 'the dependency school' " (Amin, 1996, p.59), established the concept of "underdevelopment" from the perspectives of social political economics and anthropology. According to Frank (1981), underdevelopment is a production of an unequal world economic system. For example, the primary commodities produced in the "satellite" nations are processed into industrial commodities in the "metropolis" nations, which creates an unequal exchange structure of primary and industrial commodities between the "metropolis" and the "satellite" (Frank, 1981; Ogura, 1982). Frank (1981) describes the characteristics of underdeveloped nations in view of the global power structure: "[the] character of the Third World state - dependent financially, technologically, institutionally, ideologically, militarily, in a word politically, on the international bourgeoisie(s) its metropolitan states - may be regarded as its fundamental characteristic" (p.233); therefore, "none of these countries is likely to become a metropolitan economy in the foreseeable future" (p.61). This means that the "metropolis-satellite" power structure prevents a "satellite" nation from becoming a member of the metropolitan economy.[16]

Amin (1974) analyzes the anatomy of underdevelopment in the context of the world capitalist system. While Frank separates the world into the "metropolis" and the "satellite" to explain the unequal exchange structure of primary and industrial commodities, Amin sees the world divided into the "center" and the "periphery." He insists that the problem is not the exchange system of commodities because some industrialized nations, such as Canada, are actually primary exporting countries (Amin, 1974, p.292; Ogura, 1982, p.45-49). According to Amin, the problem is in three outward features of capitalism in the periphery: (1) "unevenness of productivity as between spheres" or the gaps among different social spheres, such as an uneven growth ratio between labor productivity and profit ratio; (2) "disarticulation" or the lack of organic relationships among industrial segments; and (3) economic domination from outside (Amin, 1974, p.262; Ogura, 1982, p.47-48).[17] Due to these characteristics, "the periphery does most of its trade with the center, whereas the central economies carry out most of their exchanges among themselves" (Amin, 1974, p.292). This "center-periphery" structure keeps the periphery systematically peripheral.

Comparing dependency theory with modernization theory, Valenzuela and Valenzuela (1979) discuss the fundamental differences of theoretical assumptions. According to them, "the basic building block of the modernization perspective is the structuring of parallel ideal types of social organization and value system at two polar ends of the evolutionary process." Thus, "the use of a 'tradition-modernity' dichotomy" (Valenzuela and Valenzuela, 1979, p.34) assumes that all societies depart from one end of the "polar" to the other.[18] In this assumption of modernization theory, both traditional and modern societies are supposed to have their own characteristics,[19] and the traditional characteristics are considered as "the main obstacle in the way of modernization" (p.35).[20] In modernization theory, the difference between developed and underdeveloped nations is the speed of development, rather than the nature of the process (Valenzuela & Valenzuela, 1979, p.36).[21]

Valenzuela and Valenzuela (1979) also point out that the modernization perspective tends to focus on a nation state as an exclusive subject, rather than seeing it in the worldwide context (p.36-36). For example, modernization theory assumes that the speed of development in a nation primarily stems from the function of its domestic society, not the international structure around the society. On the other hand, dependency theory assumes that:

> [T]he development of a national or regional unit can only be understood in connection with its historical insertion into the worldwide political-economic systems which emerged with the wave of European colonizations of the world. This global system is thought to be characterized by the unequal but combined development of its different components, some of which constitute its 'centre' and other its 'periphery.' (Valenzuela & Valenzuela, 1979, pp.43-44)

While modernization theory tends to find the problems of national development within the domestic social system, dependency theory tries to grasp the worldwide picture of political economics through theoretical frameworks such as the "metropolis-satellite" structure (cf. Frank, 1981; 1996) and the "center-periphery" structure (cf. Amin, 1974). In this sense, dependency theory is more macrosociological and pays attention to the modes of production and the patterns of international trade from a global point of view (Valenzuela & Valenzuela, 1979, p.52). Moreover, in the sense that dependency theory asks "the fundamental question: development for whom?" (Amin, 1996, p.16) by considering the worldwide power structure of political economics, it can be called more normative and moralistic than modernization theory (Synder, 1980, p.744).[22]

However, I reject dependency theory's apparent claim that modernization is always evil or immoral because the concept of modernization does not always have to be understood as one side of the "two polar ends of the evolutionary process" (Valenzuela & Valenzuela, 1979, p.34). In other words, modernization is not always an equivalent concept to westernization, although they seem to be often considered correspondingly within both modernization and dependency theories. I will claim that the concept of modernization can be seen as distinct from that of westernization in the next section.

Examination of the concepts of modernization and westernization will help clarify the meaning of development in this study.

1.2.2 The meaning of "development": Modernization, westernization, and development

Although dependency theorists criticize modernization theory, they still seem to have the same assumption as modernization theorists have, that the process of modernization is equivalent to that of westernization. In other words, both dependency and modernization theories are unconscious of the difference between modernization and westernization. These two concepts might have been indistinguishable historically, especially during the colonial period; however, it is doubtful that the assumption is still valid *today*. Does the concept of development imply a certain kind of modernization which automatically promotes westernization of the society? The reexamination of this assumption is significant in order to clarify the meaning of development in this study.

Huntington (1997) claims that the concept of modernization does not always mean westernization, and that the world is going to become more modernized but less westernized: "For the first time in history global politics is both multipolar and multicivilizational; modernization is distinct from Westernization and is producing neither a universal civilization in any meaningful sense nor the Westernization of non-Western societies" (p.20).[23] He reconsiders the meaning of modernization and westernization in the context of the 1990s, and recognizes that "The balance of power among civilizations is shifting: the West is declining in relative influence... non-Western civilizations generally are reaffirming the value of their own cultures" (p.20). As will be discussed below, this world view will help clarify the meanings of modernization, westernization, and development *today*, and to find a new perspective on development.

According to his hypothesis, there are five different types of "responses to

Ch.1 History of "development": In the context of international development   23

Figure 1.1 Alternative responses to the impact of the West

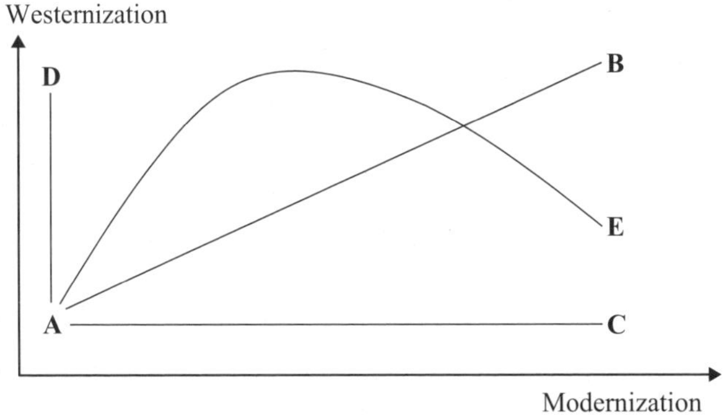

[Figure: Graph with vertical axis labeled "Westernization" and horizontal axis labeled "Modernization". Point A at origin, point D on vertical axis, point B at upper right, point C on horizontal axis, point E in middle-right. A curve rises from A through D-region to B, and a diagonal line goes from A to B, and a horizontal line from A to C, with E on the descending curve.]

(Source: Huntington, 1997, p.75, Figure 3.1)

the west and modernization": (A) *rejectionism*, (B) *Kemalism*, (C) *reformism*, (D) a "painful process of cultural Westernization without technical modernization," and (E) a general pattern (Huntington, 1997, p.72; see Figure 1.1, which will be explained below).

Rejectionism is the first response: rejecting both modernization and Westernization, as expressed at point A in Figure 1.1,[24] which does not move toward either Westernization (the vertical axis) or modernization (the horizontal axis). *Kemalism*, which assumes "that modernization is desirable and necessary, that the indigenous culture is incompatible with modernization and must be abandoned or abolished, and that society must fully Westernize in order to successfully modernize" (Huntington, 1997, p.73), is the second response, embracing both westernization and modernization, as represented by the diagonal line A-B.[25] The diagonal line A-B represents the pattern in which both westernization and modernization proceed together. *Reformism*, which attempts "to combine modernization with the preservation of the central values, practices, and institutions of the society's indigenous culture" (Huntington, 1997, p.74), is expressed as the horizontal line A-C, and is exemplified by the Chinese slogan of *Ti-Yong* or "Chinese learning for the fundamental principles, Western learning for practical use" and the Japanese slogan of *Waken Yosai* or "Japanese spirit, Western technique." Besides these three responses to the west, he cites African history and uses Mazrui's (1990) words to indicate a "painful process of cultural Westernization *without* technical modernization," which is expressed by the vertical line A-D. This pattern implies that cultural westernization proceeds but technical modernization does not happen (Huntington, 1977, p.75).

Huntington (1997) also defines a general pattern by saying that "to the extent that any general pattern of modernization and Westernization exists in the responses of non-Western societies to the West, it would appear to be along the curve A-E" (p.75). This hypothesis assumes that westernization promotes modernization in the early phase of social cultural change, but that the society becomes less westernized and more modernized in the later phase. This non-linear change happens because modernization "encourages the people of that society to have confidence in their culture and to become culturally assertive" (Huntington, 1997, p.76).[26] Huntington separates the concept of westernization from that of modernization by assuming that westernization is a cultural change while modernization is a technical change.[27] Further, he claims that westernization generally does not bring complete change non-western cultures because indigenous culture tends to revive on the way to modernization (the latter part of the curve A-E in the Figure 1.1).

Huntington's view includes two significant points about the meaning of international development. First, the differentiation of the concepts of westernization and modernization shows a possibility of modernization without westernization.[28] As Sen (2000) also insists,[29] modernization can contribute to the ultimate purpose of development, "development as freedom," which will be introduced in Chapter two, without invading or replacing indigenous and traditional cultures. Second, belief in the power of indigenous culture or that of "the people of that society" (Huntington, 1997, p.76), to which either modernization or dependency theorists have not paid enough attention, shows a possibility of autonomous social change by the people of a particular society. Existing theories of international development seem to have underestimated or overlooked the power of "the people of that society," [30] but a new perspective on development needs to take this into consideration.

All human societies have been changing inevitably over time. Therefore, a change brought about by certain external influences does not automatically necessitate cultural collapse or invasion. "Development" will bring social change in various senses. An ethical question of development is not how to avoid cultural change as a result of development, but how to define the meaning and objective of development in order to allow constructive social change.

1.3 Conclusion of the chapter: The need for a new perspective

Throughout the course of development economics after World War II, two generations have tried to find an answer for the problem of international development (Meier, 2000). Many economists have proposed theories and strategies from different standpoints under different historical political conditions (see 1.1). However, what is clear now is that an answer cannot be drawn from "a single-cause." As Adelman (2000) says, now more scholars and leaders begin to realize that "development policy requires a more complex understanding of social systems, combining economic, social, cultural, and political institutions and their changing interaction over time" (p.104-105).

The approaches to international development in the previous two generations can be compared to a "linear regression model" as Figure 1.2 shows.

There has always been one dependent variable (DV) in the model, called economic growth; and all the arguments and theories of development economics have played a role as independent variables (IV1~4) in the right side of the function. For example, in the first generation, independent variables

Figure 1.2 The regression model analogy to development economics

		The fist generation		The second generation	
DV		IV1	IV2	IV3	IV4
Economic Growth	=	Govrenmental Control	+ International Assistance	+ Investment in Human capital	+ Basic Human needs

(Created by the author)

are the control of the central government (IV1, such as Nurkse, 1953) and international assistance (IV2, such as Chenery, 1979); in the second generation, they are the investment in human capital (IV3, such as Schultz, 1971) and basic human needs (IV4, such as Streeten, 1981). Although the weights of independent variables have changed over the history of development economics (sometimes IV1 was popular and sometimes IV3 was the focus), all the models have exclusively used economic growth as the dependent variable.[31]

Sen (2000) criticizes the "narrower views of development, such as identifying development with the growth of gross national products" (p.3) and proposes a comprehensive view of development. He considers "human freedom" as the ultimate goal of development, which I will discuss further in Chapter two, and considers "economic growth" as only one instrument of development. Sen (2000) insists that "freedoms depend also on other determinants, such as social and economic arrangements (for example, facilities for education and health care) as well as political and civil rights (for example, the liberty to participate in public discussion and scrutiny)" (p.3). Following his comprehensive perspective, this study seeks a comprehensive model of human-centered development as roughly sketched in Figure 1.3.

A theoretical framework of comprehensive development will be established in Chapters two and three, and a case study of Tanzania and quantitative modeling with Tanzania's data will be conducted in Chapters four and five. The quantitative models will be interpreted in the context of policy for-

Figure 1.3 The blueprint of a new perspective on development

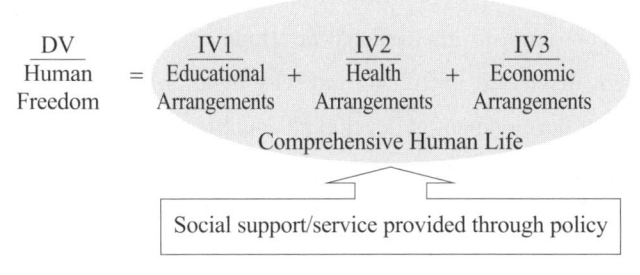

$$\underline{\text{DV}} \qquad \underline{\text{IV1}} \qquad \underline{\text{IV2}} \qquad \underline{\text{IV3}}$$
$$\text{Human} \quad = \quad \text{Educational} \quad + \quad \text{Health} \quad + \quad \text{Economic}$$
$$\text{Freedom} \qquad \text{Arrangements} \qquad \text{Arrangements} \qquad \text{Arrangements}$$

Comprehensive Human Life

Social support/service provided through policy

(Created by the author)

mulation, especially for needs assessment for human development policy in Tanzania.

In addition to the review of development economics, the comparison of modernization theory and dependency theory revealed significant assumptions about development (see 1.2.1). Dependency theorists challenge the assumption of development in modernization theory, the " 'tradition-modernity' dichotomy" (Valenzuela & Valenzuela, 1979, p.34, also see Rostow, 1960; Black, 1966; Abrokwaa, 1999), by arguing that the condition of underdevelopment is a product of the unfair world system (Frank, 1981, 1996; Amin, 1974, 1996; Synder, 1980; Gereffi & Fonda, 1992; Sangmpam, 1995). Dependency theorists also understand the issue of underdevelopment in terms of international power relations, such as the "center-periphery" structure (Amin, 1974) and the "metropolis-satellite" structure (Frank, 1981; 1996), while modernization theorists tend to consider the issue as a domestic economic problem.

This criticism of modernization theory brings two significant perspectives into the concept of development: normative and global perspectives (Synder, 1980). These perspectives on international development remind us of the significance of an ethical consideration of development in the global era (Synder, 1980). This study will reconsider the concept of development from an ethical and normative point of view in the global context today. More specifically, I will consider two questions: to what extent international assistance should be allowed to contribute to international development (a universality issue of development discussed in 2.2.1); and why developed nations should be responsible for development in developing countries (a responsibility issue of international development in the global context discussed in 2.2.2).

Finally, the consideration of meanings of modernization, westernization, and development with Huntington's model (1997) leads to two important observations. The first observation is that the process of development can bring about modernization *without* westernization. The second observation is that the power of indigenous culture or that of "the people of that society" (Huntington, 1997, p.76) can stimulate cultural revival on the way to modernization. As Sen (2000) mentions, the phenomenon of modernization can serve for the ultimate objective of development without embracing external change on the traditional culture of the society.[32]

Notes

[1] Also, Sunkel (1979) says "the subject of development started to reappear [since Adam Smith's *The Wealth of Nations* in 1776] in economic thought only in the 1950s... Hardly any book published before 1950 had the word development in its title, universities did not offer courses on the subject, special development institutes did not exist, nor did development experts" (p.19). Here he does not see the colonial period as a part of the history of international development. This position is understandable because the autonomy of colonized nations was not assumed under colonial policy, which means that international development during the colonial period can be interpreted as a history of territorial expansion, rather than a history of development. Even though international development during the Cold War still seems to be a kind of political territorial expansion (ex. the domino theory: Baldwin, 1993), international development after World War II can be differentiated from that during the colonial period in the sense that the purpose is no longer acquisition or dominance of other nations by external powers.

[2] For example, the domino theory explains how political equilibria or the balance

between anti- and pro-membership forces determine governments' stances (Baldwin, 1993).

[3] Hirschman (1958) criticizes Nurkse by suggesting the importance of "unbalanced growth" based on his hypothesis that development is the process of economic transmission from one leading-industry to other industries. Therefore, disbalance is a necessary condition to promote economic development by the catching-up incentive.

[4] Gershenkron (1966) questions Rostow's unilinear understanding of development. He insists that each developing country has a different starting point, depending on their relative levels of development. Therefore, this difference of the starting points should produce the different ways of economic growth for each country.

[5] Bauer (1971) disputes immorality of international assistance. According to him, money of foreign aid is different from that produced from domestic industry since domestic money is related to domestic laborers' quality and incentive but foreign aid is not. He insists that such money as aid, unrelated to people's incentives, can lead the central government to weaken the private sectors and impede economic growth of the country.

[6] *The First United Nations Development Decade* was proposed by former President J. F. Kennedy at the 16th United Nations General Assembly. He called on industrialized countries to provide financial assistance of 1 percent of GNP in order for developing countries to achieve the aim of 5 percent economic growth. The aim was achieved with 5.7 percent growth although the population in developing countries explosively increased at the same time (Kusano, 1997, pp.30-32).

[7] Schultz, a laureate of the Novel Memorial Prize in economic science in 1979, considers all possible factors related to human productivity such as health and mobility, not only education; while Becker, another Novel Prize laureate in economics in 1992, focuses more on the effect of education, especially schooling, on laborers' future benefit.

[8] Stewart and Deneulin (2002) explain the difference between the basic needs promoted by ILO (BN I) and that by the World Bank (BN II). According to them, BN I concerns "the actual bundle of BN goods and services provided"; while BN II concerns "the 'full life,' indicated for example by life expectancy and a measure of educational achievement" (p.62).

[9] He also shows four interpretations of basic needs (Streeten, 1981, pp.25-26):

Physical interpretation: the minimum specified quantities of such as food, clothing, shelter, water, and sanitation that are necessary to prevent ill health, undernourishment, and the like.

Subjective interpretation: the satisfaction of consumers' wants as perceived by the consumers themselves, rather than by physiologists, doctors, and other specialists.

Paternalistic/Educational interpretation: the public authorities who not only decide the design of public services such as water supply, sanitation, and education, but also guide private consumptions.

Sociopolitical interpretation: the noneconomic, nonmaterial aspects of human autonomy, embracing individual and group participation in the formulation and implementation of projects, and in some cases political mobilization.

[10] For example, the declaration of debt defaults by Mexico in 1982 (Esho, 1999, p.109, p.148).

[11] Although the droughts in the Sahel Strip had been seen since the 1970s, such as the Ethiopian famine in 1972-74 (see Sen (1981, Ch.7) for detail of the case study of the Ethiopian famine), another extreme drought hit the Sahel Strip in the mid-eighties (ex. the great Ethiopian famine in 1988-92, which killed around one third of the total population) and brought the aftereffect on economic conditions in other African countries.

[12] The four conditionalities mentioned above are (World Bank, 1988; Esho, 1999): (1) restructuring of incentives such as price rationalizations including price policy and tariff reform, (2) priority revision of public investment, (3) budgetary reform and debt management, and (4) system recreation especially for public business reform.

[13] For an actual impact of the structural adjustment in Tanzania, see Chapter four.

[14] Some might say that the basic needs approach considers "human beings," and it is true. However, the basic needs approach sees human beings as an agency of economic productivity or as a subject to be invested in. On the other hand, Sen pays special attention to individual "functionings," which reflects one's physical (ex. if the person is pregnant) and social (ex. if the person is a social minority) characteristics (Sen, 1999b, pp.6-11). The details of Sen's approach will be introduced in Chapter two.

[15] Gereffi and Fonda (1992) say that "Dependency theory [is]... in opposition to most of the claims of modernization theory" and differentiate it from modernization theory. "Whereas modernization studies tended to argue that the salvation of the periphery lay in closer investment and trade ties with the core nations, the dependency approach highlights the exploitative potential of these relationships for the periphery" (p.424).

[16] Ogura (1982) interprets Frank's works by saying that " ' underdevelopment is a creation: the development of one side in the world produced the underdevelopment of the other. Underdevelopment is neither a historical nor a traditional condition. Therefore, it is not true that the past condition of the industrialized society is equivalent to the present condition of the underdeveloped society today; because the past condition of the industrialized society has never been 'underdeveloped' even though it could have been 'undeveloped' " (p.44, translated by the author).

[17] Sangmpam (1995) also introduces a kind of capitalism called "pseudocapitalism." Pseudocapitalism has seven traits as follows: (1) the non-central position of capitalist core relations built around the capitalist and the worker; (2) the non-commdification of much peasant agriculture by the capitalist sector; (3) the marginal position of indigenous capital-

Ch.1 History of "development": In the context of international development   31

ist ownership; (4) the existence of capitalist enclaves; (5) the persistence of pre-capitalist relations; (6) extreme dependence on the world market and the West; and, (7) the smallness of the internal market (Sangmpam, 1995, p.611).

[18] Abrokwaa (1999) also describes the characteristics of the modernization theory as "an evolutionary movement along a well demarcated continuum of social change" (p.647) and "the thesis of social and economic dualism" (p.648).

[19] For example, a traditional society is characterized by "an extended kinship structure, a deferential stratification system, little outside contact" etc.; while a modern society is characterized by "a nuclear family structure, a predominance of achievement, universalistic, specific, and neutral orientations and patterns of action" etc. (Valenzuela and Valenzuela, 1979, pp.34-35).

[20] Rostow's (1960) stage theory represents this perspective on the traditional society. His theory assumes that the traditional values would prevent the society from being developed.

[21] Although Valenzuela and Valenzuela (1979) are critical of modernization theory, Black (1966) positively evaluates the role of modernization theory as a universal "yardstick" to measure the level of development in a society. According to Black (1966), "Although the problems raised by generalizations from a rather narrow base (the now modern countries) must be acknowledged, the definition of modernity takes the form of a set of characteristics believed to be applicable to all societies. This conception of modernity, when thought of as a model or ideal type, may be used as a yardstick with which to measure any society" (pp.53-54).

[22] Synder (1980) says "dependency theorists thus recognize explicitly, as modernization theorists often did not, that definitions of development and underdevelopment are essentially normative and necessarily imply the exercise of moral and political choice" (p.744).

[23] There are counter arguments that Huntington's world view is too pessimistic in the sense he overemphasizes the confrontational relations between the West and the non-West (Nagao, 1995; Ishida, 1995), and that his interpretation of "the understanding of non-Western civilization by the West" is too superficial and it produces a hermeneutic problem (Asou, 1995). These counter arguments seem to be related to his initial positioning of "clash" to consider multiculturalism in globalization. Indeed, Huntington (1997) describes his pessimistic standpoint by saying "In the emerging world, the relations between states and groups from different civilizations will not be close and will often be antagonistic" (p.183) and "A 'hate dynamic' emerges, comparable to the 'security dilemma' in international relations, in which mutual fears, distrust, and hatred feed on each other" (p.266). I do not agree with his pessimistic standpoint as I will introduce my perspective on international development in global politics in Chapter two (2.2.2), but I will buy his assumption

that modernization is not always the same as westernization. Starting from this assumption, Huntington seems to take a pessimistic way to understand the multicultural world, but I will take a different way to interpret the world from a Rawlsian point of view (see 2.2.2).

[24] An example can be seen in Japanese rejectionism from 1542 until the mid-nineteenth century. During this period in Japan, "only limited forms of modernization were permitted, such as the acquisition of firearms, and the import of Western culture, including most notably Christianity, was highly restricted" (Huntington, 1997, p.72).

[25] An example can be seen in Mustafa Kemal Ataturk's policy, which created a new Turkey out of the Ottoman Empire. However, Huntington (1997) criticizes this policy by saying that "in embarking on this course, and rejecting the Islamic past, Ataturk made Turkey a 'torn country,' a society which was Muslim in its religion, heritage, customs, and institutions but with a ruling elite determined to make it modern, Western, and at one with the West" (p.74).

[26] He also says "as the pace of modernization increase, ... , the rate of Westernization declines and the indigenous culture goes through a revival" (Huntington, 1997, p.75-76).

[27] In the definition of reformism, he exemplifies the Chinese and Japanese slogans as already cited. "Chinese learning for the fundamental principles" and "Japanese spirit" in the slogans correspond to "rejecting westernization" and "Western learning for practical use" and "Western technique" correspond to "embracing modernization" (Huntington, 1997, p.74). It implies, at least in his definition, that westernization means cultural spiritual impact and modernization means a technical practical impact on the society.

[28] He summarizes his discussion by saying that "modernization, in short, does not necessarily mean Westernization. Non-Western societies can modernize and have modernized without abandoning their own cultures and adopting wholesale Western values, institutions, and practices' (p.78).

[29] Sen (2000) recognized a role for modernization as a *means* in his definition of development, as long as modernization contributes to the ultimate objective of development or expanding human freedom: "industrialization or technological progress or social modernization can substantially contribute to expanding human freedom". (p.3).

[30] Regarding this point, Sen (2000) articulates his position as: "It is indeed possible to argue that there are more interrelations and more cross-cultural influences in the world than is typically acknowledged by those alarmed by the prospect of cultural subversion. The culturally fearful often take a very fragile view of each culture and tend to underestimate our ability to learn from elsewhere without being overwhelmed by that experience" (pp.242-243). I will introduce the details of his position in Chapter two.

[31] Figure 1.2 is a conceptual model, not a statistical model. I use only four independent variables (four major theories in development economics) in this Figure, but it does

not mean there are no other theories.

[32] As already cited in a previous section, Sen (2000) says "industrialization or technological progress or social modernization can substantially contribute to expanding human freedom" (p.3).

The need for "human development": Beyond a classical meaning of development

Chapter 2

In Chapter one, three points are found from the literature review about international development: (1) the historical review of development economics points out the need for a comprehensive perspective on development beyond the classical meaning of development limited to economic development; (2) the challenge made by dependency theorists to the unilinear sense of development insists on the significance of the global and normative perspectives on international development; and (3) Huntington's hypothesis about modernization and westernization suggests that modernization without westernization is possible under the assumption of indigenous cultural power created by "the people of that society" (Huntington, 1997, p.76).

These three findings are related to each other to shape this chapter. The first finding, the need for a new comprehensive perspective on development beyond economic development, is affected by the second and third findings. In other words, the new comprehensive perspective called for today (the first finding) needs to be considered from global and normative points of view (the second finding), with belief in the indigenous cultural power for the people's own social change (the third finding).

In this chapter, based on the findings in the previous chapter, I will introduce Sen's theory of human development as a theoretical direction for the new comprehensive perspective on development and clarify its defects (2.1). I will also respond to and compensate for the defects by using other theories

(2.2). The findings from the previous chapter will be dealt with as follows: the need for a new comprehensive perspective and a normative point of view on development will be introduced in 2.1 with Sen's theory of human development; and, the need for a global perspective and the consideration of the issue of cultural particularity and universality in development will be introduced in 2.2 by reflecting on the defects in Sen's theory. Finally, I will summarize this chapter in 2.3.

2.1 The new generation of international development

After two generations of development economics have passed (see 1.1), "the new generation must still begin with an understanding of the meaning of 'economic development'... Successful development policies need to determine not only how more rapid growth of real income can be generated but also how real income can be used to achieve the other values incorporated in 'development' " (Meier, 2000, p.24). Improving income and access to commodities is still necessary conditions in many developing counties; however, it is significant to consider the issue of development from a more comprehensive perspective. As mentioned in Chapter one, I will introduce the details of Sen's human development theory as a guiding principle of the comprehensive approach to international development today (2.1.1), and see how his theory applies to actual cases to clarify the defects of his theory (2.1.2).

2.1.1 Sen's theory of human development and human capability approach: As a guiding principle of the new generation of development

Sen's theory has been developed over the past few decades.[1] Originally, his theory started as "the entitlement approach" (Sen, 1981), which focuses on *commodity* issues concerning what one can *have*. He developed this early work into "the human capability approach" (Sen, 1992; 1997a, 1997b, 1999b, 1999c, 2002b), which emphasizes *ability* issues about what one can *be* and *do*. Recently, he has provided an alternative interpretation of development, "development as freedom" (Sen, 2000, 2002a). I will introduce: how his idea developed over time; what is the uniqueness of his theory; and, what his theory brings to the new generation of development.

(a) The entitlement approach

Sen (1981) used the concept of "entitlement" to analyze poverty and starvation in India (the great Bengal famine in 1943), and sees the famine as a "deprivation of entitlement," as explained in detail below, not simply as a natural disaster. Sen (1981) points out that there were foods available during the great Bengal famine, but the governmental policy failed to distribute them to the people in need and failed to maintain reasonable prices of foods, which resulted in three million deaths, especially among the poor (p.57-63).[2] Therefore, for Sen (1981), "Starvation is the characteristic of some people not having enough food to eat. It is not the characteristic of there being not enough food to eat" (p.1), which implies a critique of the Food Availability Decline (FAD) approach. The FAD approach assumes that "the primary cause of the famine [the great Bengal famine] was 'a serious shortage in the total supply of rice available for consumption in Bengal'" (Sen, 1981, p.57). However, according to Sen's case study of the great Bengal famine, the primary cause of the famine is not exactly a shortage of the supply, rather, "deprivation of exchange entitlement" of the poor,[3] which implies a disfunction of the "entitlement" system as explained below.

Sen (1981) supposed that an individual has "the endowment" and "the exchange entitlement." "The endowment" is a natural qualification such as labor power and the land taken over from ancestors (p.45-47), and "the exchange entitlement" is "the set of all the alternative bundles of commodities that he can acquire in exchange for what he owns" (p.3). The individual starts with one's endowment to produce a bundle of food. Therefore, when one's endowment decreases (ex. decline of labor power due to sickness) and/or when one's exchange entitlement deteriorates (ex. decline of the wage, rise of the price, and unemployment), the person will starve (Sen, 1981; Esho, 1999, pp. 197-198). This situation is called "deprivation of entitlement." Sen (1981) explains about the entitlement approach as below:

> The entitlement approach to starvation and famines concentrates on the ability of people to command food through the legal means available in the society, including the use of production possibilities, trade opportunities, entitlements vis-à-vis the state, and other methods of acquiring food... Ownership of food is one of the most primitive property rights, and in each society there are rules governing this right. The entitlement approach concentrates on each person's entitlements to commodity bundles including food, and views starvation as resulting from a failure to be entitled to a bundle with enough food. (p.45)

Sen also develops the idea of "exchange entitlement mapping," which is "the relation that specifies the set of exchange entitlements for each ownership bundle" (p.3); for example, if there is an unfair structure of exchange in the society, the relationship created from the unfair structure will deprive the person of his or her ownership bundle or entitlement to commodities. In other words, starvation is not just a question if there is enough food, but also a question of whether one's entitlement is distributed and exchanged fairly. Sen's idea of "exchange entitlement mapping" insists on the importance of "relations" which appear whenever the action of exchange happens. It also insists that a concern with "exchange entitlement" by itself is not sufficient to analyze social reality because many kinds of fair/unfair relations keep appearing in other aspects of our reality. This concern with the relations of entitlements or "exchange entitlement mapping" points out two aspects of the cause of starvation: a material shortage and a power relation over exchange entitlements, while the FAD approach considers only the first aspect.

More specifically in the case of the great Bengal famine, Sen (1981) clarifies that the price of rice, India's main food, increased more than 2.5 times in 1944 compared to that in 1941 while the daily wage of agricultural unskilled laborers increased by only 1.68 times. Therefore, the exchange ratio of wages in respect of the price of rice drops in 1944 to 65 percent of the standard in 1941 (Sen, 1981, p.66, Table 6.4).[4] He describes this kind of situation by saying that "[a person's] exchange entitlement may worsen for reasons other than a general decline of food supply. For example, given the same total food supply, other groups' becoming richer and buying more food can lead to a rise in food prices, causing a worsening of exchange entitlement" (p.4).

The entitlement approach can be called a rights-based approach,[5] and it depicts a possible power structure of the society through the concept of "exchange entitlement mapping." Sen's case studies of famines all over the world clarify how the political economic system violates the entitlements of the weak.[6] Mine (1999) evaluates Sen's work by saying that "Sen does not criticize dependency theory. Rather, he seems to catch a scent of danger that post-war development economics can be unreasonably blamed for giving governments too great a role" (p.199, translated by the author). This statement might look contradictory to the need for a new perspective in the sense that it seems to support post-war development economics. However, what Sen tries to do is, not to protect or return to post-war development economics, but to reconstruct development economics as it should be.[7] In other words, he tries to restore the ideal relationship between market systems and governments and to improve the quality of public policy for the people's well-being.[8] Sen believes in the importance of public policy in development (Mine, 1999, pp.199-200), and the significance of the revival of economics as ethics (Sen, 1987). The entitlement approach proposes normative social relations, called "the exchange entitlement mapping," although this approach is limited to the issue of commodities.

(b) The human capability approach

While Sen focuses on one's ownership of commodities in the entitlement approach, he shifts his main focus to the *ability* to realize one's own well-being in the human capability approach. In the entitlement approach, he explains "the ability [to avoid starvation]" (Sen, 1981, p.4) by depending on one's "entitlement" (ownership or command of commodities) and "exchange entitlement mapping" (the relations among exchange entitlements). However, in the human capability approach, he focuses largely on ability themselves. The entitlement approach is a commodity-based approach in the sense that the principle question is what one can have; on the other hand, the human capability approach articulates the role of entitlement as a means to the ultimate goal of human well-being. Here the shift from a tool (the entitlement approach) to a goal (the human capability approach) can be seen. Sen develops many new concepts to explain his human capability approach as follows.

In order to understand Sen's idea of human capability, at least two concepts, "well-being" and "functioning," need to be introduced. Sen (1999b) explains "well-being" as concerned with a person's achievement (how 'well' is his or her 'being'?) (p.3), and more importantly, the "person's well-being is not really a matter of how *rich* he or she is" (p.19). Sen (1999b) believes that "commodity command is a *means* to the end of well-being, but can scarcely be the end itself" (p.19). This is a warning against the confusion between end and means; in other words, between well-being as a goal of development and "commodity fetishism," which regards "goods as valuable in themselves and not for (and to the extent that) they help the person" (Sen, 1999b, p.19). Sen's well-being means "an evaluation of the 'well-ness' of the person's state of being," which includes a consideration for others, not only that for one's own well-being (Sen, 2002b, p.36; 1992, p.39).[9]

The human well-being is supposed to be judged by "functionings" (Sen, 2002b, p.37), because "living may be seen as consisting of a set of interrelated 'functionings,' consisting of beings and doings" (Sen, 1992, p.39). According to Sen, a functioning is an actually feasible choice that may contribute to one's well-being, and it converts commodities into one's utility or happiness through different kinds of functionings as described below (Sen, 1992, 1997a, 1999b, 2002b,). Sen (1999b) explains:

> A functioning is an achievement of a person: what he or she manages to do or to be. It reflects, as it were, a part of the 'state' of that person. It has to be distinguished from the commodities which are used to achieve those functionings. For example, bicycling has to be distinguished from possessing a bike. It has to be distinguished also from the happiness generated by the functioning, for example, actually cycling around must not be identified with the pleasure obtained from that act. <u>A functioning is thus different both from (1) having goods (and the corresponding characteristics), to which it is posterior, and (2) having utility (in a form of happiness resulting from that functioning), to which it is, in an important way, prior.</u> (p.7, underlined by the author)

To clarify the meaning and role of "a functioning" and "human capability" in a general form, it is explained as below:

When,
x_i = the vector of commodities possessed by the person i, where $x_i \in X_i$,[10] (e.g., a person i's ownership of a bicycle);

$c(*)$ = the function (not necessarily linear)[11] converting a commodity vector (x_i) into a vector of characteristics of those commodities (e.g., healthy body of the person i to utilize the commodity of the bicycle);

$f_i(*)$ = a personal 'utilization function' of the person i reflecting one pattern of use of commodities that i can actually make (in generating a functioning vector out of a characteristic vector ($c(*)$) with commodities possessed(x_i))[12] (e.g., commuting to school by the bicycle);

F_i = the set of 'utilization functions' $f_i(*)$, any one of which the person i can in fact choose (the aggregation of $f_i(*)$ of the person i); and,

$h_i(*)$ = the happiness function of the person i related to the functionings achieved by i [13] (e.g., the person i's comfort of commuting caused by riding the bicycle);

Then,
an achieved functioning that the person i can acquire with his or her commodity (x_i) is expressed as:

$b_i = f_i(c(x_i))$,

which reflects the person's being, such as whether well-nourished and well-clothed, and by which 'well-being' is evaluated since b_i is an indication of the kind of being he or she is achieving;

the happiness that he or she will enjoy from the function b_i is expressed as:

$u_i = h_i(f_i(c(x_i))) = h_i(b_i)$,

where it should be noted that *valuing* a life and measuring the *happiness* generated in that life are two different exercises [14];

So far the attention has been concentrated only on one utilization function fi(*) from the set Fi. The aggregation of utilization function vectors feasible for the person i is defined as:

Pi(xi) = { bi| bi = fi(c(xi)), for some fi(*) $\in$ Fi} [15]; and,

when the person's choice of a commodity vectors is restricted to the set Xi (xi $\in$ Xi), then the person's feasible functioning vectors are defined as:

Qi(xi) = {bi | bi = fi(c(xi)), for some fi(*) Fi and for some xi $\in$ Xi}. [16]

Qi(xi) represents the freedom that the person i can realize in terms of the choice of functionings, given his or her personal features Fi (conversion of characteristics into functionings), and given his or her entitlement Xi.
(Sen, 1999b, pp.6-11, and the author's additions)

Eventually, "human capability" is defined as the aggregation of "functionings." Sen (1999b) explains "Qi can be called the 'capabilities' of person i given those parameters. It reflects the various combinations of functionings ('beings') he can achieve" (p.9). The capability set Qi shows substantively possible choices or freedom to achieve one's own well-being (Sen, 1992, p.49; 2002b, p.38).[17] With these feasible combinations of choices, the person can choose to fast as a functioning, which is not just starving; "it is choosing to starve when one does have other options" (Sen, 1992, p.52).

Remembering Sen's assumptions that "living may be seen as consisting of a set of interrelated 'functionings,' consisting of beings and doings" (Sen, 1992, p.39) and that "'well-being' is concerned with a person's achievement: how 'well' is his or her 'being'?" (Sen, 1999b, p.3), his claim that "the evaluation of a person's well-being has to take the form of an assessment of these constituent elements [functionings such as escaping mortality]" (Sen, 2002b, p.36-37) makes sense. As long as we are living, we keep being and doing, hence our ultimate purpose in life is "well-being"; and, calling our actually realizable beings/doings "functionings," "capability" shows how many "functionings" we actually have.

The human capability approach can be called an approach to substantive freedom. It is for *substantive* freedom, in the sense that it takes physical, psychological, and social conditions of the person into consideration through the functions of $c(*)$, $f_i(*)$, $h_i(*)$, b_i, and u_i. Compared to his entitlement approach, which focuses on one's ownership of commodities, the human capability approach drastically broadens the perspective on the whole of human life by distinguishing different functions that are affected by various aspects of human life. Through the consideration of human capability, it becomes clear that Sen (1999b) sees substantive freedom as an issue of choice:

> To consider acts of substantial choosing as being among the relevant 'functionings,' is supportable also from the point of view that the quality of life a person enjoys is not merely a matter of what he or she achieves, but also of what options the person has had the opportunity to choose from. In this view, the 'good life' is partly a life of genuine choice, and not one in which the person is forced into a particular life - however rich it might be in other respects.[18] (pp.44-45)

His recent approach focuses more on the idea of freedom in development as explained below.

(c) Development as freedom

Through the human capability approach, Sen's concern seems to begin focusing on the question of freedom. The human capability approach shows Sen's belief in freedom as choice, but he seems not to be a blind believer in freedom. Sen (1992) points out the possibility of the conflict between freedom and well-being by saying "Indeed, sometimes more freedom of choice can bemuse and befuddle, and make one's life more wretched. There are costs of decision-making, and it may be comfortable to lie back and relax while others make the detailed choices... more freedom makes one certainly less happy" (p.59). Based on this possibility, Sen (1992) brings up two questions of freedom: (1) "whether freedom - both agency freedom and well-being freedom - can conflict with well-being, and if so, in what sense, and for what reasons"; and (2) whether "the possibly contrary effects of the expansion of some types of choices" can be observed (p.59).

In answering the first question, Sen insists that it is inevitable to separate "agency freedom" from "well-being freedom" (Sen, 1992, pp.56-58). He defines an agent as "someone who acts and brings about change, and whose achievements can be judged in terms of her own values and objectives, whether or not we assess them in terms of some external criteria as well" beyond a conventional meaning of "a person who is acting on someone else's behalf" (Sen, 2000, pp.8-19). According to his definition, "a person's agency achievement refers to the realization of goals and values she has reasons to pursue, whether or not they are connected with her own well-being" (Sen, 1992, p.56). Therefore, if a person aims at the independence of the country, the person does not always act for her own well-being, but she may be able to choose her way of life as an agent truly freely as long as her capability allows it. In short, "agency freedom" is "one's freedom to bring about the achievements one values and which one attempts to produce... seen in broader terms, including aspects of states of affairs that relate to one's agency objectives"; while "well-being freedom" is "one's freedom to achieve those things that are constitutive of one's well-being... that is best reflected by a person's *capability set*"; and, these two freedoms are thoroughly interdependent (Sen, 1992, p.57).[19]

The possibility of the conflict between freedom and well-being can be observed from these definitions of two kinds of freedom. Agency freedom does not always directly contribute to one's own well-being; in other words, one can choose a life as an agent, which is one kind of realization of one's freedom (agency freedom), but this choice may reduce one's well-being or bring difficulty in the achievement of one's well-being.[20] However, "even when freedom and well-being do not move together, it does not, of course, follow that an increase in a person's freedom would be to his or her disadvantage" (Sen, 1992, p.62). The issue to consider here is the possibility that the increased freedom could force the person to make a choice even though he or she does not want to do so. This is the question of "the possibly contrary effects of the expansion of some types of choices" that Sen addresses, as mentioned above.

Sen (1992) restates this question below:

> This question does, in fact, take us in the direction of an important issue regarding the nature of freedom, to wit, <u>whether any increase in choices that one can - and has to - make must be seen as an expansion of freedom</u>. This issue is... quite central to the assessment of social structures and public policies related to enhancing freedom. Freedom is a complex notion. Facing more alternatives need not invariably be seen as an expansion of a person's freedom to do the things she would like to do. (p.63, underlined by the author)

He answers no to the underlined question above since not all choices are always valuable to the person, and some disadvantageous choices may waste his or her time and energy in making a decision and reduce his or her freedom to enjoy making no choice.[21] The conflict is seen between "the freedom to exercise active choice over a range of (possibly trivial) options and the freedom to lead a leisured life without the nuisance of constantly having to make trivial choices" (Sen, 1992, p.64). In other words, in order to enjoy freedom without disadvantageous choices, the person has to know what is a valuable choice for him or her. Therefore, "the problem [of freedom is] related to the inescapable requirement of valuation involved in the assessment of freedom" (Sen, 1992, p.64), which implies that it is important for the person to have the ability to know what are valuable options for his or her choice in order to realize his or her substantive freedom.[22] It also implies that it is necessary for an individual to develop his or her capability to make a *good* choice for what he or she values. Only the individual can know what a valuable choice is for him or her, not anyone else; because the person may make a choice that may reduce his or her well-being by using his or her agency freedom, which may seem a ridiculous choice from others' perspective, but which may be a valuable choice for *that* person. In the sense that only *the* person can make a *good* choice, and with the assumption that "choosing is a part of living" (Sen, 1992, p.63), it can be said that development of human capability is important for everyone *and* for each individual in order to exercise her substantially meaningful freedom.

Although the argument above has focused on the "constitutive role" of human freedom, Sen (2000) also recognizes the role of freedom as an instrument: "expansion of freedom is viewed as both (1) the *primary end* and (2) the *principal means* of development. They can be called respectively the 'constitutive role' and the 'instrumental role' of freedom in development" (p.36). The "constitutive role" of freedom means "the *intrinsic* importance of human freedom as the preeminent objective of development" (Sen, 2000, p.37) to enrich one's life; on the other hand, the "instrumental role of freedom concerns the way different kinds of rights, opportunities, and entitlements contribute to the expansion of human freedom in general, and thus to promoting development" (p.37).

According to Sen (2000), the instrumental role of freedom covers broad aspects of human life, and he specifies five types of instrumental freedom: (1)

political freedoms, (2) *economic freedoms*, (3) *social opportunities*, (4) *transparency guarantees*, and (5) *protective security*, which "tend to contribute to the general capability of a person to live more freely, but they also serve to complement one another" (pp.38-40).

Political freedoms mean "the opportunities that people have to determine who should govern and on what principles" including "the political entitlements associated with democracies in the broadest sense (encompassing opportunities of political dialogue, dissent and critique as well as voting rights and participatory selection of legislators and executives)" (p.38). *Economic freedoms* mean "the opportunities that individuals respectively enjoy to utilize economic resources for the purpose of consumption, or production, or exchange" including "economic entitlements." In this definition, "distributional considerations are important, in addition to aggregative ones" because how to distribute the additional income will make a significant difference in one's economic entitlement (pp.38-39; also see "exchange entitle mapping" in 2.1.1(a)). *Social opportunities* mean "the arrangements that society makes for education, health care and so on, which influence the individual's substantive freedom to live better." They are important "not only for the conduct of private lives... but also for more effective participation in economic and political activities" (p.39). *Transparency guarantees* "deal with the need for openness that people can expect: the freedom to deal with one another under guarantees of disclosure and lucidity," which will play a role in "preventing corruption, financial irresponsibility and underhand dealings" (pp.39-40).[23] And finally, *protective security* means "a social security net for preventing the affected population from being reduced to abject misery, and in some cases even starvation and death" including "*fixed* institutional arrangements such as unemployment benefits and statutory income supplements to the indigent as well as ad hoc arrangements such as famine relief or emergency public employment to generate income for destitutes" (p.40).

As seen above, all factors Sen mentions are not new issues. Most of them have been discussed for a long time in various disciplines. However, the uniqueness of Sen's perspective can be seen in that he tries to tie all the aspects together through the concepts of *entitlement* (see 2.1.1 (a)) and *capability* (see 2.1.1 (b)) under the assumption of the intrinsic importance of human freedom, or the *primary end* of development. From his comprehensive and normative perspective on development as freedom, Sen (2000) suggests the direction for development analysis by saying: "While development analysis must, on the one hand, be concerned with the objectives and aims that make these instrumental freedoms consequentially important, it must also take note of the empirical linkages that tie the distinct types of freedom together, strengthening their joint importance" (Sen, 2000, p.38, underlined by the author). As roughly described in Figure 1.3 at the end of Chapter one (see 1.3), Sen suggests the need for a comprehensive perspective on development.

(d) Difference from human capital theory

How are Sen's human capability approach and human development theory different from the conventional human capital theory introduced in Chapter one (1.1.2)? Human capital theory has been used as a justification of educational development since the 1960s, and it also uses a language of "human capability"; therefore, it can be called a classical view of human development. It is important to identify similarities and differences between these two theories: the human capability approach (or human development theory) and human capital theory.

Schultz (1971), a founder of human capital theory, defines five major categories of human investment to improve human capabilities:

(1) Health facilities and services, broadly conceived to include all expenditures that affect the life expectancy, strength and stamina, and the vigor and vitality of a people.

(2) On-the-job training, including old-style apprenticeships organized by firms.
(3) Formally organized education at the elementary, secondary, and higher levels.
(4) Study programs for adults that are not organized by firms, including extension programs notably in agriculture.
(5) Migration of individuals and families to adjust to changing job opportunities.

(p.36)

According to Schultz, "this one-sided effort [financial aid] is underway in spite of the fact that the knowledge and skills required to take on and use efficiently the superior techniques of production are usually in very short supply in these countries [developing countries]" (p.47). For him, education as a human investment is critical to promote economic productivity. In the sense that he evaluates human capability by productivity and efficiency and that he considers education as an investment for future earnings, his perspective is limited to the economic aspects of human life.

Following and expanding Schultz's human capital theory, Becker (1993) discusses the connection between firms and schools, believing that "a school can be defined as an institution specializing in the production of training... schools and firms are often substitute sources of particular skills" (p.51). Becker's assumption concerning education is strictly economic: the needs for education originate in firms first, and these needs define the role of schools. He also focuses on the economic aspect of human activities and sees education as a tool to foster economic productivity.

From Sen's perspective, human capital theorists consider education, health, and other human investments as commodities (xi), but they do not consider "functionings (bi)" or "capability ($Qi(xi)$)," which determine one's level of "well-being." Moreover, Schultz and Becker's dependent variables are productivity and efficiency which are evaluated by the amount of earnings, and their independent variables are human investments, such as education, health, and any other factors to promote productivity. Their question is what kind of independent variables contribute to the dependent variable most efficiently. On the other hand, Sen evaluates the quality of human life by one's "capability," in other words, how many actual choices he or she can have for a better life ("well-being"). Sen's question is how to improve the "well-being" of each individual.

One important note here is that the human capability approach and human development theory never denies the value of human capital theory. Sen (1997b) says that "If a person can become more productive in making commodities through better education, better health, and so on, it is not unnatural to expect that she can also directly achieve more - and have the freedom to achieve more - in leading her life. Both perspectives put humanity at the center of attention" (p.1959).[24] The human capability approach and human development theory remind us of other aspects of human life beyond economics, and they establish human well-being as the end and economic wealth as a means, while human capital theorists assume economic productivity as the end. Tilak (2002) describes the difference between the human capital theory and Sen's human development theory, particularly in education, below:

> In the human capital approach, ... it is the economic contribution of education that mainly determines the importance that it should receive in development priorities of the economies (or even at the individual level). On the contrary, the human development approach gives more emphasis to the intrinsic value of education – it views education as a human right, as an opportunity, and as an entitlement. (p.196)

Tilak indicates that the human capability approach has a broader perspective on education than the human capital theory.

Although human capital theory use the term "human capability," this expression is limited by the concept of productivity to mean capability of economic agency. On the other hand, the term "human capability" in human development theory is limited only by the concept of constitutive freedom, to mean the capability of each individual to live a fulfilling life. These two meanings are clearly different in scope and purpose. However, "The two perspectives cannot but be related since both are concerned with the role of human beings, and in particular with the actual abilities that they achieve and acquire" (Sen, 1997b, p.1959).

(e) Why Sen's perspective?

Sen's theory of human development has been improved over time: "the entitlement approach," or the right-based approach of one's actual ownership and the relations among entitlements, has been improved into "the human capability approach," or the approach focusing on one's actually realizable choices. His recent approach, "development as freedom," includes the concepts of constitutive and instrumental freedoms, which contribute to the definition and clarification of human development:

> Development can be seen ... as a process of expanding the real freedoms that people enjoy... Development requires the removal of major sources of unfreedom: poverty as well as tyranny, poor economic opportunities as well as systematic social deprivation, neglect of public facilities as well as intolerance or overactivity of repressive states (p.3).
> The motivation underlying the approach of "development as freedom" is not so much to order all states - or all alternative scenarios - into one "complete ordering," but to draw attention to important aspects of the process of development, each of which deserves attention (p.33)... Development is indeed a momentous engagement with freedom's possibilities (p.298). (Sen, 2000, underlined by the author)

The uniqueness of his approach can be seen in its comprehensive and normative perspective on development. It is comprehensive in the sense that Sen draws our attention to a wide variety of aspects of the process of development in human life, through the concepts of capability and functionings. It is also normative in the sense that Sen defines the significance of development as the substantive freedom of each human. Due to this uniqueness, Sen succeeds in bringing a new perspective to development beyond the limitations of the classical approaches introduced in Chapter one.

2.1.2 Applications and defects of Sen's theory

How is Sen's theory interpreted and applied to the actual cases? Haq (2000) analyzes a current condition of human development in South Asia. He employs the Human Development Index (HDI), an index devised from Sen's theory (UNDP, 1990, 2003, 2004, 2005), to compare the levels of human development among some South Asian countries. He concludes his discussion with a suggestion of "massive investments in human development" (p.81) for the future of South Asia, specifically, "basic education, primary health care, family planning, safe drinking water, and nutritional programs" (p.81) to improve human development in South Asian countries. Johnson (2002) considers human development in education in southern Africa. According to him, "human development is about expanding people's choices, and the framework most likely to expand people's choices sustainably is the educational system" (p.381). He applies the idea of human development to technology education and analyzes the way to realize sustainable socio-economic development in Africa. Ahsan (2004) studies the condition of human development in Muslim countries. Through the HDI comparisons of four national categories, high and low-income Muslim and non-Muslim countries, Ahsan concludes "Muslim counties are much behind non-Muslim countries" (p.194) and suggests that Muslim countries "cut their defense budgets starting from one percent per annum" to institute "an Islamic Human Development Fund" (p.195).

In Haq's (2000) and Ahsan's (2004) research,[25] the concept of human development is statistically embodied in an indicator called Human Development Index (HDI) developed by Sen himself (Sen, 1999c; UNDP, 1990, 2003, 2004; 2005). HDI is computed by using life expectancy, adult literacy, combined primary, secondary, and tertiary school enrollment, not simply GDP per capita (UNDP, 2005, p.341). HDI is expected to work as "a measure of the same level of vulgarity as GNP - just one number - but a measure that is not as blind to social aspects of human lives as GNP is" (Haq's words to express the need for an alternative indicator of development, quoted in Sen, 1999c, p.23). Jolly (2002) notes the advantage of statistical measures of human development by citing Seers' words: "We cannot, with our own eyes and ears, perceive more than a minute sample of human affairs... So we rely on statistics in order to build and maintain our own model of the world. The data that are available mould our perceptions" (Seers, 1983, p.130), and he insists that "statisticians must abandon the common misconception that statistics have little to contribute [to human rights]... statistics can play a critical role in raising awareness and generating pressure for action" (Jolly, 2002, p.266). On the other hand, Jolly (2002) points out that HDI is a composite indicator "using arbitrary weights" (Jolly, 2002, p.268).

Panigrahi and Sivramkrishna (2002) analyze the statistical problems of HDI. According to them, "HDI-based country rankings are not robust or consistent with the choice of fixed maximum and minimum indicator values" (p.310),[26] and they propose an alternative more robust indicator, the "adjusted HDI (AHDI)." AHDI is computed by (1) creating "adjustment terms" that consider the gap between the highest and lowest values of indices all over the world and (2) dividing HDI values by the adjustment terms to produce AHDI.

These applications of Sen's theory of human development for case studies and for HDI improvement imply problems in two different ways: a problem of the statistical interpretation of Sen's theory and defects of Sen's theory itself.

The problem of statistical interpretation comes from the ways of that HDI is defined and used. Haq (2000) and Ahsan (2004) use HDI to rank countries by their levels of development. However, Esho (1999) criticizes uses of HDI by saying that "Ranking countries by HDI is not the best way to take advantage of Sen's idea ... Sen's idea should be embodied in indicators that analyze specifically what capabilities are insufficient at the level of the nation, the region, social class, and gender, in order to discover the reason for those insufficiencies" (p.216, translated by the author). A statistical application of Sen's theory is one of the constructive ways to "mould our perceptions" (Seers, 1983, p.130) and to "raise awareness and generate pressure for action" (Jolly, 2002, p.266). However, the purpose of Sen's human development theory is not to rank countries, but to arouse attention about the complexity of development. Therefore, although HDI has played a significant role as an alternative indicator to economic indicators such as GDP, there can be other statistical approaches to human development that embody the full scope of human development and that generate a diagnosis of particular societies, not for ranking or comparison. I will discuss an alternative statistical approach in Chapters five and six.

The other problem seems related to the defects of Sen's theory itself. The literature reviewed above shows how widely the idea of human development can be applied to the cases of national/regional development in various cultural contexts. At the same time, these applications expose some fundamental defects of Sen's theory.

(1) *The failure to consider the universality of the theory*: Haq (2000), Johnson (2002), and Ahsan (2004) apply the idea of human development as a universally valid value in South Asia, southern Africa, and Muslim nations respectively. Haq (2000) and Ahsan (2004) assume HDI as a universally valid

measure to compare different countries. However, Sen's theory seems not to provide warrant for an assumption of universality. Is it legitimate to consider the concept of human development as a universal value in any cultural context? Do not these applications *impose* the measure of HDI on cultural diversity?

(2) *The lack of specification of the concept*: Jolly (2002) and Panigrahi and Sivramkrishna (2002) criticize the arbitrary weights used in HDI, but they seem to accept the possibly arbitrary selection of composite indices. The problem of variable selection is also related to the issue of statistical modeling (see Chapter five), but that there is a theoretical problem that Sen's idea of human capability is not specific enough to be modeled empirically. What kind of factors should really be considered as relevant to human development? Do composite indices of life expectancy, adult literacy, school enrollment, and GDP per capita in HDI adequately reflect the concept of human development?

(3) *The lack of a perspective on international politics*: Haq (2000) insists on the need for "massive investment in human development"; Johnson (2002) insists on "investments in technology"; and, Ahsan (2004) suggests instituting "an Islamic Human Development Fund." These suggestions are inevitably related to the issue of international assistance, but Sen's theory does not provide a justification for international cooperation in international politics. Why and how can international cooperation be justified as a responsibility of developed nations?

2.2 Responding to the defects of Sen's theory

This section will respond to the three problems of Sen's theory listed above. The first and second questions will be discussed in 2.2.1 using Nussbaum's work, based on her Aristotelian essentialist defense of the universal value of human capability (1992) and her central human functional capabilities list for specification of Sen's abstract idea (2000a; 2000b). The third question will be discussed in 2.2.2 using Rawls' principles in the Law of Peoples (1999a, 1999b; Kawamoto, 2002) to propose a legitimate reason for international assistance from an ethical point of view.

2.2.1 Universality and specification:
Human capability as a universal threshold of public policy

Regarding the first question, (1) the failure to consider the universality of the theory, Nussbaum (1992) provides a justification of the universal value of human capability. From the view point of Aristotelian essentialism,[27] she proposes two essentialist assumptions.

First,

> We do recognize others as human across many divisions of time and place. Whatever the differences we encounter, we are rarely in doubt as to when we are dealing with a human being and when we are not. The essentialist account attempts to describe the bases for these recognitions, by mapping out the general shape of the human form of life, those features that constitute a life as human wherever it is. (p.215)

And second,

> We do have a broadly shared general consensus about the features whose absence means the end of a human form of life... This is really just another way of coming at the first question, of asking what the most central features of our common humanity are, without which no individual can be counted (or counted any longer) as human. (p.215)

Based on these assumptions, she insists that there should be a universal threshold of capabilities to assure all human beings a human form of life, and that public policy should achieve this threshold of *basic human capabilities* derived from Sen. She articulates her Aristotelian view toward Sen's human capability approach by saying "the Aristotelian view observes that these basic human capabilities exert a claim on society that they should be developed.

Human begins are creatures such that, provided with the right educational and material support, they can become capable of the major human functions" (Nussbaum, 1992, p.228).[28]

If the concept of human capability can be understood as a universal value, how can the concept be specified as universally valuable factors? Nussbaum's list of central human functional capability deals with the second defect of Sen's theory, (2) the lack of specification of the concept. Nussbaum (2000a) analyzes Sen's idea into a list of central human functional capabilities as "a threshold level of these human capabilities" (p.75; also see Appendix A), which can be used to formulate and to evaluate public policy (Nussbaum, 1992, p.232).[29]

The list contains ten items (Nussbaum, 2000a, pp.78-80; also see Appendix A): (1) *life*, (2) *bodily health*, (3) *bodily integrity*, (4) *senses, imagination, and thought*, (5) *emotions*, (6) *practical reason*, (7) *affiliation*, (8) *other species*, (9) *play*, and (10) *control over one's environment*. These items represent basic human capabilities or universal necessary conditions to realize one's life in a truly human way with the dignity of a human being (Nussbaum, 2000a, p.72). Therefore, "If people are systematically falling below the threshold in any of these core areas, this should be seen as a situation both unjust and tragic, in need of urgent attention - even if in other respects things are going well" (Nussbaum, 2000a, p.71). The list can work as a policy direction and a policy standard. Nussbaum says that "if all [items on the list] cannot be brought across the threshold, to this extent the ends of public policy have not been met" (1992a, p.232); and that "we could agree... that a basic social minimum in the area of the central capabilities should be secured to all citizens" (2000a, p.75). Thus, the list of human capabilities as a universal value is interpreted as a social minimum of public policy.

Nussbaum describes some characteristics of the list of special importance. First, the list is not strictly definitive: "the list remains open-ended and humble; it can always be contested and remade... the items on the list are to some extent differently constructed by different societies" (Nussbaum, 2000a, p.77). It is important to emphasize that the universal agreement concerns not a definitive list with specifically fixed items but a notion that there is a universal threshold or social minimum that should be guaranteed by public policy for *each* and *every* human being in the society. Following her notion, I will propose an interpretation of her list in Chapter three (3.2).

Second, "some items on the list may seem to us more fixed than others" (Nussbaum, 2000a, p.77). For example, the item *bodily health* may be more fixed than the item *play*. Nussbaum (2000a) categorizes capabilities into three subgroups (pp.84-86): (1) *basic capabilities* or the necessary conditions for developing the advanced capabilities and the ground of moral concern, such as the capability for speech (c.f. *bodily health* in the list); (2) *internal capabilities* or personal abilities developed with some support from the surrounding environment, such as learning language sufficiently to communicate well (c.f. *senses, imagination, and thought*, including education and literacy; see Appendix A); and (3) *combined capabilities* defined as internal capabilities combined with the environmental conditions necessary to exercise one's functionings, such as political speech under democracy (c.f. *control over one's environment*, including political participation; see Appendix A).[30]

Finally, a "part of the idea of the list is its *multiple realizability*: its members can be more concretely specified in accordance with local beliefs and circumstances" (Nussbaum, 2000a, p.77). This idea, "multiple realizability," is significant especially in the context of international development because there is often a danger of cultural and social violence caused by too culturally specific interpretations of the list, for example westernization in international development (e.g. Kitajima, 1997; Roberts, 1981; also see 1.2.2 in Chapter one). Universality without paying attention to diversity in human societies may bring cultural violation or destruction. However, Nussbaum (2000a) is sensitive to this concern: "We need to ask, then, whether it is appropriate to use a universal framework at all, rather than a plurality of different though related frameworks. And we also need to ask whether the framework we propose, if a single universal one, is sufficiently flexible to enable to do justice to the human variety we find" (p.40). Her idea of multiple realizability enables one universal framework to adjust to the plurality of global human societies.

In these ways, her theory compensates for Sen's lack of argument for universality and of specification of human capability. It thus expands and reinforces Sen's human development theory.

However, the items on her list of central human functional capabilities still seem too abstract to guide policy; for example, how should be the item *senses, imagination, and thought* considered in the policy context? How can the three hierarchical categories of human capability be applied to the ten items? In Chapter three, I will reconsider the list and the concept of capability by using hierarchical categories.

2.2.2 International relations in global politics:
From an ethical perspective

The third defect of Sen's theory, (3) the lack of the perspective on international politics, raises the question: why and how can international cooperation and the implicit responsibilities of developed nations be justified? As shown in chapter one (see 1.1), the actual rationale for international cooperation has depended on political tensions and market considerations.[31] In addition to diplomatic and economic justifications of international assistance, this study aims at adding an ethical justification for and normative reconsideration of international cooperation.

From a political philosopher's point of view, Rawls (1999b) claims that "well-ordered peoples have a *duty* to assist burdened societies" (p.106)[32] in order to realize greater political justice beyond national boundaries. He proposes an ideal global society called the "Society of Peoples[65]" in which all peoples "follow the ideals and principles of the Law of Peoples in their mutual relations" (p.3).[34] The principles are supposed to work, not to dictate actual peoples' lives in detail, but to provide a general framework within which people can find and realize their own goodness in their society.[35] The eight principles of the Law of Peoples are:

1. Peoples are free and independent, and their freedom and independence are to be respected by other peoples;
2. Peoples are to observe treaties and undertakings;
3. Peoples are equal and are parties to the agreements that bind them;
4. Peoples are to observe a duty of non-intervention;
5. Peoples have the right of self-defense but no right to instigate war for reasons other than self-defense;
6. Peoples are to honor human rights;
7. Peoples are to observe certain specified restrictions in the conduct of war; and
8. Peoples have a duty to assist other peoples living under unfavorable conditions that prevent their having a just or decent political and social regime.

(Rawls, 1999b, p.37)

It is important to note that Rawls (1999b) limits his argument to the *political* sphere (p.9, p.18), which means that he recognizes the importance of respecting the diversity of peoples' lives outside of a political sphere. Therefore, the justifications of the Law of Peoples can be different from one society to another. He defines the concept of "reasonable pluralism" as "the diversity among reasonable peoples with their different cultures and traditions of thought" (p.11). Although Nussbaum's "multiple realizability" is a similar notion, Rawls' concept of "reasonable pluralism" is restricted to *reasonable* peoples in the Society of Peoples.[36] Rawls (1999b) requires the peoples to respect human rights in order to be counted as "a decent people [37]" (p.67).

He recognizes three roles of human rights as below (p.80):
1. Their fulfillment is a necessary condition of the decency of a society's political institutions and of its legal order.
2. Their fulfillment is sufficient to exclude justified and forceful intervention by other peoples, for example, by diplomatic and economic sanctions, or in grave cases by military force.
3. They set a limit to the pluralism among peoples.

These roles of human rights imply that decent peoples should respect human rights or the principles of the Laws of Peoples in a broader sense, at least in a political sphere of life for greater mutual understanding.

However, there can be societies which "lack the political and cultural traditions, the human capital and know-how, and often, the material and technological resources needed to be well-ordered," which are called "burdened societies" (Rawls, 1999b, p.106). Rawls claims that "well-ordered peoples have a duty to assist burdened societies" (p.106; also see the eighth principle above). Such assistance is a necessary condition for peoples to be well ordered and to be members of the Society of Peoples, or the global society dedicated to greater justice and peace.[38]

Although Sen does not answer the question why and how international cooperation can be justified as a responsibility of developed nations, Rawls proposes a justification from an ethical perspective through the principles of the Law of Peoples and the concept of reasonable pluralism. However, his eight principles do not show how such ideal peoples should be developed - this is a question of education.[39] He considers the education system to be a matter of self-determination, so he would think that the question of education should not be mentioned as a part of the universal principles. However, Nussbaum's Aristotelian defense of human capability confirms that "Human beings are creatures such that, provided with the right educational and material support, they can become capable of the major human functions"

(Nussbaum, 1992, p.228). Following her standpoint, I will claim the need for basic education as a universal principle for human development in Chapter three (3.2).

2.3 Conclusion of the chapter: Human development in the global era

Following the three findings of Chapter one, this chapter introduced a new perspective on human development by relying on Sen's theory. He initially proposed "the entitlement approach" (Sen, 1981) using several case studies of famine and insists that the famines are "deprivation of entitlement" (see 2.1.1 (a)). This approach brings an ethical dimension into the definition and protection of ownership of commodities. Sen developed his idea into "the human capability approach" (1992, 1997a, 1997b, 1999b, 1999c, 2002b). While the entitlement approach focuses on a *commodity* issue, the human capability approach pays more attention to an *ability* issue. This new approach articulates the purpose of human development as the development of "human well-being," and considers one's commodities (wealth) and utility (happiness) as *means* to develop one's well-being. By proposing the concept of a "functioning," which is an actually realizable choice the person may make, and which composes the person's "capability," he describes human freedom as autonomous choice of one's life (see 2.1.1 (b)). His concern for human freedom leads him to conceptualize "development as freedom" (2000, 2002a). He examines two different meanings and roles of freedom: the "constitutive role" and the "instrumental role" of freedom. According to Sen, the "constitutive role" of freedom is realized by capability development and it should enable the person to have more functionings available for his or her well-being. In other words, it should make the person substantively freer. On the other hand, the "instrumental role" of freedom is composed of various conditions of human life such as political freedom and social opportunities that contribute for the person's constitutive freedom (see 2.1.1 (c)).

Although Sen's theory of human development brings a comprehensive and normative perspective into the classical concept of development, some applications of Sen's theory remedy the defects of his theory. In a statistical sense, the Human Development Index (HDI) seems not to embody his concept appropriately (Esho, 1999); and, in a theoretical sense, some case studies of human development in developing countries create questions about Sen's theory: (1) the lack of an argument for the universality of the theory; (2) the lack of specification of the concept; and (3) the lack of a perspective on international politics (Haq, 2000; Johnson, 2002; Ahsan, 2004; also see 2.1.2). To respond to these questions, Nussbaum (1992, 2000a, 2000b) shows the universality of Sen's capability approach and derives the "central human functional capability" list from his theory (see 2.2.1). Rawls (1999a, 1999b; Kawamoto, 2002) gives an ethical justification for international cooperation for "other peoples living under unfavorable conditions" (Rawls, 1999b, p.37) (see 2.2.2).

As discussed in Chapter one, the need for a comprehensive approach to human development is growing these days, and Sen's theory has worked as a guiding principle. For example, UNDP began to publish an annual *Human Development Report* since 1990 in order to derive from Sen's human development theory a specific theme of each year.[40] Human development theory, thus, has effected many major international organizations, and more and more practitioners and researchers all over the world have become interested in the human development approach. The comprehensiveness and complexity of human life in international cooperation, seems to require us to overcome theoretical and practical dichotomies.

Theoretically, the dichotomy between universality and particularity needs to be overcome. International cooperation in this global era has contradictory characteristics. On the one hand, it requires us to have a global standard as seen in *Universal Declaration of Human Rights* in 1948; on the other hand, it expects us to respect diversity in the world as seen in multiculturalism (cf. Banks, 2004; Grant & Lei, 2001). It seems unconstructive to argue about which is right. Rather, what we need is a theoretical framework that makes possible the coexistence of these two concepts of universality and particularity in international cooperation in our global age (I will call it "global cooperation" in the next chapter). I will claim that universality and particularity can coexist in global cooperation under Kantian liberalism in Chapter three.

Practically, the dichotomy between economic development and social development needs to be overcome. As Sen and other researchers today insist, the issue of development is highly interdisciplinary and comprehensive. The belief that economic development would lead social development automatically has now turned out to be an empty myth (see 1.1). Instead, a new belief in human development, which offers a comprehensive perspective encompassing human well-being and freedom, has begun to spread. It seems easy to accept this new belief, indeed it seems difficult to deny such highly normative claim. However, accepting and affirming this claim is a different question from specifying and realizing it in practice. I will render human development theory more specific by using Nussbaum's list of human capabilities. In particular, I will argue that basic education is an imperative need in human development policy.

Finally, it is necessary to consider the methodological possibility to realize the ideas and claims above. I will propose a conceptual model of human development in the next chapter and test it empirically in Chapters five and six.

Notes

[1] Sen's complete bibliography is available at the website of the Human Development and Capability Association (http://www.hd-ca.org/).

[2] Sen (1981) also points out the market violence under the famines: "Market demands are not reflections of biological needs or psychological desires, but choices based

Ch.2 The need for "human development": Beyond a classical meaning of development   65

on exchange entitlement relations. If one doesn't have much to exchange, one can't demand very much, and may thus lose out in competition with others whose needs may be a good deal less acute, but whose entitlements are stronger" (p.161), noting that in the 1840s the Irish government did not stop exporting wheat to foreign countries when the country was in the great famine, which killed one-fifth of the total population (p.39).

[3] Sen (1981) says "in the famine period, the worst affected groups seem to have been fishermen, transport workers, paddy huskers, agricultural laborers, those in 'other productive occupations,' craftsmen, and non-agricultural laborers, in that order" (pp.71-72). Also, it should be noted that the occupations are deeply tied to the rank of the caste in India. In addition to the Bengal case, the similar situation is observed in an Ethiopian famine, where nomadic groups are mostly affected: "they [nomadic groups in Ethiopia] were affected not merely by the drought but also by the growth of commercial agriculture, displacing some of these communities from their traditional dry-weather grazing land" (p.112).

[4] Setting the standards of the rice price and the daily wage be 100 in 1941, the rice price index in 1944 is 257 (2.57 times more than the price in 1941) and the wage index in 1944 is 168 (1.68 times more than the price in 1941). Therefore, the exchange ratio index between rice and daily wage, which is also assumed to be 100 in 1941, becomes 65 (0.65 times more or 35 percent less than the standard in 1941). Table 6.3 in Sen (1981, p.64) also shows a similar kind of analysis about the exchange ratio between agricultural wage and food grains price, where the exchange ratio drops in 1943 to 34 percent of the standard in 1940.

[5] Sen (1981) says "... the focus on entitlement has the effect of emphasizing legal rights. Other relevant factors, for example market forces, can be seen as operating through a system of legal relations (ownership rights, contractual obligations, legal exchanges, etc.)" (pp.165-166).

[6] Sen (1981) covers the cases of the Sahel region, Ethiopia, Bangladesh, and to some extent China and Ireland as well as India.

[7] Sen tries to bring an ethical perspective into economics in his work "On economics and ethics" (1987).

[8] Mine (1999) also says "As long as absolute poverty exists ... it is a critically important issue to improve the quality of public policy by learning from past failures and successes and from the failure and success of other countries... Sen seems to believe that it is necessary to pay special attention to the quality of public policy" due to his personal experience in India (p.199-200, translated by the author).

[9] Sen (2002b) says "... the effect of 'other-regarding' concerns on one's well-being has to operate through some feature of the person's own being. Doing good may make a person contented or fulfilled and these are functioning achievements of importance"

(p.36).

[10] This mathematical meaning is that "xi is a part of Xi." Sen (1999b) defines Xi as "entitlements" since Xi is a bundle of possible commodities (p.9; also see the definition of "entitlement" in 2.1.1 (a)). One has to have entitlement to the commodity, which should be legally owned by the person i, and which should be able to be freely commanded by the person i. This assumption is significant when thinking about a kind of society, where a specific sort of social subgroup is not allowed to have entitlements even to the available commodities.

[11] It is not necessarily linear because it can be quadratic, cubic, and so on, depending on individuals' inherent characteristics; in this example, those who inherently have more muscle may be able to draw on more characteristics of the bicycle than others. Also, the function $c(xi)$ may be unable to draw its characteristics from the bicycle if the person i has a physical handicap. The $c(*)$ function determines an *actual* characteristic of the commodity enjoyed by each individual.

[12] Even if the person i has an entitlement to the bicycle, and even if the physical condition of the person allows him or her to ride a bicycle, it does not mean that the person i can produce his or her utility from it. In this example of commuting to school by the bicycle, $fi(c(xi))$ may produce zero utility if the person i is an Indian girl and her family does not allow her to go to school because of her gender or because of their restricted income. Also, $fi(*)$ reflects one pattern of possible uses; for example, riding a bicycle can produce the utility of traveling, not only commuting.

[13] Even if the person i can receive utility from the bicycle, it does not always bring happiness to him or her. A girl may be uncomfortable or ashamed of commuting to school by riding a too boyishly designed bicycle, and she might think even walking to school would be better. Sen (1999b) insists on the significance of human dignity by saying "the ability to live a life without being ashamed of one's clothing, etc. is another that has been seen as important, going back at least to Adam Smith and Karl Marx" (p.31).

[14] Sen (1999b) emphasizes this differentiation and disagrees with identifying the evaluation of personal happiness with the evaluation of one's life as a whole, because happiness is a too subjective measure and because it can overlook unfairness in such case as that "a person who is ill-fed, undernourished, unsheltered and ill can still be high up in the scale of happiness or desire-fulfillment if he or she has learned to have 'realistic' desires and to take pleasure in small mercies" (p.14). It suggests that dependence only on a subjective measure of happiness may leave people in absolute poverty as long as they feel "happy" with their highly limited functions: "a poor, undernourished person, brought up in penury, may have learned to come to terms with a half-empty stomach, seizing joy in small comforts and desiring no more than what seems 'realistic' " (p.20). This kind of situation can be assumed, for example, in an Indian traditional society, where the caste hier-

Ch.2 The need for "human development": Beyond a classical meaning of development   67

archy is too strong for lower caste people to imagine the possibility to get out from their inherent caste.

[15] This shows the aggregation of all possible functionings that the person i can realize with the commodity xi; therefore, Pi(xi) tells all *possibilities* of the functions of the person i. For example, this possibility of the person i may be larger than that of the person k due to their individual physical, psychological, and social differences, which may affect c(*), fi(*), and hi(*), hence, bi and ui eventually.

[16] The definition of bi in Qi(xi) is the same as that in Pi(xi), but Qi(xi) takes the issue of entitlement into consideration; therefore, Qi(xi) reflects the *actual* freedom of the person i by considering both possible choices of fi(*) and xi.

[17] Sen (1992) also describe the differences of the capability set and the functionings by saying "a functioning combination is a *point* in such a space, whereas capability is a *set* of such points... the capability set contains *inter alia* information about the actual functioning combination chosen, since it too is obviously among the feasible combinations" (p.50). This description makes sense if one remembers that the definitions of c(*), fi(*), hi(*), bi, and ui are all vectors in the n-dimensional space.

[18] Sen (1992) also insists the importance of freedom by saying "I have discussed the scope of the idea of freedom at some length here partly because freedom is one of the most powerful social ideas, and its relevance to the analysis of equality and justice is far-reaching and strong" (p.69).

[19] Sen (1992) also adds "Depending on the context, the agency aspect or the well-being aspect might achieve prominence. It would be a mistake to expect that one of these aspects would be uniformly more relevant than the other" (p.71).

[20] Sen (1992) gives some examples such as: "Consider a doctor who is ready to sacrifice her own well-being to go and work in some terribly poor and miserable country, but is prevented from doing that because of a lack of means and opportunity to go to that faraway land. Consider next a rise in her income... and in this new economic situation she has both more well-being freedom... and more agency freedom... If she chooses the latter, it is quite possible that she would have less well-being achievement" (pp.61-62). In this case, she can exercise her freedom (agency freedom), and she may be happy about her choice (high utility), but the circumstances in the poor country may threaten her life, or prevent her from achieving her best function as a doctor due to limited medical commodities.

[21] Sen (1992) calls trivial choices, which are not very valuable for the person, "disadvantageous choices" because these choices may waste one's time and energy in making a choice. With this kind of "disadvantageous choice," people might think fewer choices would be better.

[22] I express "substantive freedom" in the sense that this freedom is not for "disadvan-

tageous choices."

[23] Remembering that the crucial issues in many developing countries such as debt default and bad governance are related to political economic transparency, and remembering that these issues have a huge negative impact on the freedom of the people in these countries, it is understandable that Sen counts transparency guarantees as one of five types of instrumental freedoms.

[24] Sen (1997b) also differentiates his human capability approach from human capital theory by saying that "The former [human capital theory] concentrates on the agency of human beings - through skill and knowledge as well as effort - in augmenting production possibilities. The latter [human capability approach] focuses on the ability of human beings to lead lives they have reason to value and to enhance the substantive choices they have" (p.1959).

[25] Haq motivated Sen to create the Human Development Index as an alternative to dominant economic indices (Sen, 1999c).

[26] HDI is a composite indicator of three different composite and non-composite indices: Life Expectancy at Birth (LEB: non-composite), Overall Education Level (EDN: composite), and Purchasing Power Parity Gross Domestic Product per-capita (GDP). The expression "fixed maximum and minimum indicator values" in Panigrahi and Sivramkrishna's analysis comes from the definition of indices used to compose HDI, such as:

$$Lj = \frac{LEBj - LEB_{min}}{LEB_{max} - LEB_{min}}$$

where Lj is the condition of life expectancy in a country j, and where $LEBmax$ and $LEBmin$ are set at 85 years and 25 years respectively. The same idea is applied to EDN and GDP.

The authors found that the fixed maximum and minimum values (85 and 25, in the example above) is inconsistent in the HDI rankings; in other words, if these values are changed arbitrarily, the rankings are also arbitrarily changed. In this sense, by using adjustment terms, AHDI is more robust than HDI. See details of the definition of adjustment terms in Panigrahi and Sivramkrishna (2002).

[27] By *Aristotelian* essentialism, Nussbaum (1992) means "internalist essentialism," not "metaphysical essentialism." We empirically know that some properties (ex. the ability to think) are more indispensable than others (ex. income) to live as human beings. Since we already know this fact empirically and historically, we do not need to presuppose an external metaphysical foundation. Nussbaum (1992) defines this kind of "historically grounded empirical essentialism" as "internalist essentialism" (p.208); in other words, she avoids metaphysical assumptions.

[28] Nussbaum (2000a) also proposes a Kantian assumption about human beings: "each

Ch.2 The need for "human development": Beyond a classical meaning of development   69

person is valuable and worthy of respect as an end, we must conclude that we should look not just to the total or the average [as utilitarian does], but to the functioning of each and every person [in Sen's sense]. We may call this the *principle of each person as end*" (p.56). Also, considered in conjunction with Sen's concept of human capability, she says that "we may thus rephrase our *principle of each person as end*, articulating it as a *principle of each person's capability*... the ultimate political goal is always the promotion of the capabilities of each person" (p.74).

[29] Nussbaum (1992) says that "if all cannot be brought across the threshold, to this extent the ends of public policy have not been met" (p.232).

[30] Nussbaum (2000a) exemplifies that "Citizens of repressive nondemocratic regimes have the internal but not the combined capability to exercise thought and speech in accordance with their consciences" (p.85). In this example, she shows only the freedom of speech (internal capability) is not enough for political participation.

[31] As already discussed, even the basic needs approach is justified by its contribution to economic growth (see 1.1).

[32] According to Rawls (1999b), "well-ordered peoples" include liberal peoples and decent peoples (p.4, p.63): liberal peoples are those who respect the principles of justice and reasonable pluralism (pp.17-19); and decent peoples are those who are nonliberal but who respect human rights and a reasonable and just law (p.59, p.64). "Burdened societies" are defined as societies which "lack the political and cultural traditions, the human capital and know-how, and often, the material and technological resources needed to be well-ordered" (p.106).

[33] Rawls (1999b) has "used the term 'peoples' and not 'states' " (p.4). He explains his reason by saying that "The term 'peoples,' then, is meant to emphasize these singular features of peoples as distinct from states, as traditionally conceived, and to highlight their moral character and the reasonably just, or decent, nature of their regimes" (p.27). By defining them in this way, he seems to focus more on the organic nature of human morality, which should grow in each human society (cf. "reasonable pluralism"), rather than the inorganic mechanism of states. However, it does not mean that he ignores the role of states, but that he differentiates the character of peoples from that of states (pp.23-30: *Why peoples and not states?*).

[34] Rawls (1999b) calls such an ideal-based approach "a realistic utopian": "Political philosophy is realistically utopian when it extends what are ordinarily thought of as the limits of practical political possibility. Our hope for the future of our society rests on the belief that the nature of the social world allows reasonably just constitutional democratic societies existing as members of the Society of Peoples" (p.6).

[35] The Law of Peoples was written as "an extension of a liberal conception of justice" based on his prior work, *A Theory of Justice* (1999a; also see Kawamoto, 2002); therefore,

the principles of the Law of Peoples largely depend on his principles of justice in *A Theory of Justice*.

[36] Reasonable pluralism is a value of liberal societies but not necessarily of other decent societies. Liberal societies accept the Society of Peoples in part because it reflects reasonable pluralism. However, liberal societies do not force other decent societies to accept the value of reasonable pluralism. Therefore, these other decent societies may accept the Society of Peoples for other reasons.

[37] The "well-ordered people" is an ideal people in the Society of People that Rawls supposes; while the "decent people" is not exactly ideal but they respect human rights and a reasonable and just law (p.59, p.64). Also see Footnote 64.

[38] Rawls (1999b) sees the concept of reasonable pluralism will bring greater justice into the society: "the existence of reasonable pluralism allows a society of greater political justice and liberty" (p.12).

[39] Rawls discusses the question of education for next generations in *A Theory of Justice* (1999a), but not in *The Law of Peoples* (1999b).

[40] For example, the theme of 2003 is "millennium development goals: a compact among nations to end human poverty"; that of 2004 is "cultural liberty in today's diverse world"; and that of 2005 is "international cooperation at a crossroads: aid, trade and security in an unequal world." (UNDP, 2003, 2004, 2005).

A modified human development theory in the global era: Two claims

Chapter 3

Based on previous chapters, I will make two claims of a modified human development theory in this chapter. The first claim is that *a universal value of human development can be consistent with cultural diversity and social particularity* (3.1) and the second claims is that *the right to basic education is a central instrumental freedom necessary to promote human capabilities for one's constitutive freedom* (3.2).

For the first claim, I will argue that Kantian liberalism, one kind of liberalism that assumes a priori human morality, will make possible the coexistence of both a universal consensus about human development and cultural particularity in this global age. This claim will turn "international development" for national development into "global cooperation" for human development. The argument for the first claim will propose a theoretical framework for considering the issue of global cooperation for the "constitutive freedom" of individual human beings (Sen, 2000; also see 2.1.1 (c)).

In order to give a practical direction to the theoretical framework of human development, a modified human development theory will pay a special attention to the function of basic education as an instrument to realize one's constitutive freedom. Therefore, the second claim focuses more on education for human development: *the right to basic education is a central instrumental freedom necessary to promote human capabilities for one's constitutive freedom* (3.2). I will reexamine the central human capability list introduced in 2.2.1 and argue that basic education is a central instrumental freedom. The argument for the second claim will clarify the role of basic education in human development in a specific way: basic education as compulsory primary school education. I will develop this idea of human capability, with a special focus on children's literacy development, into an empirical model of human development. Unlike the Human Development Index introduced in 2.1.2, it is a model, not an index, which means that it yields not a single statistical value but a conceptual relationship among indices for each individual society. This model will be examined empirically in Chapter five.

3.1 Claim one: A universal value of human development is consistent with cultural diversity and social particularity under Kantian liberalism

Before arguing for basic education as an instrumental freedom and modeling the concept of human development in 3.2, a theoretical framework of human development will be considered in this section. As discussed at the end of the last chapter (see 2.3), international development in this global era contains both universal and particular aspects; in other words, both universal consensus and social particularity need to be respected. What kind of theoretical framework makes possible the coexistence of these two concepts of universality and particularity in international development (or "global cooperation" as claimed later) in our global era?

Under the phenomena called globalization, there are more opportunities and even necessity for seeking a world-wide consensus [1]; at the same time, more and more people recognize the significance of protecting social particularity against unitary universal values (cf. multiculturalism in Banks, 2004; Grant & Lei, 2001). I explained, in Chapter one, how modernization theory had justified a single universal value of economic development (see 1.1) and how dependency theory had resisted it (see 1.2.1). I also introduced Huntington's (1997) perspective to distinguish modernization from westernization, and explained his claim that the cultural indigenous power of "the people of that society" (p.76) can promote modernization *without* westernization (see 1.2.2). In this section, first of all, I will reconsider Huntington's claim by taking Sen's perspective into consideration to defend development as social change driven by "the people of that society" with respect to their social particularity (3.1.1). Second, I will claim a universal value for human development, namely, the constitutive freedom of human beings, by reconsidering Sen's and Nussbaum's claims about the human capability approach (3.1.2). Third, I will propose Kantian liberalism as a possible theoretical framework for integrating these two seemingly contradictory concepts, universality and particularity, within a conception of human development (3.1.3). Finally, I will propose a modified human development theory as a guiding principle of *global* cooperation, rather than *international* development (3.1.4).

3.1.1 Development as social change driven by social particularity

Is the concept of "development" as a universal value in conflict with social particularity? Roberts (1981) and Kitajima (1997) argue that western modern values have caused the destruction of indigenous cultures in non-western societies. Cummings (1986) also criticizes the theory of developmental strategies in 1960s and 1970s, which gave "a lower-priority ranking" (p.19) to African traditional agriculture. July (1983) insists on the independence of African culture from the west, and Sherman (1990) expects African universities to resolve a conflict between "the traditional African environment and the modern Western sector" (p.384) in African society. These perspectives criticize the concept of development as modernization/westernization (see 1.2.2).

However, in doing so, these critics seem to assume that modernization is equivalent to westernization. As noted in Chapter one, Huntington (1997) insists that westernization can be differentiated from modernization. Rather, he claims that the indigenous cultural power of the people may revive and cultivate their own culture by taking advantage of modernization (see 1.2.2). Sen (2000) also says:

> While there is some danger in ignoring uniqueness of cultures, there is also the possibility of being deceived by the presumption of ubiquitous insularity. It is indeed possible to argue that there are more interrelations and more cross-cultural influences in the world than is typically acknowledged by those alarmed by the prospect of cultural subversion. The culturally fearful often take a very fragile view of each culture and tend to underestimate our ability to learn from elsewhere without being overwhelmed by that experience. (pp.242-243)

As Huntington shows in his model of cultural revival in the process of modernization, Sen also believes in the potential of indigenous culture to learn from others without being overwhelmed. From this standpoint, Sen does not oppose modernization of the society, saying that "industrialization or technological progress or social modernization can substantially contribute to expanding human freedom" (Sen, 2000, p.3). In Sen's view, the problem of cultural subversion that often accompanies modernization is not caused by development itself but by giving too much priority to a certain interpretation of development.

Social change itself is a substantive and inevitable part of the dynamics of human history. The difference between social change as historical dynamics and that as cultural subversion arises from ignoring the people's *choices* within a fair decision-making process. Social change can be stimulated externally. For example, the phenomenon today called globalization has promoted external stimulation around all over the world. If a society can *choose* by itself to accept, accept only partially, or reject the external stimulation, the choice would trigger a society's own social change. In Huntington's classification (1997; also see 1.2.2), *Rejectionism, Kemalism,* and *Reformism* are different types of results of choices that each society may make; however, when the society has no choice, as exemplified in the African colonial era, cultural subversion or a "painful process of cultural Westernization" occurs (Huntington, 1997, p.75; also see 1.2.2).

Recalling Huntington's model (see Figure 1.1 in 1.2.2), a society could be affected by both westernization and modernization in an early phase of social change (the first half of the bell curve A-E in Figure 1.1). This means that although a society has had social change imposed by a relatively stronger external power, the society can revive itself in a later phase of social change (the latter half of the bell curve A-E in Figure 1.1). As Sen (2000) articulates above, moreover, we might sometimes unnecessarily underestimate the ability of the people of the society "to learn from elsewhere without being overwhelmed by that experience" (pp.242-243).

These claims of Huntington and Sen may seem too optimistic since there is indeed an unbalanced structure of political, economic, and social power working in favor of so-called developed nations in the world. Therefore, I would not claim that indigenous cultures are *always* strong enough to revive themselves. Instead, I would claim that cultures can revive themselves under a condition of a fair decision-making process. This condition includes two parts:

1. *Political condition*: The society has a democratic decision-making system.
2. *Educational condition*: The people of the society enjoy basic education that enables them to participate in the decision-making process.

These conditions may be contrary to some societies' cultures. However, as Rawls (1999b) limits his argument about the eight principles of the Law of Peoples to the *political* sphere, I would also limit these conditions only to the political sphere of the society. Although it may be inevitable for these conditions to influence the culture of that society, they need not drastically change the whole culture as long as their role is limited to the political sphere.

Moreover, the purpose of setting these two conditions is not to change the culture of a society but to protect its original culture and to help the society to develop its culture in its own way.

Regarding the first condition, the democratic regime of the society will help the society develop its cultural particularity in utilizing external influences; at the same time, it will help the society resist inimical external forces. A "democratic regime" here does not always mean a complete democracy, where *only* the result of the deliberation dictates a final decision, but it can include a semi-democracy, in which the central decision-makers can make the final decision by taking deliberative outcomes into serious consideration.

When the society is subject to an external influence, a democratic society could launch the deliberation process to decide whether to accept, reject, or modify it. In case that the deliberation reaches a consensus of accepting it, the people of that society will make an effort to digest it in their own way; eventually, the change caused by the acceptance will become a part of the indigenous culture because it is their own choice. The democratic principle of participation brings a sense of ownership in the decision to each participant, and this sense of ownership stimulates self-respect, which becomes a seed of cultural revival. Huntington (1997) says that reestablishing cultural confidence in the second phase of the bell curve (see Figure 1.1 in 1.2.2) leads to cultural revival. This claim implies the significance of developing self-respect for cultural revival when facing external influences, and democratic deliberation promotes self-respect through the ownership of participation.

In the case where the deliberation reaches a consensus to reject an external influence, this decision will preserve the society's original culture. The process of deliberation provides an opportunity for participants to reevaluate their culture. In a semi-democratic society, the decision-makers may choose a result that conflicts with the deliberative outcome. Even if it is the case, having a democratic deliberation system is important because at least the people have been consulted in the decision-making process. By consulting with the people, decision-makers are in a position to reconsider their decision if, for example, they encounter difficulties in attempting to implement a decision that is contrary to the deliberative consensus. It is critically important for the society to retain the possibility of reconsidering a social decision, even though complete democracy may be inconsistent with the political traditions of some societies.

As Sen (2000) insists above, the society has the ability to learn something new from the outside and to digest it in its own way without being overwhelmed by that experience. However, Sen's claim is true only when decision-makers listen to various voices of the people of that society because it is the people who actually learn, digest, and create culture and tradition in the society. Therefore, ignoring the voice of the people leads directly to cultural subversion and cultural submission to external influences. In other words, a democratic decision-making system is a necessary condition for developing and protecting cultural particularity by utilizing or resisting external stimulation.

The second condition is naturally implied by the first condition. In order for the people to participate in a democratic decision-making procedure, the people have to know what they want and how to understand others. The latter, how to understand others, is especially important to reach a consensus in a diverse society, and hence to sustain the democratic decision-making procedure among the people who have different values. How to understand others is also important in order for there to be a widespread sense of participation in deliberation: when the people feel that they do not understand others' opinions, their sense of participation may diminish. On the other hand, when the people feel that they understand others very well, their sense of participation would increase, and a deep sense of participation motivates people to develop or protect their own culture/society.

The more information that becomes available today from all over the world, the greater variety of options people may have. Social complexity will require better understanding of others in the decision-making process. In other words, less understanding will weaken both possibilities to develop social particularity and to resist external power because these possibilities are motivated by a sense of participation. For this reason, for better understanding of others, basic education becomes more important since it can equip children, the future participants in deliberation, with tools to understand others, such as literacy. I will discuss this issue of basic education more in detail in 3.2 later.

Particularly in our global era, societies are inevitably affected by each other. People inevitably need to understand and respect the differences among societies. As noted in 2.2, Nussbaum (2000a; also see 2.2.1) proposes the concept of "multiple realizability" and Rawls (1999b; also see 2.2.2) introduces the concept of "reasonable pluralism." As these concepts imply, an external stimulation for social change can be realized in different ways that reflect the uniqueness of societies. Development as social change can be promoted by the people's choice as influenced by their cultural particularity.

3.1.2 Human development for constitutive freedom as a universal value

Although development can and should be realized in unique ways, I also claim that human development is a *universal* value. As discussed in 2.2.1, Nussbaum (1992) defends the universal value of Sen's human capability theory from an Aristotelian viewpoint. As an Aristotelian essentialist, she accepts "others as human across divisions of time and place" (Nussbaum, 1992, p.215) and proposes the items in the central human capability list (see 2.2.1 and Appendix A) as necessary conditions for all human beings to live as humans. This perspective on human beings insists on the universal value of human development as represented by the central human capability list.

When central human capabilities are a necessary condition or a universal value for all human beings, would this alter Sen's concept of human development for substantive freedom? Remembering Sen's argument in 2.1.1, he differentiates instrumental freedom from constitutive freedom and explains that instrumental freedoms "tend to contribute to the general capability of a person to live more freely, but they also serve to complement one another" (Sen, 2000, p.38). By taking Nussbaum's interpretation of human capability into consideration (see 2.2.1), the relationship among the concepts of constitutive freedom, instrumental freedom, and central human capabilities can be interpreted as follows.

Constitutive freedom is the ultimate purpose of development, and instrumental freedoms contribute to this purpose. Instrumental freedoms have at least five aspects according to Sen (2000) – *political freedoms, economic freedoms* (cf. "economic entitlement" in 2.1.1 (a)), *social opportunities, transparency guarantees,* and *protective security* as introduced in 2.1.1 (c). Instrumental freedoms can be realized in different ways: for example, a national health insurance system may be considered as a social opportunity in one society (e.g. in a socialist society), but not in another society (e.g. in a liberal society). Therefore, it seems to be impossible to define a universal form of instrumental freedoms. Rather, this is a question of social particularity.

However, instrumental freedoms include the idea of human capability. According to Nussbaum (1992, 2000a), human capabilities are universal values, and according to Sen (2000), instrumental freedoms and human capabilities complement each other. This could be interpreted to mean that the central human capabilities include the most fundamental part of instrumental freedoms, which are universally necessary conditions for all human beings to live as humans regardless of the cultural particularity of the society. On this interpretation, the central human capabilities are the basis of instrumental freedoms and therefore the foundation of constitutive freedom. The details will be explained and visualized in Figure 3.3 later in 3.2.

Is it possible to define constitutive freedom as a universal value? It might be impossible to propose a universal realization of constitutive freedom because "only an individual can know what a valuable choice is for him or her, not anyone else," as discussed in 2.1.1 (c). However, I would insist on the existence of *a universal priority order*: constitutive freedom should universally have the first priority no matter how it is embodied. In other words, constitutive freedom as an ultimate goal of development is universally prioritized over other goals. I would justify this claim as follows: if we recognize human life as "consisting of a set of interrelated 'functionings,' consisting of beings and doings" (Sen, 1992, p.39; also see 2.1.1 (b)), and if functionings are a set of actually realizable choices (Sen, 1999b; also see 2.1.1 (b)),[2] then a richer life means a more realistically *choosable* life. Expanding constitutive freedom through instrumental freedoms, which include central human capabilities as their basis, will expand the possibility for each individual to realize the life he or she chooses to live.[3] Choice of life is a basis of human dignity. Therefore, human development to expand constitutive freedom is a universal value or a universal priority of development.

3.1.3 Theoretical framework for a modified human development theory

I made two claims about development above: development can be driven by cultural particularity (3.1.1) and development that provides the conditions of constitutive freedom is a universal value (3.1.2). How is it possible to integrate these seemingly contradictory concepts? What kind of theoretical framework can synthesize them? I propose Kantian liberalism as a theoretical framework to answer these questions.

(a) Overview: Liberalism, democracy, and communitarianism

Before discussing why Kantian liberalism can become an appropriate framework for human development theory, I will review three major standpoints of political philosophy: liberalism, democracy, and communitarianism. Bull et al (1992) introduce these three standpoints and examine how each political stance works to resolve educational conflicts. Through these case studies, they analyze the characteristics of each political standpoint.

The characteristics of liberalism can be described by such key words as personal liberty, neutrality, fair outcomes, and equal opportunity. A liberal society makes a decision by following a priority order which assumes that personal liberty to realize each person's own conception of the good life is most important. Therefore, conflicts in a liberal society are solved by following this priority. For example, a conflict between two persons is solved by giving advantage to the one whose liberty is at risk since personal liberty has the highest priority in a liberal society (Bull et al, 1992, Ch.2).

On the other hand, the characteristics of democracy can be described by such key words as fair procedure, individual opinions, and the right to participate. While liberalism articulates a priority of values, democratic theory does not. Instead, democratic theory respects the fair deliberative procedure of decision-making, and the fair procedure in a democratic society is assured by the principles of non-discrimination and non-repression. A democratic society would accept any outcome of deliberation as long as the procedure is fair to all. Thus, in a democratic society, fair procedure is the only criterion of decision-making since there is no independent priority of values to be followed. Therefore, a conflict in a democratic society is solved by following the result of fair deliberation (Bull et al, 1992, Ch.3).

Finally, the characteristics of communitarianism can be described by such key words as association, culture, history, and tradition. While both liberal and democratic societies consider the role of reason in decision-making, a communitarian society considers the community's network of relationships based on its culture, history, and tradition, rather than reason. For example, in a liberal society, an individual has to use his or her reason to define his or her own conception of good life and in a democratic society, reason guides deliberation. However, in a communitarian society, an individual is expected to maintain the existing tradition. A communitarian decision is justified by its consistency with the culture, history, and tradition of the society, or with the social morality legitimated by the tradition and the people of the society. Therefore, a conflict in a communitarian society is resolved by following the obligation to maintain the community tradition, or by following the morality created by the community tradition (Bull et al, 1992, Ch.4).

(b) Why liberalism in international development in the global era?

In light of the previous discussion, one of the most important features of international development is plurality and diversity. Therefore, the theoretical framework of international development needs to be consistent with pluralism. In terms of the tolerance of others implied in pluralism, liberalism can be the most advantageous of all three political stances because of its clear priority order and its emphasis on toleration of diversity. I will begin this discussion from a liberal standpoint; however, I have to emphasize that I do not completely agree with liberal theories, and I will explain this in more detail below in 3.1.3 (c). Nonetheless, in this section, I will examine the problems of democratic and communitarian theories in the context of international development.

First, why cannot democracy be consistent with human development theory? The problem of democratic theory is its emphasis on deliberative procedure without any priority of values to be achieved. Even though fair deliberation can be an ideal *political device* to reach a consensus, it is difficult to consider it as an independent *theoretical framework* for human development because human development theory proposes constitutive freedom as an absolute value of human life (see 2.1.1 (c) & (d) and 3.2.1 (a) later). Although democratic deliberation is critically important as a *political device* for social development to prepare a social foundation of human development as claimed in 3.1.1, it is difficult to consider democracy as a *theoretical framework* all by itself. The problem of democratic theory is that it cannot endorse the universal value of constitutive freedom. Especially in the context of international development, it is necessary to share a certain kind of universal value as a criterion of political morality, since power politics indeed exist among nations and since our global society today increases the possibility of conflict because of increasing diversity. Following a democratic theory without a universal criterion of political morality could result in powerful nations coercing other nations. Having a moral criterion is one of the ways to compensate for such reality of the world. Therefore, the theoretical framework of human development needs to embrace a universal value, namely constitutive freedom.

Second, why cannot communitarianism be consistent with human development theory? The problem of communitarianism is its emphasis on cultural tradition. Since a communitarian society respects the cultural tradition of the community, it requires the concept of "bare community," which is "a network of traditions that unite a group of individuals" (Bull et al, 1992, p.84). "Bare community" tries to constitute an individual as a member of the community and to tie the members to one another by a shared cultural tradition. This communitarian system aims at maintaining the cultural tradition of the society rather than developing the individuals' constitutive freedom. Moreover, it prioritizes cultural tradition over constitutive freedom. In addition, the more diverse the society becomes, the more difficult it would become to unify a group of people culturally. At this point, a communitarian theory would be the least tolerant of pluralism, which is a fundamental standpoint when thinking of international development. These limits of communitarianism are problematic when applying communitarian theories to human development theory since human development theory posits constitutive freedom as the highest priority and takes pluralism as its standpoint.

(c) Kantian liberalism as a theoretical framework of human development

Now I will examine the limitations of liberalism as an ideal theoretical framework of human development. Two problems of liberalism will be considered here: (1) the needs for the Kantian priority order; and (2) the needs for democratic procedure and communitarian respect of cultural tradition. At the same time, considering these problems will define Kantian liberalism as a theoretical framework appropriate for a modified human development theory.

(1) Needs for the Kantian criterion of morality

I claimed above the importance of a priority order as a criterion of political morality in international development, but what kind of order is appropriate for human development theory? Classical liberalism proposes the priority of personal liberty, but this priority allows an individual to consider others as an instrument for realizing his or her own good as long as the individual does not violate others' liberty. This standpoint is known as classical utilitarian liberalism. However, Nussbaum (1999b) notes [4]:

> There is danger in speaking so generally about "liberalism"... "Liberalism" is not a single position but a family of positions; Kantian liberalism is profoundly different from classical Utilitarian liberalism... Many critiques of liberalism are really critiques of economic Utilitarianism, and would not hold against the views of Kant or Mill. (p.57)

Three main thinkers on whom I rely on in this study - Sen, Nussbaum, and Rawls - identify themselves as Kantians, and Kantian philosophy underlies their theories. Kantian philosophy requires that others be treated as ends, not merely as means (cf. Kant, 1997, p.46 & 53; 2002, p.103 & 120; Ishikawa, 1995, p.165). Thus, it claims to consider the existence of other human beings as valuable in themselves.[5] In Kantian morality (cf. Kant, 1997, p.53 & 54; 2002, p.42 & 120 & 122; Ishikawa, 1995, p.163 & 164; also see Footnote 77), a *right* choice reflects a human's *autonomous will*,[6] even if it reduces an individual's utility. Kantian morality considers the individual truly autonomous only when he or she makes the right choice following a universal moral principle (the categorical imperative); otherwise his or her choice is controlled by other teleological concerns (hypothetical imperatives).[7] Under Kantian liberalism, a modified human development theory is activated as a universal moral principle.

Sen's concept of human capability and Nussbaum's central human capability list are consistent with Kantian philosophy because they challenge economic utilitarianism, which considers human capital to be a tool of economic development (see 2.1.1 (d)).[8] I will reexamine Nussbaum's list of central human capabilities in 3.2.2 to specify a theoretical model of human development, and I claim here that Sen's concept and Nussbaum's list of human capabilities work as a priori criteria of a Kantian political morality of international development.[9]

(2) Needs for democratic procedure and communitarian respect for cultural tradition

Other limitations of liberalism are its lack of mechanism to modify social decisions and its lack of attention to cultural tradition. Regarding the former limitation, Bull et al (1992) point out that "the liberal approach to decision making provides no mechanism for changing a decision once it has been taken" (p.46). However, a modified human development theory requires a democratic decision-making system (see 3.1.1), and the important function of democracy as a *political device* is already confirmed in 3.1.3 (b). In addition, current liberals mention the right to participate in the decision-making process as political liberty, not as personal liberty. For example, Rawls (1999b) recalls "the fact of democratic unity in diversity" and "the fact of liberal democratic peace" (pp.124-125); Nussbaum (2000a) includes "political control over one's environment" in her central human capability list (p.80). They consider the right to political participation as a political liberty; while classic liberalism has exclusively focused on personal liberty.

Regarding the latter limitation of liberalism, the lack of attention to cultural tradition, Bull et al (1992) assert that "the highly individualized perspective of liberalism fails to capture the social and historical dimensions of ... other citizens' beliefs" (p.46). However, a modified human development theory respects social particularity (see 3.1.1), and social particularity is created by the cultural tradition of the society. Therefore, the failure to appreciate and tolerate cultural tradition contradict a modified human development theory. Rawls (1999b) and Nussbaum (2000a) solve this contradiction by using the concept of "multiple realizability" and "reasonable pluralism" respectively (see 2.2). Although a modified human development theory does not use cultural tradition as a conclusive criterion of decision-making as communitarianism does, it does not ignore the significance of respecting the cultural tradition of each society.[10]

3.1.4 Conclusion of claim one: From international development to global cooperation under Kantian liberalism

I have described in this section a possible framework of a modified human development theory. Kantian liberalism as a political liberalism with a democratic deliberation system and respect for cultural tradition can be consistent with a modified human development theory, and it renders the universality of the value of human development consistent with cultural diversity and social particularity in the real world. This theoretical framework suggests a new justification for international development.

International development began as financial aid for reconstruction from World War II, and grew as international aid for economic development as explained in Chapter one. Since then, the justification of international development has been understood as national economic growth. This justification has promoted economics-focused indices, such as GDP per capita to measure the level of development, and this focus on national economic development has paid much less attention to the individuals in developing countries. The issue of development has often been understood as an inter*national* matter, rather than as a matter of individual human lives. Such problems as cultural subversion in international development reflect the limitations of this perspective of national economic development.

I introduced Sen's perspective on development in Chapter two to improve - not deny - the classic conception of development and to propose a new perspective beyond the classical meaning of national economic development. After reexamining Sen's human development theory and its defects, I proposed a modified human development theory that shifts the justification of development from the issue of national economics to the issue of human freedom, and from the issue of nations to the issue of peoples.

However, this does not mean that human development theory ignores the economic aspect of development. Sen (2000) himself says "to be *generically against* markets would be almost as odd as being generically against conversations between people... they [the freedom to exchange words, or goods, or gifts] are part of the way human beings in society live and interact with each other" (p.6), and he claims that economic problems need to be solved "not by suppressing the markets, but by allowing them to function better and with greater fairness, and with adequate supplementation" (p.142).[11]

Also, in international relations, it is unrealistic to disregard the function of international development assistance. bi-lateral aid and multi-lateral aid is now indispensable for the national budgets of most developing nations. In addition, as introduced in 2.2.2, Rawls (1999b) says that "well-ordered peoples have a *duty* to assist burdened societies" (p.106). Human development theory recognizes the significant role of international economics and does not deny classical approaches to international development. Rather, it can work as a guiding principle of global cooperation, which is constructed by relationships among peoples, rather than among nations, and which aims at individual human development, not only national economic development.

As already noted, human development theory is getting more and more attention these days, especially after the 1990s. More and more international organizations and donor governments are beginning to consider the idea of human development as the goal of their policies of international assistance, as UNDP has advocated since 1990.[12] Following this trend, "comprehensiveness" (see 1.3) is becoming a key word in developmental strategy today, as seen in Millennium Development Goals in 2000.[13] Beyond national governmental donors, more and more nongovernmental organizations also conduct projects for human development at the grassroots level. Not only in practical contexts, but also in academics, such societies as *the Human Development and Capability Association* have been established[14] and the idea of human development has been spreading across different disciplines.

Since these movements have only a short history, there does not seem to be a well-developed philosophical and theoretical warrant for human development theory. A modified human development theory proposed in this study aims to contribute to improving human development theory as a guiding principle of *global cooperation* beyond international development.

3.2 Claim two: The right to basic education is a central instrumental freedom to promote human capability for one's constitutive freedom

I have been constructing a theoretical framework for a modified human development theory so far. In this section, I will examine the factors that are included in a modified human development theory and how these factors are related to each other under the theoretical framework of human development. In particular, I will focus on the function of an educational factor as a central instrumental freedom, and consider how it advances the ultimate purpose of human development, namely "constitutive freedom" (see 2.1.1). In addition to consideration of human development factors, I will propose a conceptual model of these factors to be examined empirically in Chapter five. Modeling is necessary for a policy purpose because an abstract theory needs to be translated into a specific model for application to the policy context.

In this section, I will represent a modified human development theory proposed in 3.1 as a conceptual model of human development. Simultaneously, this is a preliminary step toward a quantitative analysis in Chapter five. I will reconsider Nussbaum's list of central human capabilities (2000a), paying particular attention to three factors of education, health, and material wealth (3.2.1 (a)), and I also focus on the role and definition of basic education for human development (3.2.1 (b)). Based on these considerations and definitions, I will propose a conceptual model of human development with description of the model characteristics (3.2.2).

3.2.1 Reconsideration of the central human capability list
(a) Three factors of instrumental freedom: education, health, and material wealth

Remembering Nussbaum's (2000a) list of central human functional capabilities (pp.78-80; also see 2.2.1 and Appendix A), she analyzes Sen's concept of human capability into a ten-item list. Nussbaum (2000a) also finds that "some items on the list may seem to us more fixed than others" (p.77) and

Figure 3.1 Hierarchy of human capability

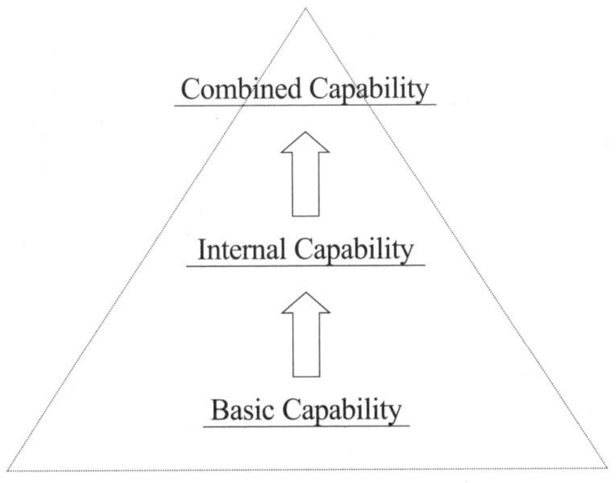

Combined Capability
⇑
Internal Capability
⇑
Basic Capability

(Based on Nussbaum, 2000a, created by the author)

proposes three hierarchal subgroups among the human capability items (see Figure 3.1), which Sen does not mention in his capability approach.

As briefly introduced in 2.2.1, the most fundamental level, the bottom of the hierarchy called *basic capability*, is defined as "the innate equipment of individuals that is the necessary basis for developing the more advanced capabilities, and a ground of moral concern" (Nussbaum, 2000a, p.84). Capability at this level can be called a prerequisite of human development. Nussbaum (2000a) says that "they [basic capabilities] are very rudimentary, and cannot be directly converted into functionings" (p.84). The second level subgroup, called *internal capability*, is defined as the capabilities which are developed "with support from the surrounding environment, as when one learns to play with others, to love, to exercise political choice" (Nussbaum, 2000a, p.84). Capability at this level requires external nurturance. As Nussbaum claims at the basic capability level, a basic capability by itself cannot always be directly converted into functionings. It often needs to be developed through *education* in a broader sense. In Nussbaum's conception, *education* includes *learning, love*, and *exercising political choice*. The third level subgroup, the top of the hierarchy called *combined capability*, is defined as "internal capabilities com-

Figure 3.2 Hierarchy of human capability factors

Combined Capability
achieved by *three Factors*

⇧

Internal Capability
developd by *An Educational Factor*

⇧

Basic Capability
developd by *Health and Material Factors*

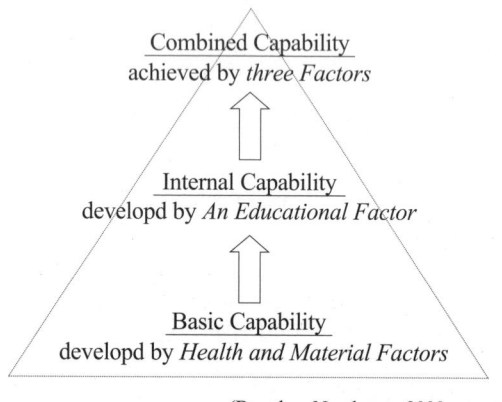

(Based on Nussbaum, 2000a, created by the author)

bined with suitable external conditions for the exercise of the function" (Nussbaum, 2000a, pp.84-85). Capability at this level can be realized through developing individual's internal capabilities as well as receiving environmental supports working in favor of the individual's exercising his or her internal capabilities.

Nussbaum (2000a) states that all the items in her list are *combined capabilities* (p.85). However, when viewing the list analytically, it can be seen that, for example, *bodily health* is more basic than *political control over one's environment*. I would see three fundamental factors in the items: *educational*, *health*, and *material factors*. An educational factor is defined as basic education as I will discuss in the next section, and health and material factors are specified as vital conditions for human life. I would classify the items in Nussbaum's list into three factors as follows (also see Figure 3.2): *life* and *bodily health* are basic capabilities which are developed by a health factor; *material control over one's environment* is also a basic capability which is developed by a material factor. *Senses, imagination, and thought, emotions, practical reason*, and *play* are internal capabilities which are nurtured by an educational factor. The rest of items, *bodily integrity, affiliation, other*

Figure 3.3 Hierarchy of human development

Constitutive Freedom
by Combined capability

Instrumental Freedom
Internal Capability by *An Educational Factor*

Basic Capability by
Health and Material Factors

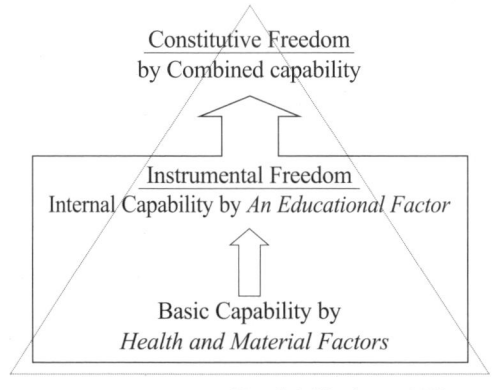

(Based on Nussbaum, 2000a, created by the author)

species, and *political control over one's environment*, are combined capabilities which are achieved by combinations of all three factors and adequate environmental supports. Health and material factors help develop basic capability at the first level of the hierarchy, and an educational factor helps develop internal capability at the second level.

When applying Sen's distinction between instrumental freedom and constitutive freedom to Nussbaum's hierarchy of human capability, it can be said that basic and internal capabilities function as instrumental freedoms to realize constitutive freedom through developing combined capability. In other words, instrumental and constitutive freedoms are realized through human capability development, and human capability is developed by three factors (*education*, *health*, and *material wealth*). Moreover, these three factors should have a universal value since they are abstractions from the items in the human capability list.[15]

These three factors, *education*, *health*, and *material wealth*, are consistent with the definition of Human Development Index (HDI), too (see 2.1.2 for details of HDI). HDI is composed of three indices: overall education level, life expectancy, and GDP. Each of them seems to represent education, health, and economic wealth respectively. I would call the third factor, material wealth, instead of economic wealth, because economic activity cannot always be evaluated in monetary terms. For example, a farm household can be rich enough to support its family members' lives without producing large monetary earnings, while an employment income household, which has no farm or livestock, can have a more difficult life than a self-sufficient farm household. Thus, the material factor should include an economic factor, but also non-economic material wealth as well.

(b) Basic education as a central instrumental freedom

I would claim that an educational factor has a central function among the three factors introduced above; particularly, basic education has a significant role in realizing constitutive freedom. To describe the educational factor, I will use the term *basic* education, rather than *primary* education. This is because primary education seems to be too closely tied to the existing school education system. Primary education implies an "educational ladder" leading toward secondary education and tertiary education: primary education is considered as the first step of the ladder. On the other hand, I interpret the expression basic education as an education encompassing the basis of human life such as literacy. No matter what way of life a person will choose for the future and regardless of what kind of culture to which he or she belongs, basic education is a universal foundation of human life or a fundamental ability to live as a human. Therefore, even though I will claim the importance of primary school education later, I use the term *basic education* in order to avoid confusion with a conventional understanding of primary education.

(1) Purposes of basic education for human development

Before describing a specific content and form of an ideal basic education, two purposes of basic education will be examined. This examination will answer the question: why can basic education be called a *central* instrumental freedom?

First, basic education aims at helping children become democratic citizens. I claimed two conditions of development in 3.1.1, where the second condition says: "the people of the society enjoy basic education that enables them to participate in the decision-making process." Gutmann (1999) proposes the concept of "conscious social reproduction" to explain the importance of education in a democratic society. Conscious social reproduction is "the ways in which citizens are or should be empowered to influence the education that in turn shapes the political values, attitudes, and modes of behavior of future citizens" (p.14). Society is developed through reproduction of values, norms, and cultures over generations, and the intellectual power of citizens is necessary for this dynamic process of social reproduction. It may be unreasonable to force all children to climb the educational ladder toward higher education, but from the viewpoint of "conscious social reproduction," at least basic education can be compulsory for all.

Not only as citizens, but also as members of the society, all children need to develop their ability to understand others. As stated in 3.1.1 and 3.1.3, the more diverse a society becomes, the more the ability to understand others becomes critical because social diversity and complexity require tolerance and understanding for creating consensus in political deliberation. Such ability as literacy can promote other abilities to think reasonably, to search for necessary information, and to understand others' written opinions. These abilities need to be provided to *all* children through basic education as claimed later.

Second, basic education aims at helping children develop advanced human capabilities. As Nussbaum (1992, 2000a) says, basic capability is needed to acquire more advanced human capabilities (2000a, p.84), and all human beings need to be provided with the right education to become capable of the major human functions (1992, p.228). In this sense, basic education as a foundation of human life has a *central* function in developing human capabilities. It is important to have a healthy body and some income, but an individual needs to convert them into capabilities for realizing the life that the individual wants to live, such as becoming an athlete with his or her healthy body or going to secondary school by using his or her income. The ability developed through basic education can help individuals find what is important to realize in their own lives.

(2) A definition of basic education for human development

How can the ideal form of basic education for human development be described? I would define it as *compulsory public primary* education.

First, *compulsory public* education can distribute educational opportunity equally because people can claim governmental support for this opportunity as long as it is compulsory. Equality is important in basic education. Since basic education is a basis of human life, the opportunity to enjoy basic education needs to be considered as a fundamental human right to live as a human. Therefore, this opportunity for basic education needs to be equally guaranteed for all. *The Convention of the Rights of the Child* (UNICEF, 2002) articulates the right of the child to education in Article 28 (underlined by the author):

> 1. States Parties recognize the right of the child to education, and with a view to achieving this right progressively and <u>on the basis of equal opportunity</u>, they shall, in particular:
>
> a. <u>Make primary education compulsory and available free to all</u>; ......
>
> 3. <u>States Parties shall promote and encourage international co-operation in matters relating to education</u>, in particular with a view to contributing to the elimination of ignorance and illiteracy throughout the world and facilitating access to scientific and technical knowledge and modern teaching methods. <u>In this regard, particular account shall be taken of the needs of developing countries.</u>

However, making an educational opportunity available to all children does not always secure actual educational access for all children because some adults prioritize children's labor over their education.[16] The compulsory nature of basic education protects children from adults' arbitrariness and will enable children to take advantage of their right to education. In other words, the compulsory nature of basic education is one kind of environmental support needed to develop children's internal human capability.

To ensure equality of opportunity, compulsory education needs to be distributed through public policy, not through the market. Gutmann (1999) observes "how schooling should not be distributed: not by the market -- children of poor and uninterested parents will not receive it; not by unconstrained democratic decision [17] – children of disfavored minorities will be relegated to inferior schools" (p.127). The first purpose of basic education is "conscious social reproduction" (Gutmann, 1999, p.14), and thus it can be understood as a public investment. The public nature of basic education is also an environmental support needed to distribute educational opportunity to all children regardless of their financial condition or social status.

Second, *primary* education can contain the critical essence of basic education; in other words, basic education can be a universal foundation of different conceptions of primary education. As discussed above, basic education aims at developing children's internal capability and citizenship at the early stage of life, through cultivating basic abilities such as literacy. Literacy can be attained, for example, through daily life not through schooling. However, the compulsory and public nature of basic education would require institutionalized education for the reason of equality. In particular, primary education is one of the most effective institutional forms to realize the compulsory and public nature of basic education, and it provides broader accessibility than secondary and higher education.[18]

(3) Literacy as basic education for human development

Different societies will realize their own conception of compulsory public primary education by reflecting their own social needs. For example, instruction about malaria and HIV/AIDS may be considered as necessary parts of primary education in some societies (e.g. Taasisi ya Elimu Tanzania, 1999, pp.34-45), but other societies may have different needs. However, any conception of primary education requires basic literacy (UNESCO, 2005a). Literacy is a necessary condition both for living as human and for climbing up the "educational ladder." In the example above, literacy helps children to learn how to protect themselves from malaria or HIV/AIDS (basic education for life) as well as to pass the examinations and proceed to secondary education (primary education for claiming the educational ladder).

The association of literacy with health, nutrition, and other social goods has been widely accepted by governments, and "high rates of literacy have taken generations to achieve" (Wagner, 1990; 1992, p.21). Even though there is an argument over the oral nature in the African culture (Silagan, 1986), Bhola (1990) warns that "we may be making too much of the so-called orality of the African culture," insisting that the oral cultural tradition in Africa does not imply that there is no need for literacy in current Africa. UNESCO (2005a), a leading sponsor of literacy development programs, declared on international literacy day, September 8, 2005, that "literacy is inseparably tied to all aspects of life and livelihood. Literacy is at the heart of learning, the core of Education for All and central to the achievement of the Millennium Development Goals." In this sense, literacy can be considered as a critical part of basic education and thus as a universal foundation of primary education. In other words, literacy can play a significant role in promoting children's internal capability, which develops other future capabilities.

3.2.2 Conclusion of claim two: The conceptual model of human development

As Figure 3.3 in 3.2.1 (a) shows, the purpose of human development, or constitutive freedom, is realized by exercising instrumental freedom to follow one's own conception of the good life. Each individual develops his or her capabilities to achieve constitutive freedom, and I claimed that basic education, specifically literacy, plays a significant role in developing internal capability. Although I defined basic education as compulsory public primary education, it does not mean that I believe that public policy can directly contribute to the realization of individuals' constitutive freedom. Since constitutive freedom is a result of the unique combinations of each individual's capabilities, what public policy can do is to improve environmental conditions to promote instrumental freedoms, not to directly develop one's constitutive freedom. In particular, I focused on literacy; public policy can contribute to improving environmental conditions to promote literacy, one of the most necessary internal capabilities, through compulsory public primary education.

When thinking of public policy, it is critically important to assess people's needs to develop their internal capabilities. Again, human development is a highly comprehensive concept; therefore, the capability approach requires educational, health, and material factors as seen in this chapter. In order to assess such comprehensive needs, quantitative modeling can be useful for following reasons. First, it is generalizable for creating public policies, and it will help define the needs of people. Second, even though it is impossible for a model to capture the whole complexity of reality, the model can provide some guidance in analyzing that complexity. In Chapter five, I will construct a quantitative model based on a modified human development theory developed in this chapter.

Before developing a quantitative model with the existing data, it is important to consider the characteristics of the model conceptually. The purpose of modeling a modified human development theory by using actually existing data is to show a practical application of this theory. The model will pay attention to school-age children and it will include an indicator of literacy as an outcome variable to represent children's internal capability. This model is expected to function for needs assessment to improve children's literacy. Three major characteristics of the model are described as below:

1. *Comprehensive perspective*

    As repeated in this study, the model sustains a comprehensive perspective on human development. Specifically, explanatory variables in the model represent three factors of instrumental freedom: education, health, and material wealth. The model assumes that all three factors contribute to children's literacy.

2. *Hierarchical structure*

    The model pays attention to differences between the individual and district levels. Individual lives can be affected by district differences. For example, the needs of the people living in affluent districts can be different from that of those living in needy districts even if their individual conditions are the same. The model considers the variance among districts, not only among individuals.

3. *Literacy as a "promoter" of human development*
The model takes literacy as an outcome variable, assuming that literacy develops other capabilities to promote one's instrumental freedom and eventually to achieve one's constitutive freedom. An outcome variable in this model is not a goal but a start toward human development.

Based on these characteristics, the model at the individual level considers how children's schooling life contributes to their literacy; at the district level, it considers how their environmental conditions as indicated by public services (educational, health, and material wealth factors) contribute to their literacy. Conceptually, the model is represented as below:

Although the individual level in Figure 3.4 does not include health and material wealth factors, there is a limitation of data availability as discussed later in Chapters five and six. Therefore, the individual level in this model considers only educational issues, which are represented by schooling experience and book possession. This seems to be a critical limitation of the model capacity to reflect human development theory. However, the question whether one has schooling experience often reflects the children's health condition and the question whether one owns books often reflects the household's economic condition. Thus, this individual-level model can be

Figure 3.4 The conceptural relation between the individual and district levels

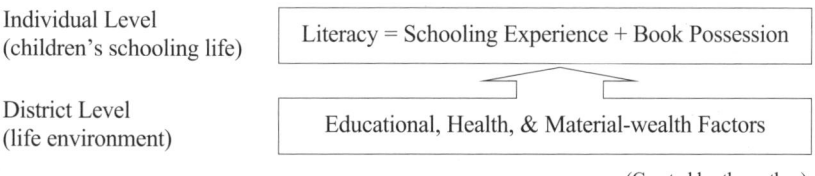

Individual Level (children's schooling life)	Literacy = Schooling Experience + Book Possession
District Level (life environment)	Educational, Health, & Material-wealth Factors

(Created by the author)

said to represent the other two factors indirectly.

A statistical methodology, called Hierarchical Generalized Linear Modeling (HGLM), allows one to examine data from different levels. The details of HGLM and the model interpretations will be discussed in Chapters five and six, after introducing the history and present condition of Tanzania as a case study in Chapter four.

Notes

[1] There are several examples of a world-wide consensus in education: The World Conference on Education for All in Jomtien, Thailand in 1990 supported the goal of "Education For All"; The World Education Forum in Dakar, Senegal in 2000 adopted "The Dakar Framework for Action Education For All"; The United Nations General Assembly in 2000 adopted "Millennium Development Goals"; and The G8 Summit in Kananaskis, Canada, in 2002 proposed the "Basic Education for Growth Initiative." These declarations have been functioning as a world-wide consensus for international cooperation.

[2] It is important to remember that human capability is defined as aggregation and combination of functionings. See 2.1.1 (b) for details.

[3] The choice of the person's life does not always depend on what he or she *wants*, but on what he or she *values*. A human may choose what he or she does not want when the person values it or when the person thinks it is inherently right. Sen (1992) also mentions the possibility that one's freedom may conflict with one's well-being (see 2.1.1 (c)).

[4] Nussbaum states this in the context of critiques of liberalism in gender theory. Although the discussion here is not about gender theory, I judge that her understanding of liberalism in general is appropriate here to be quoted.

[5] Kant (1997) proposes "three aforementioned ways of presenting the principle of morality":

1. A form, which consists in universality, and in this respect the formula of the moral imperative requires that maxims be chosen as though they should hold as universal laws of nature.
2. A material (i.e., an end), and in this respect the formula says that the rational being, as by its nature an end and thus as an end in itself, must serve in every maxim as the condition restricting all merely relative and arbitrary ends.
3. A complete determination of all maxims by the formula that all maxims which stem from autonomous legislation ought to harmonize with a possible realm of ends as

with a realm of nature.
(p.53)
He also articulates "the universal formula of the categorical imperative the basis," which is the basis of all three above: "act according to the maxim which can at the same time make itself a universal law" (p.54).

[6] In the sense that the choice is made by one's *autonomous* will, the person is considered truly free. Kant (2002) says "whereas freedom is indeed the *ratio essendi* [reason for being] of the moral law, the moral law is the *ratio cognoscendi* [reason for cognizing] of freedom" (Footnote 25 in Kant, 2002, p.5; also see Kant, 1997, pp.57-58; 2000, p.18; Ishikawa, 1995, p.171-174).

[7] There is a difference between following two statements: (1) I study because I want to pass the exam; (2) I study because I think I should. Statement (1) is a hypothetical imperative since the study is motivated by a teleological concern (to pass the exam); on the other hand, statement (2) is a categorical imperative since the study is motivated only by the individual's moral duty.

[8] However, I note that Nussbaum's Aristotelianism does not assert a priori value as Kantian philosophy does. Aristotelians rely on empirical experience as the basis for values rather than attempting to deduce them a priori. However, in the sense that I see basic capabilities as universal values, which are determined empirically not metaphysically, it can be said that Nussbaum's list is consistent with the universal but not the a priori character of Kantian philosophy.

[9] Nussbaum (2000a) calls her list "a threshold level of these human capabilities" (p.75; also see 2.2.1), but I interpret her list as "an external a priori criterion of political morality," in a broader sense than "a threshold level."

[10] Rawls (1993, 1999b) confirms that non-liberal societies such as communitarian societies can be considered as "decent societies" when they respect human rights.

[11] Sen (1987) considers that the economic action in human society is based on sympathy and morality among people. He is strongly influenced by the philosophy of Adam Smith (cf. Raphael & Macfie, 1982; Smith, 2004a, 2004b) and criticizes contemporary economic theory: "other parts of Smith's writings on economics and society, dealing with observations of misery, the need for sympathy, and the role of ethical considerations in human behavior... have become relatively neglected as these considerations have themselves become unfashionable in economics... Indeed, it is precisely the narrowing of the broad Smithian view of human beings, in modern economics, that can be seen as one of the major deficiencies of contemporary economic theory" (p.28).

[12] UNDP started to publish an annual report, *Human Development Report*, since 1990.

[13] The United Nations General Assembly in 2000 adopted the Millennium Development Goals, which contains eight goals of development: poverty eradication, uni-

versal primary education, gender equality, child mortality reduction, maternal health improvement, disease reduction, environmental sustainability, and global partnership development (United Nations, 2005).

[14] *The Human Development and Capability Association* was established in 2004 by welcoming Sen and Nussbaum as the founding presidents. (see http://fas.harvard.edu/~freedoms/)

[15] The universal value of the human capability list is argued by Nussbaum (2000a; also see 2.2.1).

[16] Following *the Convention of the Rights of the Child*, UNICEF (1996) features the issue of child labor in its annual report. It reports that one child (5-14 years old) out of three is working in Africa.

[17] Gutmann (1999) constrains democracy with principles of non-repression and non-discrimination (pp.71-75) because unconstrained democracy can neglect social minorities.

[18] For example, in Tanzania, the primary school enrolment rate is 63 percent for both males and females (gross, 1997-2000), while the secondary school enrolment rate is 6 percent for males and 5 percent for females (gross, 1997-2000) (UNICEF, 2003, 2004).

Part II
Empirical analysis of human development

Case study: Tanzania

Chapter 4

In this chapter, I will shift from a theoretical study to an empirical analysis and adapt a modified human development theory to the real world, emphasizing policy considerations. I will try to model the idea of human development with Tanzania's data in the next chapter (Chapter five). Prior to this data analysis, it is necessary to understand Tanzanian society and history. In this chapter, I will provide an overview of Tanzanian society from two different perspectives. First, I will review the history of Tanzania's educational and social policies to determine whether Tanzania's original post-independence policies dealt with the essence of human development (4.1). I will also show that the externally imposed structural adjustment policy redirected the original policy and philosophy (4.1). Second, I will describe Tanzanian society in the 1990s by using statistical data to show that there is a significant gap of life circumstances between the rural and urban areas, which was deepened by structural adjustment in the 1980s (4.2). Through these overviews of Tanzanian society, I will argue for a similarity between Tanzania's original philosophy and the concept of human development and expose its inconsistency with Tanzania's policy of "socialist vision and capitalist practice" (Samoff, 1990, p.262). I will conclude that needs assessment for human development policy based on the theoretical model of human development is necessary for social development in Tanzania (4.3).

Why Tanzania? As will be seen in this chapter, Tanzania has had a unique experience among developing counties in the world. After independence in 1964, founding Prime Minister Nyerere proposed a Tanzanian socialist policy based on the Tanzanian original philosophy of *Ujamaa* or 'familyhood,' although Capitalism had been the dominant trend in the rest of the world (Block, 1984; Buchert, 1994, Cameron, 1980; Cliff, 1969; Cunninghum, 1968; Mbilinyi, 1982; Mbunda, 1982; Morrison, 1976; Nyerere, 1969a, 1969b, 1969c, 1969d, 1982a, 1982b; Omari, 1983; Samoff, 1990; Svendsen, 1976; Thompson, 1968). Although Tanzanian social and educational policies have been affected by this world trend and by external political and economic influences, it still can be said that "the Tanzanian experience suggests both the potential and the limits for nonrevolutionary noncapitalist development and its accompanying educational reform" (Samoff, 1990, p.210). Moreover, because of Prime Minister Nyerere's strong leadership and philosophy of development, Tanzania's education policies, especially *Education for Self-Reliance* in1967, have been widely cited and "provided inspiration and guidance in many other countries" (Samoff, 1990, p.210). Therefore, the case study of Tanzania, especially its educational policies, can serve as a model for other African countries.

4.1 History of Tanzania's educational and social policies

Tanganyika attained political independence from England on December 9, 1961 (Cliffe, 1969), and in 1964, it became the United Republic of Tanzania, composed of mainland Tanganyika and the island of Zanzibar. Tanganyika was colonized by Germany in 1884, and after the First World War, it was governed by England as a trust territory until its independence in 1961. Zanzibar was governed by England as a protectorate from 1890 until its independence in 1963. In the year following Zanzibar's independence, the United Republic of Tanzania was born, and, since then, Tanzania has had two distinct governments in Tanganyika and Zanzibar. In this chapter, I use the term Tanzania to refer to the mainland and its government, excluding Zanzibar.

In this section, I will begin the historical review by describing an educational situation in Tanzania during the British colonial period from 1922 until its independence as the United Republic of Tanzania in 1964 (4.1.1), and will describe its unique its unique post-independence philosophy (4.1.2 (a)), education policies (4.1.2 (b)), and the dilemma of "socialist vision and capitalist practice" (Samoff, 1990, p.262) adopted under external influences in the 1980s (4.1.2 (c)).

4.1.1 Tanzanian education during the British colonial period: From 1922 to Independence

Full legislative, executive, and judicial power in Tanganyika was handed over to the British administration in 1922 after 38 years of German administration. The British administration adopted the previous German system of *direct* rule at the beginning; however, conflicts of interests among immigrant communities, specifically between white settlers and Indian immigrants, later promoted an *indirect* system of rule in Tanganyika (Buchert, 1994, p.8-9). Consequently, Tanganyika became "a prime site of the system of indirect rule, which was established over virtually the whole territory by 1931" (Buchert, 1994, p.9). The British indirect ruling system involved the integration of the indigenous political system into the central British administrative structure; for example, the local administration was run by tribal chiefs and village headmen, although they were supervised by the district or provincial officers of the British administration (Buchert, 1994, p.9). The British government established the Colonial Office to supervise local administration, and each Executive and Legislative Council under the Colonial Office contained representatives of the main interest groups - agriculture, commerce, missionary organizations, and the heads of the British government departments. However, there was no Tanzanian representation on either the Executive or Legislative Council until 1945, and even then the majority of those organizations consisted of representatives of the British government (Buchert, 1994, p.9).

Even though Tanzania was ruled by the indirect system, the institutional framework for the formulation and implementation of educational policies was largely controlled by the British government officials and Christian missionaries (Morrison, 1976, pp.47-48). In particular, Christian missionaries largely determined the formal schooling system (Buchert, 1994, p.15; Thompson, 1968, p.16). In 1925, about 115,000 children, out of estimated 800,000 school-age population, were in missionary schools, while only 5,000 were in governmental schools (Thompson, 1968, p.24). Moreover, the few governmental schools were controlled by the colonial government (Morrison, 1976, pp44-47), which means that there was little opportunity for Tanzanians to build their own schooling system.

The mission-inspired and government-backed the Phelps-Stokes Commission visited East and Central Africa in 1924 in order to inquire into educational problems and to recommend solutions. In African schools, the Commission observed that "with full appreciation of the European language, the value of the Native tongue is immensely more vital, in that it is one of the chief means of preserving whatever is good in Native customs, ideas and ideals, and thereby preserving what is more important than all else, namely, Native self-respect" (Thomson, 1968, p.19). However, the Commission actually supported the use of dominant vernacular, Swahili, despite the fact that there were six million people speaking 120 distinct vernaculars. Such a situation caused some observers to argue that "the school system... is an alien thing, torn from a European environment and set down in a society to which it is unrelated" (Thompson, 1968, p.15); and that "African parents did not accept formal education eagerly... The people were naturally suspicious of the European missionaries who denounced traditional ways and beliefs and preached a new religion; thus the initial recruits for schools came primarily from families of freed slaves and social outcasts" (Morrison, 1976, p.44).

"Education for Adaptation" (Buchert, 1994) to modern British culture was advanced through education policies that reflected both conflict and cooperation. The first policy paper of the Colonial Office Advisory Committee on Education, *the Education Policy in British Tropical Africa*, was published in 1925 (Buchert, 1994, p.17; Thompson, 1968, p.18). This memorandum described the task of education as:

> [T]o raise the standard alike of character and efficiency of the bulk of the people, but provision [was] also to be made for the training of those who [were] required to fill posts in the administrative and technical services... As resources permit, the door of advancement, through higher education... must be increasingly opened for those who by character, ability and temperament show themselves fitted to profit by such education. (Quoted in Buchert, 1994, p.17; Thompson, 1968, p.18)

According to Thompson (1968), this memorandum, as well as the Phelps-Stokes report, is based on "the principle of adaptation." The major task of education was to create an elite class of Tanzanians who were willing to adapt to the British administration system and to support and work for the system. Therefore, the colonial government provided limited secondary education only for the students of the colonized elites "to socialize a new leadership and to nurture a sense of social class" (Samoff, 1990, p.242).

However, Thompson (1968) also points out that the initial policy of adaptation evolved. The memorandum in 1943 titled *Mass Education in African Society* set a new goal for education.

> [The goal includes] the development of political institutions and political power until the day arrives when the people can become effectively self-governing... Mass education should, as it spreads, be able to give this knowledge and at the same time call out the ability and the

will to share in the direction and control of the social, economic and political forces. (Quoted in Thompson, 1968, pp.21-22)

Here, the shift of emphasis from higher education for creating an elite class to mass education for empowerment can be seen. Moreover, the 1948 memorandum on *Education for Citizenship in Africa* restated the task of education:

> [The] advance towards political freedom will not and must not be delayed. But if political freedom is to benefit all the people and not merely the favored few, then all the people must be guided to use it for the common good. This is the task of education. (Quoted in Thompson, 1968, p.22)

Indeed, school enrolment dramatically increased after the 1943 memorandum on *Mass Education in African Society*, as shown in Figure 4.1 below.

Although school enrollments increased, Thompson (1968) evaluates Tanzanian education policies during the British colonial period negatively:

> "In the past, attempts at adaptation of education in this country have been consistently regarded with suspicion by the people. The educated 'elite' have been suspicious of the motives behind them, impatient of the gradualistic assumptions upon they were based and increasingly resentful of the failure of the colonial government to take their views

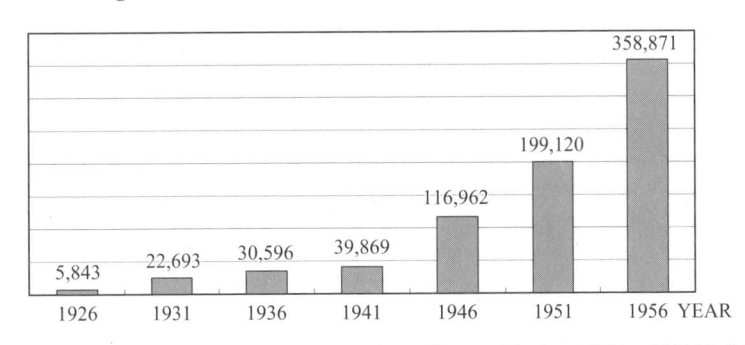

Figure 4.1 Enrolment in African schools, 1926-1956

Year	Enrolment
1926	5,843
1931	22,693
1936	30,596
1941	39,869
1946	116,962
1951	199,120
1956	358,871

(Source: Morrison, 1976, p.45, Table 2.1)

more fully into account and to involve them more effectively in the policy making process" (p.31).

Therefore, "In the past the school has been an inadequate instrument for the accomplishment of the broader tasks allotted to it... In the past the school has tended to carry a wholly disproportionate share of the blame for the existence of social problems" (p.32). According to him, colonial education policies were nothing beyond "Education for Adaptation," and he considers the post-independence education policy adopted in 1967, *Education for Self-Reliance*, which will be introduced in the next section (4.1.2 (a)), as a policy "ripe for effective adaptation" (Thompson, 1968, p.32).

According to Morrison (1976), colonial educational policies brought significant political and social changes in Tanzania, especially in developing a sense of "social class": "differences in educational provision among races, regions, tribes, and religious communities made social cleavages more obvious and heightened the potential for political conflict based on social structure" and "a widening gap and gradually solidifying differences between educated and uneducated Africans led to the emergence of yet another dimension of political interaction centered on class" (Morrison, 1976, p.64). However, Morrison (1976) also recognizes that these negative social changes motivated educated Tanzanians: "schools and colleges, although hardly designed as instruments of nationalism, contributed markedly to increased resistance to colonialism and a growth in national consciousness," and eventually, "the emergence of articulate spokesmen for African interests and, later, of organized action to secure independence forced an opening of the process of educational policy-making" (p.64).

Remembering Huntington's (1997) conception of the indigenous power of "the people of that society" and Sen's (2000) caution concerning our tendency to underestimate the ability to learn from outsiders without being overwhelmed, a real example of these phenomena can be seen in Tanzanian colonial history. "Education for Adaptation" and the social changes brought by the Adaptation all the better motivated the people in Tanzania to gain independence; however, this did not mean a return to the pre-colonial era. Instead, there developed a progression toward "effective adaptation" (Thompson, 1968, p.32), in which the people of a society digest the outside effects in their own way, and create their own society based on the colonial experiences.

4.1.2 Tanzanian education since 1964

Right after independence in 1964, the new Tanzanian government issued *the First Five-Year Plan (FFYP) for Economic and Social Development 1964-1969*. A major educational focus of this policy was on "high-level skills training by the educational system, particularly secondary schools and the university" (Samoff, 1990, p.269). Following this policy, secondary school fees were abolished. Buchert (1994) describes Tanzania's educational situation, "reorientation of the efforts" (p.93), immediately after independence:

> During this period, Education for Manpower Development was stressed in order to fulfill expressed goals of increased economic growth and to meet the demands for an Africanisation of the middle- and high-level posts as a manifestation of politico-economic independence. The wider framework for the manpower planning approach was the human capital theory which was developed particularly by American economists in the late 1950s and the early 1960s. Manpower development dominated international thinking on education all over the world at the time. (Buchert, 1994, p.93)

However, founding Prime Minister Nyerere, the first president of the political party Tanganyika African National Union (TANU),[1] shifted the direction of FFYP into Tanzania's own.

(a) Arusha Declaration in 1967

In 1967, Prime Minister Nyerere published two major social and educational policies. The *Arusha Declaration* clarified Tanzania's philosophy of social development and *Education for Self-Reliance* emphasized mass education, especially primary education focusing on development of children's agricultural skills (Samoff, 1990, p.270). The *Arusha Declaration* articulated a new goal for Tanzania's national development, which "centered on equality and participation by the mass of the population in local and national development efforts as the basis for the construction of a socialist society" (Buchert, 1994, p.90). Attention to the rural sector was also articulated in this Declaration. Following the direction of the *Arusha Declaration*, an education policy named *Education for Self-Reliance* emphasized "the socio-cultural and political purposes of education in addition to economic ones" (Buchert, 1994, p.94). This education policy has been widely cited and has influenced and inspired other African countries (Samoff, 1990, p.210). Cliff (1969) evaluates the *Arusha Declaration*[2]:

> The Arusha Declaration was a document of significance to Tanzania, and indeed all of Africa, not merely because it sought to draw up a program for development on an egalitarian, co-operative basis. Earlier we isolated, in addition to the very limited spread of development, a second set of problems of the colonial economy Tanzania had inherited - its dependence on the world economy. Under the heading of "Self-Reliance," the Declaration suggested a new strategy for the country's own resources with foreign assistance regarded as an extra bonus rather than the main determinant of what should be done... Tanzania has thus embarked on the final stage of decolonization. (p.256)

The *Arusha Declaration* was based on the Tanzanian original philosophy of *Ujamaa* or "familyhood," and the idea of the Declaration was embodied in an educational policy *Education for Self-Reliance*, as will be introduced next.

(1) Ujamaa: *Tanzanian socialism*

The philosophy of Tanzania's national development stated in *the Arusha*

Declaration is well explained by the concept of *Ujamaa*, a Swahili word literally translated as "familyhood" and generally used to mean "Tanzanian socialism" (Samoff, 1990, pp.212-214). Prime Minister Nyerere said that "the basic difference between a socialist society and a capitalist society does not lie in their methods of producing wealth, but in the way wealth is distributed" (quoted in Buchert, 1994, p.91). Under the Nyerere administration, therefore, the plantations developed during the colonial period were taken over by the state and the capitalist farms were also turned into state farms over time in order to "promote social equality among the African population in terms of socio-economic, rural-urban and rural-rural differences" (Buchert, 1994, p.91).

It has to be noted that *Ujamaa* or Tanzanian socialism has a particular meaning different from socialism in a general sense. The government party Tanganyika African National Union (TANU) articulates their principles as follows.

(a) All human beings are equal;

(b) Every individual has a right to dignity and respect;

(c) Every citizen is an integral part of the nation and has the right to take an equal part in Government at local, regional and national level;

(d) Every citizen has the right to freedom of expression, of movement, of religious belief and of association within the context of the law;

(e) Every individual has the right to receive from society protection of this life and of property held according to law;

(f) Every individual has the right to receive a just return for his labor;

(g) All citizens together possess all the natural resources of the country in trust for their descendants;

(h) In order to ensure economic justice the state must have effective control over the principal means of production; and

(i) It is the responsibility of the state to intervene actively in the economic life of the nation so as to ensure the well-being of all citizens and so as to prevent the exploitation of one person by another or one group by another, and so as to prevent the accumulation of wealth to an extent which is inconsistent with the existence of a classless society. (Nyerere, 1969b, p.184)

These principles recognize and appreciate people's political participation, freedom of speech and freedom of conscience, human rights, and respect for law. More importantly, according to Nyerere (1969a), these principles are not imports from so-called western philosophy:

> "*Ujamaa*" then, or "Familyhood," describes our socialism. It is opposed to capitalism, which seeks to build a happy society on the basis of the exploitation of man by man; and it is equally opposed to doctrinaire socialism which seeks to build its happy society on a philosophy of inevitable conflict between man and man. (Nyerere, 1969a, p.165)

He also characterizes *Ujamaa* socialism as an extended version of the Tanzanian indigenous philosophy, and at the same time, as a kind of cosmopolitanism that extends beyond African society.

> We, in Africa, have no more need of being "converted" to socialism than we have of being "taught" democracy. Both are rooted in our own past - in the traditional society which produced us. Modern African socialism can draw from its traditional heritage the recognition of "society" as an extension of the basic family unit. But it can no longer confine the idea of the social family within the limits of the tribe, nor, indeed, of the nation. For no true African socialist can look at a line drawn on a map and say, "The people on this side of that line are my brothers, but those who happen to live on the other side of it can have no claim on me"; every individual on this continent is his

brother... Our recognition of the family to which we all belong must be extended yet further - beyond the tribe, the community, the nation, or even the continent - to embrace the whole society of mankind. This is the only logical conclusion for true socialism (Nyerere, 1969a, p.165-166)

Specifically, the Nyerere administration promoted rural agriculture in the belief that "in a socialist Tanzania ... our agricultural organization would be predominantly that of co-operative living and working for the good of all" (Nyerere, 1969d, p.258). The government pointed out the problem that the colonial experience modified the Tanzanian traditional agricultural style into one that worked "in competition and not in co-operation with their neighbors," (Nyerere, 1969d, p.250) aimed at producing commercial crops. In order to transform the agricultural system again, the Nyerere administration proposed a three-stage approach: the first stage persuades people to move their houses into a single village and to plant food crops in places easily reachable for all households in the same Ujamaa village; the second stage persuades a group of households in an Ujamaa village to start a small communal activity such as starting a community farm and sharing the harvest; and the final stage fully realizes the Tanzanian socialist village, in which people would be willing to invest all their effort for the village in cooperation with neighbors (Nyerere, 1969d, pp.263-264).

(2) Education for Self-Reliance

In order to promote the Ujamaa philosophy and to realize Ujamaa socialist villages in Tanzania, the Nyerere administration relied on education as its primary tool (Buchert, 1994, p.91). Soon after independence, the Nyerere administration made three significant changes in Tanzanian education: complete integration of the separate-racial education system created during the colonial period; critical expansion of the educational facilities available; and a change from a European to a Tanzanian curriculum (Nyerere, 1982a, p.238).

A month after *the Arusha Declaration*, Prime Minister Nyerere published an education policy titled *Education for Self-Reliance*. According to Cameron (1980), this policy document is "unlike the [Arusha] Declaration, it is a [Nyerere's] personal pamphlet" (p.106), which implies that this policy document reflects Nyerere's personal voice and belief. The policy document begins with a fundamental question: why education in newborn Tanzania for what purpose?

> ... we have never really stopped to consider why we want education - what its purpose is. ... It is now time that we looked again at the justification for a poor society like ours spending almost 20 per cent of its government revenues on providing education for its children and young people, and began to consider what that education should be doing. (Nyerere, 1982a, p.235)

The document criticizes colonial education for departing from the Tanzanian ideal of education based on *Ujamaa*: "[Colonial education] emphasized and encouraged the individualistic instincts of man, instead of his co-operative instincts. It led to the possession of individual material wealth being the major criterion of social merit and worth" (Nyerere, 1982a, p.237). The document describes the goals of Tanzanian education:

> Our village life, as well as our state organization, must be based on the principles of socialism and that equality in work and return which is part of it. This is what our educational system has to encourage. It has to foster the social goals of living together, and working together, for the common good. It has to prepare our young people to play a dynamic and constructive part in the development of a society in which all members share fairly in the good or bad fortune of the group, and in which progress is measured in terms of human well-being, not prestige buildings, cars, or other such things... Our education must therefore inculcate a sense of commitment to the total com-

munity, and help the pupils to accept the values appropriate to our kind of future, not those appropriate to our colonial past. (Nyerere, 1982a, p.240)

In order to realize Tanzanian ideal education to foster Ujamaa, the document articulates four problems to be overcome (Nyerere, 1982a, pp.241-244). The first problem is that Tanzanian education has been basically designed as an elitist education to meet the interests and needs of a limited segment of the population. The second is that Tanzanian education has divorced its participants from the society; in other words, schools have not been a part of the community. The third problem is that Tanzanian education has put a biased emphasis on knowledge from books and 'educated people'; in other words, it has fostered the young people's attitude not to respect 'uneducated farmers' and their experience-based wisdom. The final problem is that fewer and fewer young people have been willing to do physical work. The document also provides three ways to overcome these problems: (1) curriculum change to give additional emphasis to agricultural skills development at school farm; (2) reorganization of the school system to promote its relationship with community; and (3) an increase of the entry age of primary school to seven years to produce more responsible young workers and citizens after primary school completion and to reduce the number of primary school leavers (Nyerere, 1982a, pp.244-252).[3]

Notwithstanding the significant impact of this education policy on other neighbor countries, the idea of *Education for Self-Reliance* was not always understood as originally intended. Miscommunication between the Ministry of Education and local schools caused alternative interpretations of this policy: "some implemented it by focusing on the idea of economic independence, others by endeavoring to increase the output of the schools' 'productive activities' (agricultural, handicrafts, etc.), commodities, and some, thinking that it was a policy for raising the schools' prestige as an end in itself, provided

118   Part II. Empirical analysis of human development

activities of no relation whatsoever with those of the community at large" (Mbunda, 1982, p.91). This miscommunication and misinterpretation explained the gap between the policy direction at the government level and practical implementation at the school level. As Goodin & Klingemann (1996) says, "Policy-making rarely looks like the textbook discussions of the policy cycle. Sometimes a solution goes looking for a problem" (p.568). *Education for Self-Reliance* was splendid as a policy, but its implementation produced problems.

However, this education policy still played a significant role in clarifying the direction that new Tanzanian education should have followed; indeed, it stimulated Tanzanian society to make some significant changes in its education system. A year after *Education for Self-Reliance* in 1967, new textbooks were introduced, which focused on development for rural living skills such as farming, poultry keeping, and other agricultural projects. In addition, Swahili became a teaching language throughout primary school (Mbunda, 1982, p.92). *The Education Act of 1969* terminated mission participation in public education and placed Tanzanian education in the control of the Tanzanian

Figure 4.2   Number of pupils enrolled in Tanzania, 1967-1975

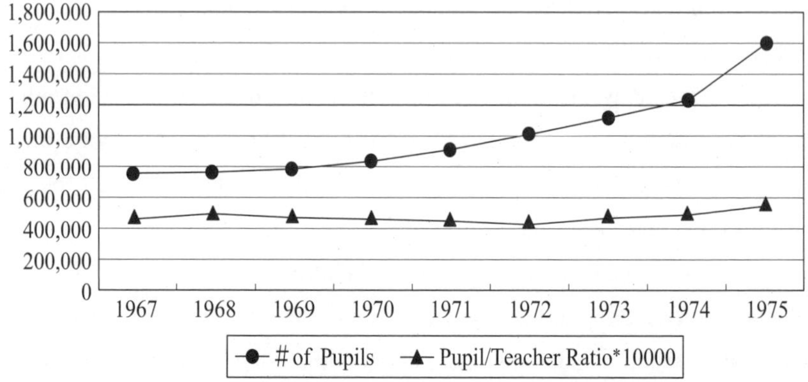

━●━ # of Pupils   ━▲━ Pupil/Teacher Ratio*10000

(Source: Mbunde, 1982, p.93, Table 4.5)

government. In 1972, primary school fees were abolished, which increased primary school enrollment. Figure 4.2 shows a stable pupil/teacher ratio, which indicates that the number of teachers also increased following the increase of pupils enrolled. It kept a ratio of 40 to 60 pupils per teacher constantly.

(b) Musoma Resolution in 1974: The path to Universal Primary Education

Regardless of the constant increase of primary school enrollment, the assessment in 1973 for the result of *Education for Self-Reliance* showed that more than half of Tanzanian children were out of primary schools (Mbunda, 1982, p.93)[4] and that the secondary and post-secondary education were limited only to "the elites" and constrained by financial resources available rather than the number of qualified candidates (Block, 1984, p.106-107).[5] The government party TANU held *the National Educational Conference* at Musoma in November 1974 to publish *the Musoma Resolution*.

The Musoma Resolution spoke to both primary and higher education (Block, 1984, pp.106-110; Mbunda, 1982, pp.93-95; Samoff, 1990, p.216). Regarding higher education, realizing that "socialist education is not worthy of this distinction if work is not integrated into it at all levels" (Block, 1984, p.107), a minimum of two years work experience after second school became required for entry to university.[6]

Regarding primary education, the Resolution "addressed elitism among students and led to the acceleration of the achievement of universal primary

Table 4.1 Additional teachers and classrooms needed for UPE

Year	Expected number of pupils enrolled*	Grade C teachers	Grade A teachers	Total teachers	Classrooms
1975/76	829,993	1,947	1,493	3,440	6,075
1976/77	848,293	4,546	1,222	5,768	9,298
1977/78	867,793	2,914	999	3,913	10,913

* Assuming 100% enrollment

(Source: Mbunda, 1982, p.94, Tables 4.6 & 5.7)

Table 4.2 Teacher training system in Tanzania*

Teacher's grade	Primary schooling (years)	Secondary schooling (years)	Teacher education (years)	Total (years)
C	7(8)**	–	2	9(10)
B***	8	2	2	12
A	7(8)	4	2	13(14)
Diploma	7(8)	6	1	14(15)
B.A.	7(8)	6	3	16(17)
Post-Graduate	7(8)	6	3+1	17(18)

* This is the system in the 1970s
** Numbers in parenthesis refer to the period before 1967 when primary education was 8 years. After the 1967 Education for Self-Reliance policy, primary education became 7 years.
*** Grade B training was abolished; Grade B was qualified by promotion on merit from Grade C.

(Source: Mmari, 1982, p.122, Table 4.11)

education" (Samoff, 1990, p.216). Following the Resolution, the goal of *Universal Primary Education* (UPE) was set by 1977; seven years of primary schooling became compulsory; and additional needs to achieve this goal were estimated as below.

In order to satisfy these additional needs, teacher training was no longer limited to teachers colleges. Secondary schools began providing certain elements of pedagogy, and those who completed them at the secondary school were qualified to help teach in nearby primary schools to fill the shortage of teachers (Mbunda, 1982, p.94). In addition, a distance teacher training program was launched mainly for qualifying primary 7 leavers as Grade-C UPE teachers (Cooksey & Riedmiller, 1997). Although such "quantity-focused" policies caused quality problems, Prime Minister Nyerere said: "We cannot protect the excellence of education for the few by neglecting the education for the majority. In Tanzania, it is a sin to do so" (quoted in Omari, et al., 1983, p.41).

The Resolution also recognized that too much emphasis had been placed on academic subjects and examinations, which meant that the school curriculum was not always relevant to pupils' lives. Considering that "the aim of primary school education in Tanzania is to improve the economic and social conditions in the rural area where about 90 per cent of our people live" (Mbunda, 1982, pp.94-95), new curriculum was introduced that focused on six main topics: (1) literacy and numeracy; (2) intermediate technology including mathematics and science; (3) agriculture including animal husbandry; (4) business education that involved pupils in the activities of village co-operatives; (5) development studies including civics, history, health, and sanitation; and (6) cultural activities (Mbunda, 1982, p.95). Following this new curriculum, the primary school leaving examination was decentralized to make it more relevant to the pupils' life circumstances (Mbunda, 1982, p.95). After the UPE policy was published, "the schools seemed the obvious site for this sort of educational practice... Schooling was to become *education for Tanzanian socialism*" (Samoff, 1990, p.230). After *Education for Self-Reliance* clarified the significant role of primary education in a conceptual way, the UPE specified its conception as a form of "schooling."

Through *the Arusha Declaration, Education for Self-Reliance, the Musoma Resolution*, and UPE, Tanzanian education specified its philosophy, definition, and implementation. All were based on the belief in equality. These documents imply that the Tanzanian government has pursued an education policy based on *Ujamaa* since its independence.

(c) Structural adjustment in the 1980s: Redirection of education policy

Although the Tanzanian government desired to create an Ujamaa socialist nation, the wave of modernization and the international economy did not fully allow Tanzania to maintain that policy. In the early 1980s, an international economic depression affected most developing countries all over the world. As noted in Chapter one (1.1.2), many Latin American countries suffered from a severe debt problem; and natural disasters, in addition to economic disasters, hit African countries. Two major lending institutions, the World Bank and the International Monetary Fund (IMF), launched the structural adjustment program to overcome economic difficulties in this so-called "lost decade" (see 1.1.2).

The Tanzanian government had to give up its former long-term economic plans during this decade and to introduce some short-term economic policies under pressure from lending institutions as reported in: *The Structural Adjustment Program* of 1982; *The Economic Recovery Program* of 1986; and *The Economic and Social Action Program* of 1989-1992 (Buchert, 1994, p.145). The Tanzanian economy in the 1980s restructured "with renewed attention to the standard of living of the upper strata, greater receptivity to foreign investment and development advice, and a willingness to slow, or postpone, social transformation" (Samoff, 1990, pp.219-220), which were the reverse of what the government had pursued since independence - equality based on *Ujamaa* philosophy, self-reliance and independence from foreign aid, and social transformation to a socialist nation through primary education. Following this redirection of the national policy, Prime Minister Nyerere stepped down from the presidency in 1985 (Buchert, 1994, p.146).

Although the Nyerere administration had given a high priority to the education sector, especially primary education, under the structural adjustment program, the educational sector became less important, and the first priority was shifted to the economic sector (Buchert, 1994, pp.147-151; Cooksey & Riedmiller, 1997, p.121; Samoff, 1990, pp.219-220). This priority change redirected education policies. Buchert (1994) notes that the 1982 government's plan of Tanzanian future education towards the year 2000 excluded the original idea of *Education for Self-Reliance* and emphasized "the academic quality of education, its costs and its training role, particularly at the post-primary level, rather than the previous issues of access, equity and 'relevance' related to mass education reforms" (p.147).[7]

Again, this change in Tanzanian education seems almost opposite to its original direction. Because of the decreased attention to the issues of access, equity and 'relevance' for mass education, "the majority rural poor have increasingly turned away from formal schooling, while the urban middle class continue to compete through education for the limited number of modern-sector jobs" (Cooksey & Riedmiller, 1997, p.121). This redirection of education policy increased the rural-urban gap and enforced social stratification between the rural uneducated poor and the urban educated elite.

The subordination of the education sector was immediately reflected in educational expenditure: approximately 5 percent of GDP for total educational expenditure in 1982 dropped to about 2 percent in 1988; and approximately 12 percent of the total recurrent budget spent for education in 1981/82 dropped to about 6 percent during 1985/86-1989/90. Such financial difficulty brought another political problem to Tanzanian education: more dependency on foreign aid. Samoff (1990) says that "since funds for schooling are chronically tight, proponents of new programs commonly look to external assistance. In doing so, they must find a match between their own goals and those of potential donors" (p.241). Excessive financial dependency on foreign investments reduced the autonomy of Tanzania in education: "where the educational system relies heavily on external funding and advice, schools are unlikely to be primarily concerned with promoting social transformation or laying the foundation for Tanzanian socialism" (Samoff, 1990, p.268). In general, redirection of education policy in the 1980s contradicted the original philosophy of Tanzanian education.

In summary, while Tanzanian policies in the 1970s aimed at social equality through mass primary education, reorientation in the 1980s focused on the post-primary elite education, which resulted in increasing the gap between the urban educated and the rural uneducated. How does this gap created in the 1980s appear Tanzanian society in the 1990s? The next section (4.2) will answer this question.

4.2 Tanzanian education and society today: Reality in the 1990s

As noted in 4.1, Tanzanian society recognized, especially in the 1970s, a significant role for primary education in spite of the world trend based on human capital theory, which focuses on post-secondary education for manpower development. Moreover, the Tanzanian government traditionally has given a high priority to public primary schooling as mass education. Remembering the second claim in Chapter three (3.2), in which I defined basic education as a central instrumental freedom (*basic education for human development*), and in which I specified basic education as a *compulsory public primary* education (3.2.1 (b)), the original education policies of the post-independent Tanzania seem to encompass of basic education for human development.

However, the situation that Tanzanian society had to face during the structural adjustment period in the 1980s increased the gap between the rural uneducated poor and the urban educated elite. Reducing the rural-urban gap is one of the most fundamental necessary conditions for realizing the Tanzanian philosophy of Ujamaa; and it will help Tanzania regain human development in its own way.

How does the increased rural-urban gap of the 1980s appear in the life of school-age children in the 1990s? In this section, I will analyze how the rural-urban gap affected Tanzanian society in that decade, particularly focusing on the school-age population. I will describe the data collected by the World Bank in 1993 called the *Tanzania Human Resource Development Survey* (THRDS) (4.2.1) and examine descriptive statistics based on these data (4.2.2). I will also use this dataset for modeling in the next chapter.

4.2.1 Description of the data: The Tanzania Human Resource Development Survey

To describe the rural-urban gap in Tanzanian society from the perspective of basic education for human development, comprehensive data, which includes "three factors of education, health, and material wealth," are necessary as claimed in Chapter three (3.2.1 (a)). Also, in order to describe people's life at the local level, survey data are necessary, rather than national macro data. The *Tanzanian Human Resource Development Survey* (THRDS) (The World Bank, 1993, 1997; The World Bank & University of Dar es Salaam, 1993) is one of the most comprehensive survey datasets, compared to *the Household Budget Survey* in 1991 and *the Cornell/ERB survey* in 1991 which include "only economic information" (Ferreira & Griffin, 1996, p.7), and compared to *the Demographic and Health Survey* in 1992, *the Health Financing Survey* in 1991, and *the Tanzanian National Nutrition Survey* in 1991 which include "data on specific nutrition, demographic, and health outcomes, as well as use of some social services," but which "do not contain essential economic information about the household or detailed data on the use of the education system" (Ferreira & Griffin, 1996, p.7). In a recent survey in 1998, UNICEF (1998) conducted the *Multiple Indicator Cluster Survey*, which includes questionnaires on households, individual women, and children under-five, but this survey also focuses mainly on nutrition and health outcomes, lacking the essential economic information and data on the school-age population. Other recent survey data, such as *the Sumve Survey on Adult and Childhood Mortality Tanzania* in 1995, *the Demographic and Health Survey* in 1996, and *the Reproductive and Child Health Survey* in 1999, have the same problem: they do not contain all three factors and are not comprehensive enough for the purpose of this study.

On the other hand, THRDS contains a variety of variables on education, health, and material possessions, which are necessary factors to consider basic education from the perspective of "human development" (cf. Chapters two and three). In addition, the main object of THRDS is "to assess household welfare, ... and to evaluate the effect of various government policies on the living conditions of the population" (Grosh & Glewwe, 1995, p.2), which is consistent with the purpose of this study.

Mason and Khandker (1996) and Lambert and Sahn (2002) used THRDS for their research.[8] Mason and Khandker (1996) analyze the direct and opportunity costs of primary and secondary schooling. For the direct cost, they focus on such variables as the *monthly direct expenditure of primary and secondary schools per student* and the direct costs of *uniforms, books and supplies*, and *school fees and contributions*. For the *monthly direct school expenditure*, they report the average by school level and grade; for other direct costs, they report the average by school level and gender. Regarding the opportunity cost, they consider the hours of children working in school and not in school, and measure the opportunity cost by "the average predicted market wage, given the age, education level and the gender of the child" (Mason & Khandker, 1996, p.8). They report the average by age group and gender. Taking both direct and opportunity costs into consideration, they calculate "full private costs" of primary and secondary schooling, and analyze the "full private costs" by school levels and genders to find:

(1) At the primary level, where the direct costs of schooling are highly subsidized in Tanzania, the opportunity cost of children's time is from two-and-half to three times greater than the value of direct expenditures on education, on average, accounting for as much as 75 percent of the costs household face when they send a child to school.

(2) At the secondary level, the direct costs households face are significantly higher than at the primary level (approximately 5 times higher); but so is the opportunity cost of children's time. At this level, the value of children's work foregone still makes up from 50 to 80 percent of the average direct costs of secondary schooling, depending on whether the student is a male or female.

(Mason & Khandker, 1996, p.9-11 & p.14-16)

This study is unique because the researchers pay special attention to the opportunity cost, which is often ignored in policy makers' consideration. This study also shows that the opportunity cost at the primary level is about three times greater than the direct cost. Their findings can be the basis for strong policy recommendations for the educational sector in Tanzania. However, they do not take the rural-urban gap into consideration "assuming that the opportunity cost of children's time is roughly similar across income groups" (Mason & Khandker, 1996, p.10), which does not sound reasonable when considering the fact that most of the rural population are not wage earners but self-sufficient farmers. A study of human development needs to be sensitive to the rural-urban difference.

Lambert and Sahn (2002) use THRDS, particularly the data on health and education expenditure, to calculate different kinds of Gini coefficients and to draw Lorenz curves in order to analyze equality of distribution of public expenditures for health and education services in Tanzania. Gini coefficients and Lorenz curves can show how equally the expenditure is distributed between the poorest and the richest [9]: the Gini coefficient of completely equal distribution is 0 while that of exclusive possession by the richest is 1 (Takagi, 1996, pp.26-29). Regarding income distribution equality, Lambert and Sahn (2002) calculate a Gini coefficient and find high inequality (Gini coefficient=0.41) "despite Tanzania's espousal of socialist ideals with the primary objective to improve social welfare through economic justice and opportunity for all" (p.115). They also present concentration curves and Gini coefficients for "health and education" (Lambert & Sahn, 2002, p.130-131) by using variables of expenditures for *primary education, secondary education* and *hospitals*, and find high inequality again particularly in *secondary education* (Gini coefficient=0.29). For Gini coefficients of "primary education" (p.133), they use variables of *primary education expenditure* by rural-urban areas and by genders to find that gender does not matter and that rural services are more progressive than those in urban areas. In the same way, they examine Gini

128 Part II. Empirical analysis of human development

coefficients for "schooling-related subsidies" by using such variables as *books and supplies, uniform,* and *food* (p.135) and "access to water, electricity, and public sector employment" by using such variables as *water, public job,* and *electric* (p.137). Overall, they find that "among the various possible education and health sub-sectors, the most progressive public spending would be on primary schooling and non-hospital care, particularly in rural areas" (Lambert & Sahn, 2002, p.153).

The researchers' approach is a unique and significant examination of the issue of domestic equality in Tanzania and the issue of progressive allocation of health and educational public services. Since their analysis is sensitive to rural-urban differentials, their suggestions can be significant influence on budget design for health and education services in both rural and urban Tanzania. However, their analysis is limited to the financial aspects of health and education services. This study for human development will bring a more comprehensive perspective into the analysis and modeling in the next chapters.

4.2.2 Statistical description of the rural-urban difference

Since THRDS contains many sub-datasets, it is necessary to select and merge data to be used for this study. THRDS is composed of 19 sub-datasets:

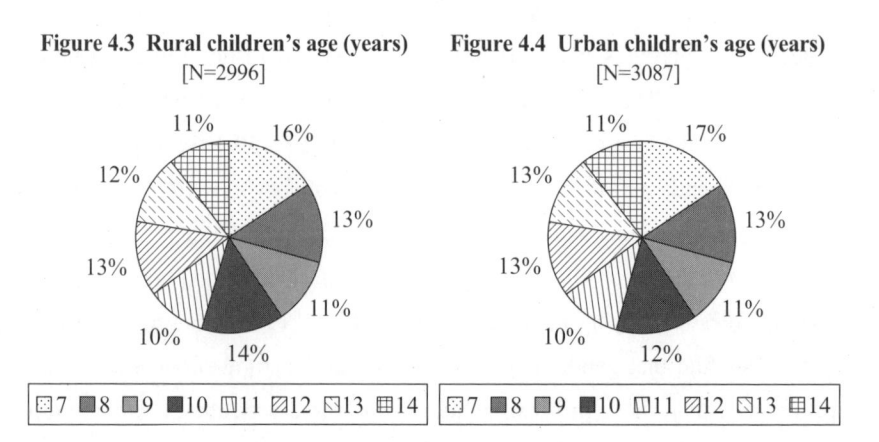

Figure 4.3 Rural children's age (years)
[N=2996]

11%, 16%, 12%, 13%, 13%, 10%, 14%, 11%

☒7 ■8 ■9 ■10 ▥11 ▨12 ▧13 ⊞14

Figure 4.4 Urban children's age (years)
[N=3087]

11%, 17%, 13%, 13%, 13%, 10%, 12%, 11%

☒7 ■8 ■9 ■10 ▥11 ▨12 ▧13 ⊞14

Figure 4.5 Children's gender

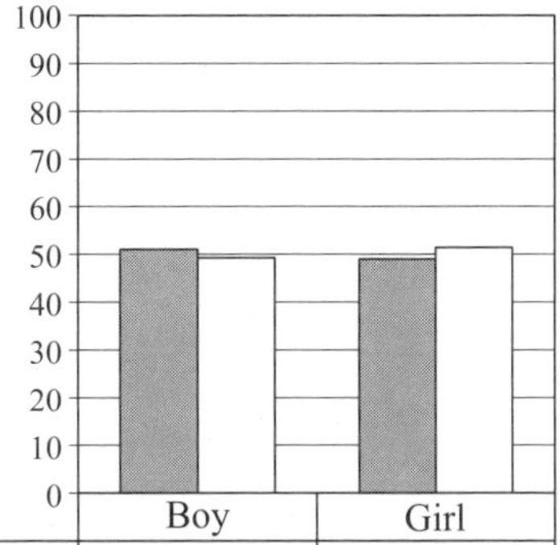

	Boy	Girl
■ RURAL%	51	49
□ URBAN%	49	51

one dataset of survey execution notes containing household identification code, regional/cluster/village/district codes and the like; 12 datasets of the household and individual information; three datasets of the result from the contingent tests; one dataset of the result from the Sabot's test; one dataset of material prices; and one district-level dataset. For the analysis in this section, focusing on the 7-14 year old school-age children, I will use the variables from some household and individual datasets. The data to be examined here is from 6083 respondents (7-14 year old: 2996 living in rural districts, 3087 living in urban districts).

In terms of demographic information of the samples, the age and gender of 6083 children by rural-urban areas are distributed as below.

No large numerical differences between rural and urban samples can be seen in these age and gender variables. I will analyze the data from the perspectives of "three factors of instrumental freedom for human development" introduced in Chapter three (3.2.1 (a)), which are composed of educational, health, and material wealth aspects of life.

(a) Education

As an educational factor, children's responses to three questions on litera-

Table 4.3 Questions on literacy and numeracy

Questions \ Answers	RURAL (%) Yes	No	URBAN (%) Yes	No
Can you read?*	47	53	60	40
Can you write?**	41	59	53	47
Can you do arithmetic?***	45	55	57	43
Have you ever been to school in the last 12 months?****	61	39	67	33

* Rural N=2985; Urban N=3063
** Rural N=2985; Urban N=3062
*** Rural N=2985; Urban N=3064
**** Rural N=2987; Urban N=3060

(Created by the author from the World Bank, 1997, the THRDS)

cy and numeracy and one question on schooling experience are seen as below.

Urban children are more likely to be literate and numerate than rural children. In other words, only 41 percent, 47 percent, and 45 percent of rural children can write, read, and do arithmetic respectively, while 53 percent, 60 percent, and 57 percent of urban children can write, read, and do arithmetic.[10] The same tendency can be seen in schooling experience too: only 61 percent of rural children have been to school in the last 12 months, while 67 percent of urban children have.[11]

(b) Health

As a health factor, water-related variables are used here. Means of *the time to fetch water in a day* and *the distance to drinking water* for rural and urban areas are shown as below.

Rural children generally take more time to fetch water per day than urban children.[12] This may be partially because the source of drinking water in rural districts is generally located farer from home than that in urban districts is. This point becomes clearer when looking at *source of drinking water*. The difference between rural and urban areas is found as follows.

In rural districts, *river, lake, spring, or pond* is the most common source of

Ch.4 Case study: Tanzania *131*

Table 4.4 means of water-related variables

	RURAL				URBAN			
	Mean	SD	Min	Max	Mean	SD	Min	Max
Time to fetch water (min)	27.97	58.35	0	600	13.97	37.28	0	360
Distance to drinking water (m)	5307.89	60332.51	0	1500000	1446.03	19714.75	0	500000

(Created by the author from the World Bank, 1997, the THRDS)

Figure 4.6 Source of drinking water (Rural)
[N=2988]

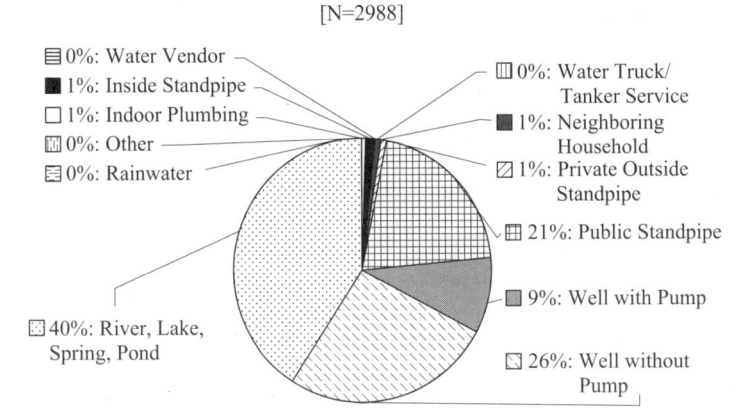

- 0%: Water Vendor
- 1%: Inside Standpipe
- 1%: Indoor Plumbing
- 0%: Other
- 0%: Rainwater
- 40%: River, Lake, Spring, Pond
- 0%: Water Truck/ Tanker Service
- 1%: Neighboring Household
- 1%: Private Outside Standpipe
- 21%: Public Standpipe
- 9%: Well with Pump
- 26%: Well without Pump

Figure 4.7 Source of drinking water (Urban)
[N=3077]

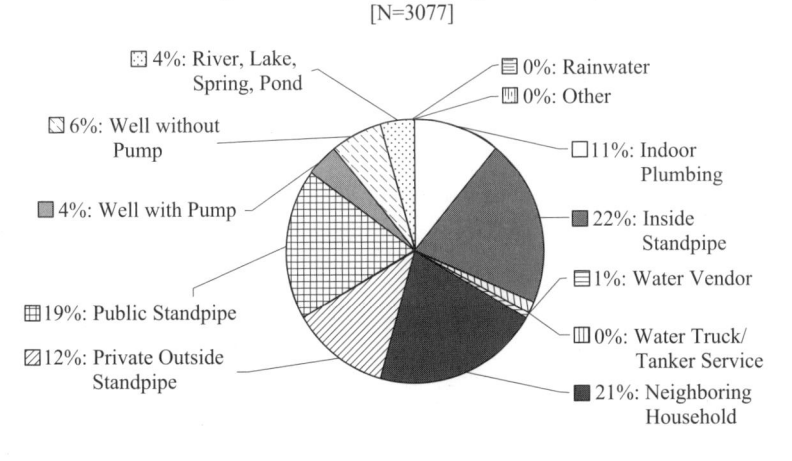

- 4%: River, Lake, Spring, Pond
- 6%: Well without Pump
- 4%: Well with Pump
- 19%: Public Standpipe
- 12%: Private Outside Standpipe
- 0%: Rainwater
- 0%: Other
- 11%: Indoor Plumbing
- 22%: Inside Standpipe
- 1%: Water Vendor
- 0%: Water Truck/ Tanker Service
- 21%: Neighboring Household

drinking water followed by *well without pump*, *public standpipe*, and *well with pump* in that order. On the other hand, in urban districts, *neighboring household* and *inside standpipe* are the two major sources followed by *public standpipe*, *private outside standpipe/tap*, and *indoor plumbing*. This difference shows that rural children may be more likely to drink unsanitary water. In addition, this difference of source may affect children's time to fetch water, which can affect children's time for schooling and doing school work. In this sense, water access can be related to education, and also it can be considered as a material factor too since sanitary water requires equipment such as standpipe.

(c) Material wealth

As a material wealth factor, the responses to four questions on material possessions are seen as below.

For all materials, urban children own more than rural children.[13] While only 71 percent rural children own shoes, 93 percent urban children own them: possession of shoes can be related to children's health too since bare feet pose a greater risk of injury and thanatophidia. While only 30 percent rural children own at least one book, 39 percent urban children do: book possession can be related to children's education too, especially to their literacy. While only 13 percent rural children have electricity, 85 percent urban chil-

Table 4.5 **Questions on material possessions**

Questions / Answers	RURAL (%) Yes	No	URBAN (%) Yes	No
Do you have shoes?*	71	29	93	7
Do you have any book?**	30	70	39	61
Do you have electricity?***	13	87	85	15
Do you have a bank account?****	14	86	44	56

* Rural N=2992; Urban N=3070
** Rural N=2990; Urban N=3066
*** Rural N=2994; Urban N=3086
**** Rural N=2987; Urban N=3074

(Created by the author from the World Bank, 1997, the THRDS)

dren have it: availability of electricity can be related to quality of public services at the district level. While only 14 percent of rural children's households have a bank account, 44 percent of urban children's households have it: possession of a bank account indicates that the household participates in the market economy and that the household may be relatively affluent economically.

In general, it can be said that there is a rural-urban gap in all these aspects of education, health, and material wealth of life.

4.3 Conclusion of the chapter:
Significance of needs assessment for human development policy

In this chapter, the historical transition of educational and social policies in Tanzania was reviewed (4.1), and Tanzanian children's life circumstances in the 1990s was described by using the database called *Tanzania Human Resource Development Survey* (THRDS). The historical review considered the national-level policies; the statistical description showed the local-level individual life.

The historical review of Tanzania's policies showed that Tanzania has struggled with the contradiction between its "socialist vision and capitalist practice" (Samoff, 1990, p.262). Since independence in 1964, Tanzania's original philosophy of *Ujamaa* or "familyhood" has aimed at constructing an *Ujamaa* socialist nation through primary education for the masses (4.1.2 (a) & (b)). *Ujamaa* made Tanzanian policies unique among neighboring countries by introducing "nonrevolutionary noncapitalist development" (Samoff, 1990, p210), and Tanzania's unique policies, especially its education policies focusing on primary schooling for self-reliance, inspired many other countries (Samoff, 1990) when the post-secondary education played a dominant role for national economic development in the 1960s (cf. human capital theory such as Schultz, 1971; Becker, 1967, 1993; Becker & Murphy, 1990). These policies effectively provided more relevant education to children's daily life and succeeded in increasing the number of pupils enrolled (Mbunda, 1982). However, the world trend toward capitalism prevented Tanzania from achieving its own goal through primary education particularly during the 1980s. Eventually, structural adjustment policies widened the domestic gap between rural and urban districts in contravention of Tanzania's ideal of *Ujamaa* socialism (4.1.2 (c)).

The existence of this rural-urban gap was demonstrated by the statistical data THRDS collected in 1993 (4.2). All "three factors of instrumental freedom" (education, health, and material wealth) showed gaps between rural and urban schooling-age children (4.2.2). In education, urban children are more likely to be literate and numerate; in health, rural children more likely to spend their time on fetching water and to drink unsanitary water; and in material wealth, urban children are more likely to enjoy materials which will support their health and education. Although the urban condition is not particular satisfactory, the descriptive statistics clarified that there is a rural-urban gap in all three factors and that the rural children's life conditions are generally more difficult than urban children's.

Since the rural-urban gap was found in all three factors, it is natural to assume that there can be different needs in rural and urban districts. Resources are always limited; therefore, it is a key for policy analysis to find and propose an appropriate priority order of such needs. Which factor actually matters in rural and urban areas respectively? In the next chapter, I will try to answer this question by applying a modeling method called Hierarchical Generalized Linear Modeling for the THRDS data.

Why does the rural-urban gap matter for Tanzanian society and for education policy for human development? As stated in section 4.2, Tanzania's original philosophy *Ujamaa* and its subsequent policy implications aspire to the goals implied by the concept of human development. For example, the Tanzanian government has given a high priority, both financially and ideologically, to public primary schooling as mass education, even when post-secondary education, supported by human capital theory, was dominant in neighbor countries. The Tanzanian government also has specifically focused on children's life-skill development since its independence in1964, far before the world declaration *Education for All* in 1990.[14] This is consistent with the idea of "basic education as a central instrumental freedom" introduced in 3.2.1 (b). In addition, Founding Prime Minister Nyerere said that "progress [of development of a society] is measured in terms of human well-being, not prestige buildings, cars, or other such things" (Nyerere, 1982a, p.240), which is also consistent with the idea of human development introduced in Chapter two (2.1.1).

Moreover, it is important to note that this direction of Tanzania's education policies does not deny external influence. As claimed by Sen (2000) in 1.2.2, Tanzania has "learn[ed] from elsewhere without being overwhelmed by that experience" (Sen, 2000 p.243). In other words, it accepted a form of schooling as a distribution method of education but maintained the purpose of schooling, creation of an *Ujamaa* society. Especially after the Universal Primary Education policy was adopted in1974, "the schools seemed the obvious site for this sort of educational practice... Schooling was to become *education for Tanzanian socialism*" (Samoff, 1990, p.230), which meant that Tanzania used the school system in its own way and for its own purpose.

Therefore, achievement of Tanzania's original goal, constructing an *Ujamaa* society through primary education, can be called the Tanzanian conception of human development. However, it has never been achieved at the actual policy level. For promoting the Tanzanian conception of human development and for implementing its educational and social policies for human development, the first and most fundamental step is to reduce the rural-urban gap because both purposes require domestic equality: *Ujamaa* aims at social equality (see 4.1.2) and human development theory assumes the universal value of all (see 3.1.2).

This chapter described the similarity between Tanzanian original philosophy and the concept of human development at the theoretical level and the dilemma of Tanzanian society struggling between the *Ujamaa* ideal and capitalist urgency at the actual policy level. The possible direction that Tanzanian society needs to take is to span the divide between the theoretical and actual policy levels. Here is the significance of needs assessment for human development policy that contributes to reducing the rural-urban gap and promoting the theoretical model of human development at the actual policy level. The next chapter will challenge this problem by testing the theoretical model of human development empirically using Tanzania's data and by assessing rural and urban needs for human development policy.

Notes

[1] Tanganyika African National Union (TANU) was established in 1954 as a national territorial movement to represent Tanganyika local interests to the colonial government (Buchert, 1994, p.57). The political goal of TANU is to build a socialist nation.

[2] Of course, criticisms of the *Arusha Declaration* have also been made. For example, Svendsen (1969) points out the Declaration's inconsistency between a socialist agricultural policy and insufficient provision for social control of the economy (pp.209-218).

[3] The entry age of primary school was five or six years old, but Nyerere (1982a) considered that it was too low: "Nor can we expect those finishing primary schools to be useful young citizens if they are still only 12 or 13 years of age" (Nyerere, 1982a, p.245). This statement may be based on the fact that only around 10 percent of the primary graduates go to secondary school (from the 1960s to present) and hence the primary graduates are considered as citizens.

[4] The Statistics Section in Planning Division in Tanzanian Ministry of National Education (1967-1975) collected and published the actual numbers of enrolled pupils, teachers, and primary schools, but not the enrollment ratio. Therefore, even though Figure 4.2 shows increase of enrolled pupils and teachers, it did not include even half of children in Tanzania.

[5] The government party TANU held the National Conference in September 1973 and noted that the primary school enrollment ratio was 48.6 percent (Mbunda, 1982, p.93).

[6] However, this requirement caused an argument with the Umoja Wa Wanawake

Tanganyika (the Union of Tanganyika Women). The Union argued that "the Resolution's two-year work prerequisite discouraged or disqualified women from entering the university" (Block, 1984, p.108). According to Block (1984), the female enrollment at the University of Dar es Salaam in year 1974/75 was 13 percent; however, in the first year when the Resolution was endorsed (1975/76), it dropped to 10 percent. The Union's argument won the women's waiver of the Resolution requirement in 1977/78.

[7] This reorientation was reflected in the acknowledgement of English as the medium of instruction at the post-primary level, whereas Kiswahili was maintained at the primary level (Buchert, 1994, p.147).

[8] There are some studies using the data from the World Bank's *Living Standards Measurement Surveys* (LSMS), which includes the survey in Tanzania, THRDS. Pisani and Pagan (2004) use one of the LSMS sources called the *Nicaragua National Household Living Standards Survey* in 1993 and 1998 to analyze self-employment phenomena in Nicaragua. Thang and Popkin (2003) use one of the LSMS data collected in Vietnam called the *Vietnam Living Standard Survey* in 1992-93 and 1997-98. They use logistic regression models with dichotomous outcome variables of stunted (if a child is stunted or not) and underweighted (if a child is underweighted) to analyze child malnutrition in Vietnam.

[9] Gini coefficient is defined by the proportion of the areas drawn by the Lorenz curve and the diagonal line divided by the areas below the diagonal line (Takagi, 1996, pp.26-29).

[10] Chi-square tests show statistically significant differences between the rural and urban children in all three questions (Kirk, 1999, pp.355-358; Tabachnick & Fidell, 2001, p.55): χ^2 of *reading* (1, n = 6048) = 100.719, $p<0.01$; χ^2 of *writing* (1, n = 6047) = 92.742, $p<0.01$; and χ^2 of *arithmetic* (1, n = 6049) = 86.688, $p<0.01$.

[11] Chi-square test shows statistically significant difference between the rural and urban children in schooling experience: χ^2 (1, n = 6047) = 23.089, $p<0.01$.

[12] Analysis of Variance (ANOVA) can assure statistical significance of difference among multiple groups in single continuous variable. However, the variables *time to fetch water* and *distance to drinking water* here violate statistical assumption of normal distribution (Kirk, 1999, pp.479-480), and hence correct results cannot be expected from ANOVA for these variables. Therefore, no statistical test is conducted for them.

[13] Chi-square tests show statistically significant differences between the rural and urban children in all four questions: χ^2 of *shoes* (1, n = 6062) = 506.149, $p<0.01$; χ^2 of *book* (1, n = 6056) = 48.759, $p<0.01$; χ^2 of *electricity* (1, n = 6080) = 3100.021, $p<0.01$; and χ^2 of *bank account* (1, n = 6061) = 635.006, $p<0.01$. However, the cross tabulation of shoes contains the cell showing less than 5 percent (3.51 percent of those who own no shoes living in the urban area). Therefore, the interpretation of χ^2 of shoes may be prob-

lematic.

[14] The world declaration *Education for All* in 1990 shifted the emphasis of educational development into basic education from manpower creation through higher education. After this declaration, more and more intensive attention has been paid to basic education, and basic education today plays a central role in educational development. However, before this declaration, the post-secondary education was a dominant tool for national manpower development in most of developing countries.

Modeling a modified human development theory

Chapter 5

Why is quantitative modeling of a modified human development theory useful? As previously discussed, there are three answers. First, as mentioned in Chapter two (2.1.2), we need a more comprehensive way to capture the concept of human development beyond the Human Development Index (HDI). Although Panigrahi and Sivramkrishna's (2002) invention of the "adjusted HDI (AHDI)" improved the accuracy of HDI as an indicator, it is still provide country rankings only. As Esho (1999) observes:

> Ranking countries by HDI is not the best way to take advantage of Sen's idea ... Sen's idea should be embodied in an indicator that analyzes specifically what kinds of capabilities are insufficient at each level of nation, region, social class, and gender; and to seek for its reason. (p.216, translated by the author)

Human development theory is not a standard for ranking one country as more or less developed than an other. Rather, it should produce a diagnosis of each individual country to allow the people of that society to achieve more easily their "constitutive freedom" (see 2.2.1). In order to apply human development theory in its full meaning, it is necessary to construct a model that goes beyond rakings to diagnose factors of human development in each society.

Second, as considered in Chapter three (3.2.2), a modified human development theory needs to be specified as a practically meaningful idea, particularly as a needs assessment model for people's internal capability development. Since human development theory is a highly comprehensive concept, it tends to end in an abstract theory. As Khoi (1991) argues, however, quantitative studies can confine the range of complex phenomena and clarify abstract concepts (p.224). A quantitative model can make a complicated reality manageable and analyzable. Even though it is impossible for a quantitative model to capture the whole complexity of a real society, and even though it is inevitable for a quantitative model to miss some qualitative aspects of the phenomena, the model will give us guidance for approaching the complex problems associated with human development.

Finally, because this study is a policy analysis, I cannot ignore issues of generalization and feasibility of human development theory. In order to create a bridge between abstract theory and practical policy recommendations, empirical research needs to guarantee a certain level of generalizability; interviews of a few individuals would be unlikely to represent the whole population and hence provide an unreasonable basis for generalizing to a national policy recommendation. When considering compulsory public primary education as a tool to promote instrumental freedom, as discussed in 3.2.1 (b), and when taking the national population into consideration for public policy formulation, a quantitative approach becomes necessary to allow for generalization of the analysis. Although quantification alone does not necessarily allow generalization, this is a useful way to depict a large picture. In addition, quantitative language tends to be sharable with practitioners, which can enhance the practicality of the study. In order for an abstract concept to be useful in the actual context of policy formulation, it is necessary for policy studies to share a common language with practitioners.

For these three reasons, in this chapter, I will empirically test the theoretical model based on the modified human development theory developed in Chapter three. The next section (5.1) will lay the groundwork for modeling, including reconfirmation of the conceptual model (5.1.1), selection of the modeling method (5.1.2), and definition of the variables to be used in the model (5.1.3). In section 5.2, I will apply Hierarchical Generalized Linear Modeling (HGLM) to examine the theoretical model. The substantive interpretation of the models and their application to policy will be discussed in the next chapter.

5.1 Preparation for modeling

In this section, I will provide an overview of the conceptual model of the modified human development theory developed in Chapter three and clarify the hypotheses to be tested in this chapter (5.1.1). I will also discuss the appropriate modeling method for this study (5.1.2), and define the variables to be used from the *Tanzania Human Resource Development Survey* (THRDS) introduced in Chapter four (5.1.3).

5.1.1 Reconfirmation of the conceptual model

In Chapter three, I reconsidered Sen's theory of human development and modified it by employing the idea of Kantian liberalism (3.1.3) and Nussbaum's hierarchy of human capability (3.2.1). Through this reconsideration, I brought a philosophical idea of human development into the field of education, asserting that:

> Literacy functions as a central internal capability, especially for children to develop their instrumental freedom to achieve their constitutive freedom in the future; therefore, compulsory public primary education is expected to guarantee the opportunity for all children to obtain literacy. (Summary of claim two; see 3.2)

Based on this theoretical conclusion, the model to be considered here is represented in Figure 5.1:

Theoretically, the entire model assumes that improvement of individual literacy contributes to developing one's instrumental freedom, which eventually helps individuals achieve their constitutive freedom (see 3.2). However,

Figure 5.1 The theoretical & empirical model of human development

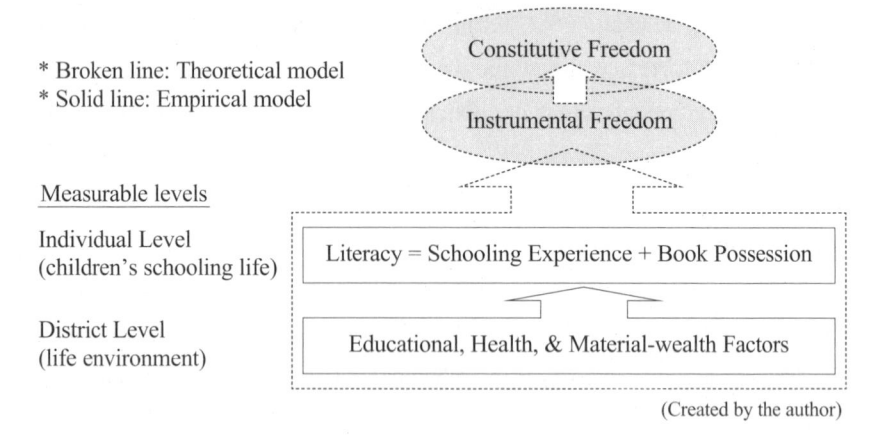

* Broken line: Theoretical model
* Solid line: Empirical model

Constitutive Freedom

Instrumental Freedom

Measurable levels

Individual Level
(children's schooling life)

Literacy = Schooling Experience + Book Possession

District Level
(life environment)

Educational, Health, & Material-wealth Factors

(Created by the author)

due to the limitations of the available data, it is not possible to test the entire model. Therefore, the model to be tested in this chapter is limited to the model indicated by the solid lines in Figure 5.1: individual children's schooling life and life environment at the district level. The individual-level model assumes that children's schooling life contributes to their literacy development. Although there are other possibilities of variables to measure *literacy* besides *schooling experience* and *book possession*, this model focuses on these variables due to data limitation. The district-level model assumes that children's environmental conditions including educational, health, and material factors contribute to creating opportunities for children to develop their literacy. The variables to represent the three factors will be introduced in 5.1.3. In sum, the model to be tested in this chapter will focus on the process of central internal capability development, or literacy development, for the realization of freedoms.

An empirical model built on a modified human development theory is expected to function as a *needs assessment* that can contribute to improving children's literacy and eventually their instrumental and constitutive freedoms. It is worth repeating the three major characteristics of the model, introduced in Chapter three:

1. *Comprehensive perspective*

    The model sustains a comprehensive perspective on human development. Specifically in an empirical model, explanatory variables at the district level represent three factors of instrumental freedom: education, health, and material wealth. The model assumes that all three factors contribute to children's literacy.

2. *Hierarchical structure*

    The model pays attention to differences between the individual and district levels. Individual lives can be affected by district differences; for example, the needs of some people living in an affluent district can be different from those living in a needy district even if their individual conditions are the same. An empirical model considers variance among districts, not only among individuals, through hierarchical modeling.

3. *Literacy as a "promoter" of human development*

    The model takes literacy as an outcome variable, assuming that literacy contributes to the development of advanced capabilities needed to promote one's instrumental freedom and eventually to achieve one's constitutive freedom. Since literacy is a tool for achieving freedom, an outcome variable in this model is not literally an "outcome" but a necessary condition of human development. This assumption is not testable by modeling; however, it is theoretically important when considering the meaning of the models (see Chapter six).

When testing this model, I hypothesize that:

1. General conditions affect individual lives: Effects of the life environment at the district level may have significant impacts on children's schooling life at the individual level.

2. Individual needs differ between rural and urban areas: As shown by descriptive statistics in 4.2, there are significant differences between rural and urban districts. These differences may result in different needs in the rural and urban areas.
3. Comprehensive needs extend beyond educational factors: As human development theory claims comprehensiveness of development, non-educational factors, such as health and material wealth factors, may also contribute to children's literacy, in addition to educational factors.

Given the extensive attention that has been paid to girls' education in Africa (UNESCO, 2003), and to women's needs in Nussbaum's own work (1999, 2000a, 2000b), it is important to clarify why gender does not enter the model proposed below. I do not hypothesize different needs between genders in this study for two reasons. First, historically the Tanzanian government has focused on equality of educational access and it may be the reason why the gender gap in Tanzania is relatively small among African countries. Second, as a result of this policy emphasis, Tanzania's Gender Parity Index (GPI) in primary education is officially reported as 0.99 (in 2000, UNESCO, 2003, p.326), which indicates that there is almost no gender gap in primary education.[1]

5.1.2 Selection of the modeling method: HGLM vs. SEM

There are two possible methods appropriate to model a modified human development theory: Hierarchical Generalized Linear Modeling (HGLM) and Structural Equation Modeling (SEM). The first method, SEM "attempts to explain the relationships among a set of observed variables in terms of a generally smaller number of unobserved variables" (Long, 1983, p.11). SEM is composed of a measurement model part and a structural model part: (1) "the measurement part, linking observed variables to latent variables [or unobserved variables in Long, 1983] via a confirmatory factor model" and (2) "the structural part, linking latent variables to each other via systems of simultaneous equations" (Kaplan, 2000, p.5). SEM can analyze complicated relations among observed variables as well as unobserved latent variables.

The advantages of SEM are that: (1) SEM can deal with conceptual variables, called latent variables, to represent educational, health, and material wealth factors; and that (2) SEM can analyze direct effects and indirect effects separately, for example, it can examine the effects of education-related variables on literacy as *direct* effects and the effects of health-related variables on literacy as *indirect* effects. SEM would be advantageous for modeling human development theory because it can accurately reflect the conceptual relations of a modified human development theory, particularly the relations and influences of the three factors identified above. In addition, SEM would be useful for articulating theoretical assumptions by differentiating direct and indirect effects among variables in the model.

In contrast to SEM, H(G)LM aims to examine "relations between variables at different layers in a hierarchical system" (Snijders & Bosker, 2003, p.6). In H(G)LM, the explanatory variables are nested. For example, they may include both individual student-level variables and classroom-level variables that affect each student in a given classroom. Therefore, H(G)LM is appropriate for examining the effects of variables at different levels and the interactions across different levels. HGLM in particular, aims to analyze data with using a non-linear model, as elaborated in 5.2 below. In HGLM, the outcome variable is non-continuous, for example it may be binary data, count data, ordinal data, or multinominal data (see Raudenbush & Bryk, 2002, pp.291-335). The technical details of HLM and HGLM will be explained later in 5.2.

Thus, the advantages of HGLM for modeling a complex theory such as that of human development are that: (1) HGLM can deal with nested structured data, containing the variables from different levels such as an individual level and a district level; and that (2) HGLM can use a dichotomous outcome variable in a statistically robust manner. Because of its ability to capture the hierarchical structure of the theoretical model, HGLM is useful for policy purposes, such as examining the effects of the district-level public services on individual children's literacy. HGLM is also appropriate for this study since the outcome variable *literacy* is dichotomous in the database.

A third advantage of HGLM is that it requires fewer statistical assumptions than alternative methods. The database being used, the *Tanzania Human Resource Development Survey* (THRDS) is not robust enough to satisfy strict statistical assumptions. Although SEM may be a better way to reflect the conceptual aspect of the human development theory, there is a practical limitation of this method. According to Kaplan (2000), data employed in SEM must meet strict statistical assumptions. These include multivariate normality, no systematic missing data, sufficiently large sample size, and correct model specification (pp.79-105). The multivariate normality assumption is particularly problematic for this study since many variables in THRDS violate this assumption. HGLM is a robust method in this sense. Since HGLM is a non-linear modeling method, a normality assumption is not required for this method. The model in this study will have two levels, individual and district levels, and Raudenbush and Bryk (2002) articulate that "estimation of the fixed effects will not be biased by a failure of the normality assumption at level 2" (p.274), in addition to level one.

In addition to this practical limitation of the data, in order to propose policy recommendations for Tanzania's human development policy, HGLM is more appropriate than SEM because the dataset THRDS contains both individual-level data and district-level data. HGLM can take the best advantage of this data structure and examine how the district-level public services affect children's literacy. By analyzing the district-level effects on the individual-level literacy, the models will allow me to discuss what may be significant

factor(s) that might improve children's literacy.
For these reasons, I will use HGLM in this study to analyze THRDS.

5.1.3 Definition of the variables:
From the Tanzania Human Resource Development Survey

For this study, the rural and urban samples (7-14 years old school-age children) from the *Tanzania Human Resource Development Survey* (THRDS) are used with the variables as follows. Table 5.1 shows the final selection of the variables from THRDS. This section will explain why and how these variables were selected.

Table 5.1 Description of variables

LEVEL-1 VARIABLES (Individual children age 7-14)	
Writing	Whether the children can write a letter or not (yes=1, no=0)
Book	Whether the children own a book or not (yes=1, no=0)
Schooling	Whether the children have attended school during the past 12 months (yes=1, no=0)
LEVEL-2 VARIABLES (District)	
TCHR	Number of teachers per 10,000 people
PRIM	Number of primary schools per 10,000 people
DISP	Number of dispensaries per 10,000 people
AID	Number of staff of maternal and child health aid per 10,000 people
WAT	Percentage of the population with clean water
BRANCH	Number of national banks (community branches) per 10,000 people

(Ferreira & Griffin, 1996; World Bank, 1993)

(a) Individual level (outcome variable): Literacy

UNESCO (2005a) defines "literacy" as "the ability to read and write, with understanding, a short simple sentence about one's everyday life" (p.127); and fundamental literacy and numeracy skills are often defined as the "3Rs" which comprise reading, writing, and arithmetic (Thomas, 2004, p.237; UNICEF, 1998a). The THRDS datasets contain variables of *reading* (if able to read a newspaper; yes = 1, no = 0), *writing* (if able to write a letter; yes =

Table 5.2 Correlations among writing, reading, and arithmetic: Rural

Simple Statistics				Pearson Correlation Coefficients (** p<.0001)		
Variable	N	Mean	Std Dev	1.	2.	3.
Reading	2985	0.47069	0.49922	1. Reading –	0.878**	0.838**
Writing	2985	0.40804	0.49155	2. Writing	–	0.876**
Arithmetic	2985	0.44556	0.49711	3. Arithmetic		–

(Analyzed by SAS 9.13)

Table 5.3 Correlations among writing, reading, and arithmetic: Urban

Simple Statistics				Pearson Correlation Coefficients (** p<.0001)		
Variable	N	Mean	Std D	1.	2.	3.
Reading	3093	0.59941	0.49010	1. Reading –	0.863**	0.873**
Writing	3062	0.53168	0.49908	2. Writing	–	0.8795**
Arithmetic	3064	0.56527	0.49580	3. Arithmetic		–

(Analyzed by SAS 9.13)

1, no = 0),[2] and *arithmetic* (if able to do written calculations; yes = 1, no = 0). High correlations are found among these three variables as seen in Tables 5.2 and 5.3.

Correlations among these three variables are all more than 0.8 (p<0.01); therefore, it may be reasonable to use one of these variables, especially either *reading* or *writing*, as a proxy of literacy. The frequency of children's *read-*

Table 5.4 Frequency of reading and writing conditions

RURAL					URBAN				
			Cumulative	Cumulative				Cumulative	Cumulative
Condition	Frequency	%	Frequency	%	Condition	Frequency	%	Frequency	%
0	1578	52.88	1578	52.88	0	1220	39.86	1220	39.86
1	189	6.33	1767	59.22	1	214	6.99	1434	46.85
2	1215	40.72	2982	99.93	2	1621	52.96	3055	99.80
9	2	0.07	2984	100.00	9	6	0.20	3061	100.00

* Frequency Missing = 12   * Frequency Missing = 26

Condition 0: cannot read or write
Condition 1: can read but cannot write
Condition 2: can read and write
Condition 9: cannot read but can write - unreasonable condition

(Analyzed by SAS 9.13)

ing and *writing* are as follows.

The results show that those who can read are not always able to write (Condition one=189 in rural, 214 in urban), but that those who can write report almost always being able to read. Although there are a few exceptions to Condition nine, children with writing ability but no reading ability (2 out of 2984 in the rural sample and 6 out of 3061 in the urban sample), it seems unreasonable to assume that those who cannot read can write. Since there are only 2 and 6 exceptions out of 2984 and 3061 respectively, I will assume that children with writing ability have reading ability. Therefore, I will define a variable of writing as proxy for children's literacy, and use it as an outcome variable in the model.

(b) Individual level (explanatory variables): Schooling experience and book possession

It is a common assumption in the scholarly literature that participation in schooling has an impact on children's literacy (Fuller et al., 1999; Haidara, 1990; Muller & Murtagh, 2002; Smith, 1970). I also assume that schooling experience contributes to literacy development. Moreover, as pointed out in Chapter four, education policy in Tanzania has emphasized schools as a site for literacy development: "the schools seemed the obvious site for this sort of educational practice... schooling was to become *education for Tanzanian socialism*" (Samoff, 1990, p.230). The datasets contain a variable of *schooling* (if attending school during the past 12 months; yes = 1, no = 0). I will use this variable as an explanatory variable of the model.

Elley (2000) argues that books have a significant role in literacy development by introducing "the Book Flood approach," an approach to reducing illiteracy by providing books to schools. He conducted experimental design analyses in primary schools in Niue, Fiji, Singapore, Sri Lanka, South Africa and Solomon Islands that show the success of this approach. Although Elley's study focuses on second language literacy, it should be applicable for literacy development in general. Moreover, considering the multi-lingual social situation in Tanzania, where most children have a mother language besides the teaching medium language, Swahili, it is reasonable to apply Elley's findings to the Tanzanian case. Following Elley's argument, I assume that possession of books contributes to children's literacy. The datasets contain a variable of *own-a-book?* (if owning a book; yes = 1, no = 0). Therefore, I will use this variable as an explanatory variable of the model.

However, it is necessary to note that the variable *book possession* may not correctly reflect the reality in Tanzania. In Tanzania, books are very expensive, and textbooks are not required and not free in most primary schools. Thus, many teachers and students do not own textbooks themselves (Murakami, 2002). An ideal variable for this study should be not *book possession* but *book access*, indicating whether the child has any access to books including borrowing them from friends or schools. Since no variable for book access exists in the THRDS, I will use the variable *book possession* to represent children's access to books.

The correlation between these two explanatory variables is shown in Tables 5.5 and 5.6 below.

There are significant correlations between *schooling* and *book* in both rural and urban data, but their correlations (Φ_{rural} = 0.47, Φ_{urban} = 0.47) does not indicate multicollinearity.[3]

About multicollinearity, Tabachnick and Fidell (2001) say that from a technical point of view "the statistical problems created by singularity and multicollinearity occur at much higher correlations (.90 and higher)" (p.84). The sociological and educational literature that employs H(G)LM provides little guidance on this issue, leaving it unexplained (see Roderick & Camburn, 1999; Schiller & Muller, 2000). In this study, I will take a conservative approach and check correlation matrices among the variables in advance in case there might be extremely high correlations. While not technically neces-

Table 5.5 Chi-square test and Phi coefficient: Rural

book	Freq(%) Row(%) Col(%)	schooling 0	schooling 1	total (%)
	0	1122 / 37.63 / 54.05 / 96.81	954 / 31.99 / 45.95 / 52.33	2076 (69.62)
	1	37 / 1.24 / 4.08 / 3.19	869 / 29.14 / 95.92 / 47.67	906 (30.38)
total (%)		1159 (38.87)	1823 (61.13)	2982 (100.00)

Statistic	df	value	p
Chi-square	1	662.642	<.0001
Likelihood ratio Chi-square	1	811.365	<.0001
Continuity adj. Chi-square	1	660.541	<.0001
Phi coefficient		0.471	
Contingency coefficient		0.426	
Crame's V		0.471	

* Frequency missing = 14   (Analyzed by SAS 9.13)

Table 5.6 Chi-square test and Phi coefficient: Urban

book	Freq(%) Row(%) Col(%)	schooling 0	schooling 1	total (%)
	0	941 / 30.86 / 50.59 / 93.63	919 / 30.14 / 49.41 / 44.96	1860 (61.00)
	1	64 / 2.10 / 5.38 / 6.37	1125 / 36.90 / 94.62 / 55.04	1189 (39.00)
total (%)		1005 (32.95)	2044 (67.04)	3049 (100.00)

Statistic	df	value	p
Chi-square	1	670.888	<.0001
Likelihood ratio Chi-square	1	788.809	<.0001
Continuity adj. Chi-square	1	688.843	<.0001
Phi coefficient		0.469	
Contingency coefficient		0.425	
Crame's V		0.469	

* Frequency missing = 38   (Analyzed by SAS 9.13)

sary, this will help reduce the introduction of unnecessary variables into the model. I will not keep the variables strongly correlated to other variables for purposes of parsimonious modeling.

The relationships between *writing* and *schooling* and between *writing* and *book* are presented in Tables 5.7 and 5.8.[4]

The tables above suggest the effects of book possession and schooling experience on children's writing ability, although the interpretation of these

Table 5.7 Chi-square test for writing: Rural

Freq(%) Row(%) Col(%)		book		total
		0	1	(%)
writing	0	1122 37.63 54.05 96.81	954 31.99 45.95 52.33	2076 (69.62)
	1	37 1.24 4.08 3.19	869 29.14 95.92 47.67	906 (30.38)
total (%)		1159 (38.87)	1823 (61.13)	2982 (100.00)

* Frequency missing = 16
$\chi^2(df = 1) = 667.4002$ (p<.0001)
Phi coefficient = 0.4732

Freq(%) Row(%) Col(%)		schooling		total
		0	1	(%)
writing	0	1122 37.63 54.05 96.81	954 31.99 45.95 52.33	2076 (69.62)
	1	37 1.24 4.08 3.19	869 29.14 95.92 47.67	906 (30.38)
total (%)		1159 (38.87)	1823 (61.13)	2982 (100.00)

* Frequency missing = 19
$\chi^2(df = 1) = 1036.7775$ (p<.0001)
Phi coefficient = 0.5901

(Analyzed by SAS 9.13)

Table 5.8 Chi-square test for writing: Urban

Freq(%) Row(%) Col(%)		book		total
		0	1	(%)
writing	0	1228 40.24 85.87 65.95	202 6.62 14.13 16.97	1430 (46.85)
	1	634 20.77 39.09 34.05	988 32.37 60.91 83.03	1622 (53.15)
total (%)		1862 (61.01)	1190 (38.99)	3052 (100.00)

* Frequency missing = 35
$\chi^2(df = 1) = 699.3384$ (p<.0001)
Phi coefficient = 0.4787

Freq(%) Row(%) Col(%)		schooling		total
		0	1	(%)
writing	0	935 30.72 65.75 93.88	487 16.00 34.25 23.78	1422 (46.71)
	1	61 2.00 3.76 6.12	1561 51.28 96.24 76.22	1622 (53.29)
total (%)		996 (32.72)	2048 (67.28)	2977 (100.00)

* Frequency missing = 43
$\chi^2(df = 1) = 1322.7340$ (p<.0001)
Phi coefficient = 0.6592

(Analyzed by SAS 9.13)

tables may be problematic because these tables contain cells with less than 5 percent frequency. These effects of book possession and schooling experience will be examined more precisely in HGLM.[5]

(c) District level (explanatory variables): Educational, health, and material wealth factors

In order to consider district level variances, I need to create another dataset that contains the district level information. From one subset of THRDS,[6] the variables listed in Tables 5.9 and 5.10 seem related to educa-

Table 5.9 District level variables: Rural

Variable	N	Miss	Mean	Std Dev	Skewness	Kurtosis
Educational Factor						
Number of primary schools [PRIM]*	65	1	5.20	1.11	0.20	0.68
Number of class rooms [CLASS]*	65	1	27.44	11.38	0.59	0.59
Number of teachers [TCHR]*	64	2	48.61	20.76	1.32	3.11
Health Factor						
Number of dispensaries [DISP]*	65	1	1.26	0.53	-0.03	0.08
Number of staff of maternal and child health aid [AID]*	62	4	1.40	0.55	0.25	0.29
Material Wealth Factor						
Branches of community bank [BRANCH]*	61	5	0.06	0.06	2.80	10.33
Population with clean water (%) [WAT]	65	1	35.36	20.22	0.79	0.96

* Divided by the district population and multiplied by 10,000 to measure people's *accessibility* to these services. The child population and teacher population by districts are unavailable.

(Analyzed by SAS 9.13)

Table 5.10 District level variables: Urban

Variable	N	Miss	Mean	Std Dev	Skewness	Kurtosis
Educational Factor						
Number of primary schools [PRIM]*	42	0	4.36	1.72	0.43	0.85
Number of class rooms [CLASS]*	42	0	29.65	20.73	2.88	9.84
Number of teachers [TCHR]*	41	1	58.59	29.74	1.67	3.55
Health Factor						
Number of dispensaries [DISP]*	42	0	1.73	1.24	1.53	2.58
Number of staff of maternal and child health aid [AID]*	42	0	2.32	1.88	2.07	5.67
Material Wealth Factor						
Branches of national bank [BRANCH]*	40	2	0.20	0.18	1.67	3.37
Population with clean water (%) [WAT]	42	0	40.80	27.02	1.20	1.45

* Divided by the district population and multiplied by 10,000 to measure people's *accessibility* to these services. The child population and teacher population by districts are unavailable.

(Analyzed by SAS 9.13)

tional, health, and material wealth factors respectively (also see Appendix B for their histograms).

The number of primary schools (PRIM), the number of class rooms (CLASS), and the number of teachers (TCHR) are categorized as educational factors; the number of dispensaries (DISP) and the number of maternal and child health aid staff (AID) are categorized as health factors; and, the number of national bank branches (BRANCH) and the population with clean water (WAT) are categorized as material wealth factors.[7] Educational factors represent children's schooling environment, and health factors represent health service availability. Regarding material wealth factors, I did not take a household-income type index to represent a material wealth factor because some household economies are based on agricultural self-sufficiency, and it is difficult to measure their economic condition by a currency-based index. In this sense, the number of bank branches (BRANCH) is still a problematic index, but this index will represent the level of participation in the market economy of that district. On the other hand, clean water is a necessary material condition of people's life regardless of the modes of their household economies.

In the model, I have adjusted the WAT variable in order to address a problem with its interpretation. The original data of WAT include values exceeding 100 percent of the population having access to clean water for the maximum of 160.34 percent in the rural data and that of 237.86 percent in the urban data. In all likelihood, the districts that exceed 100 percent access to clean water are those in which water is consumed by non-human uses, such as by industry. Because the model being considered here focuses on human development, it is sufficient to know that 100 percent of the population has access to clean water. Access exceeding 100 percent does not indicate any direct contribution to material well being, though we can imagine an indirect effect through other material factors. Therefore, I have set the maximum value of WAT as 100 and define WAT as an index to measure sufficient level of water supply in a given district. Although this modification still may include non-human consumption, it becomes conceptually interpretable.

In general, those variables represent conditions of public services from the points of view of education, health, and material wealth. Although there may be other possibilities to use other variables that might represent these factors, due to data limitations, these available variables were selected to represent each factor. The issue of the limitation of data availability will be discussed in the next chapter.

Some strong skewness and kurtosis can be seen in both rural and urban data (see Tables 5.9 and 5.10), such as BRANCH in the rural data (skewness: 2.80, kurtosis: 10.33) and AID in the urban data (skewness: 2.07, kurtosis: 5.67). Although there are methods to transform data closer to a normal distribution (Tabachnick & Fidel, 2001, pp.80-82), the estimation of Hierarchical Generalized Linear Modeling "will not be biased by a failure of the normality assumption at level 2" (Raudenbush & Bryk, 2002, p.274).[8] Since data transformation tends to make interpretation difficult,[9] I did not transform such data for this analysis.

As stated in 5.1.3 (b), I will check correlations among the explanatory variables. Correlations in the rural data are presented in Table 5.11.

Table 5.11 Pearson correlation coefficients: Rural

	1.	2.	3.	4.	5.	6.	7.
1. PRIM	---	0.61 **	0.49 **	0.24	0.34**	-0.02	-0.12
2. CLASS		---	0.75 **	0.09	0.17	0.05	0.11
3. TCHR			---	0.19	0.39**	0.25	0.12
4. DISP				---	0.46**	0.19	-0.09
5. AID					---	0.31*	0.11
6. BRANCH						---	0.04
7. WAT							---

** $p<.01$
* $p<.05$
$r>.60$

(Analyzed by SAS 9.13)

Significantly high correlations are found between PRIM and CLASS (r =.61, p<.01) and between CLASS and TCHR (r =.75, p<.01). These high correlations may happen because the number of primary schools determines the number of classroom, and the number of classroom determines the number of teachers. However, the correlation between PRIM and TCHR is not so high (r =.49, p<.01). This may be because teachers do not always teach in a school building. For example, when a school building cannot accommodate students or when there are not enough schools in a district, teachers have classes outside. From these findings, I will use PRIM and TCHR as representatives of an educational factor, and use DISP and AID as health factors and BRANCH and WAT as material wealth factors. By deleting a variable CLASS, there is no high correlation left among these six variables.

Correlations among variables in the urban data are presented in Table 5.12.

In the urban data, a significantly high correlation is also found between CLASS and TCHR (r =.78, p<.01). The same reason as that in the rural data may be assumed: the number of classroom determines the number of teachers. Since there is no strong correlation between PRIM and TCHR (r =.19, p =.23) as in the rural case, I will use PRIM and TCHR as representatives of an

Table 5.12 **Pearson correlation coefficients: Urban**

	1.	2.	3.	4.	5.	6.	7.
1. PRIM	---	0.19**	0.19	0.12	-0.10	-0.09	0.08
2. CLASS		---	0.78**	0.49**	0.79**	0.60**	0.49**
3. TCHR			---	0.36**	0.59**	0.48**	0.37*
4. DISP				---	0.60**	0.40*	0.28
5. AID					---	0.60**	0.38**
6. BRANCH						---	0.32
7. WAT							---

** p<.01
 * p<.05
 r>.60

(Analyzed by SAS 9.13)

educational factor. After deleting the variable CLASS, there is no high correlation left among these six variables. Although some correlations are close to .60, r =.60 will not cause a multicollinearity problem (Tabachnick & Fidell, 2001, p.84). Therefore, I will use DISP and AID as health factors and BRANCH and WAT as material wealth factors.

In sum, for both rural and urban models, I will use *writing* as an outcome variable to represent literacy; *schooling experience* and *book possession* are the individual-level explanatory variables.[10] As the district-level explanatory variables, PRIM and TCHR will represent educational factors, DISP and AID will represent health factors, and BRANCH and WAT will represent material wealth factors.

5.2 HGLM: Technical introduction and model building

This section will introduce the details of Hierarchical Generalized Linear Modeling (HGLM) (5.2.1) and explain how to apply it (5.2.2). Finally, HGLM will be applied to the THRDS data to test the theoretical model of human development by using the variables defined in the previous section (5.2.3).

5.2.1 Why and what HGLM?

(a) Hierarchical Linear Modeling (HLM)

Hierarchical Liner Model (HLM) has been developed to analyze multi-level-structured data or the data collected from different sampling levels, such as an individual level and a group level that contains the individuals in it (c.f. Luke, 2004; Raudenbush & Bryk, 2002; Raudenbush et al., 2004; Snijders & Bosker, 2003). For the analysis in this study, the data contains both individual-level variables such as schooling experience and district-level variables such as the number of primary schools. Individual samples in this data live in a specific district; in other words, they are *nested* into a specific district and share the district-level information among other individuals living in the same district. When analyzing this kind of nested or multilevel-structured data, HLM is an appropriate method.

Why use a hierarchical modeling for the multilevel-structured data? Luke (2004) identifies two issues with applying non-hierarchical models to multilevel-structured data (pp.6-7). First, in non-hierarchical models, all of the unmodeled information is pooled into a single individual error term even if the unexplained information may come from a different level. Even though that the error caused at the individual level can be different from those caused at the group level (e.g. districts where children live), a non-hierarchical model reports these different errors in a single individual-level error term. This miscounting of error may violate a statistical assumption of the independence of errors because children at the individual level, who belong to the same district, may have correlated errors caused at the district level. Another problem is in the interpretation of regression coefficients. The coefficients in a non-hierarchical model are considered equally applicable to all groups even if there is large variability from one group to the other. In the case of this study, ignoring group differences by using a non-hierarchical model means ignoring differences among districts. Figure 5.2 provides a visual representation of

Figure 5.2 Concept of the hierarchical model

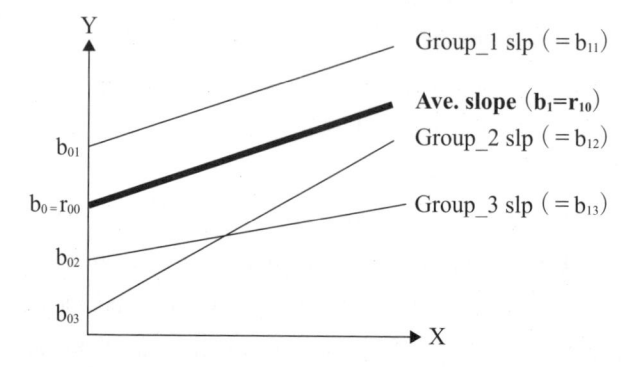

Group_1 slp $(=b_{11})$
Ave. slope $(b_1 = r_{10})$
Group_2 slp $(=b_{12})$
Group_3 slp $(=b_{13})$

b_{01}
$b_0 = r_{00}$
b_{02}
b_{03}

this problem. Here, I will provide a general explanation about HLM first, and then a specific example.

The non-hierarchical model created from the data of groups one, two, and three:

$$Y = b_0 + b_1 * X + e \qquad \ldots (0)$$

ignores the contextual differences among three groups, which have different intercepts (b_0, b_{01}, b_{02}, and b_{03}) and slopes (b_1, b_{11}, b_{12}, and b_{13}). HLM can reflect these group contextual differences by defining the model as follows.

$$\text{Level one: } Y_{ij} = b_{0j} + b_{1j}*X_{ij} + e_{ij} \qquad \ldots (1)$$
$$\text{Level two: } b_{0j} = r_{00} + r_{01}*W_{0j} + u_{0j} \qquad \ldots (2)$$
$$b_{1j} = r_{10} + r_{11}*W_{1j} + u_{1j} \qquad \ldots (3)$$

where W_{ij}-s represent the variables at the group level and u_{ij} is the error term created in modeling the group-level variables. Equation (2) defines the intercept in equation (1), which is measured by a group-level variable W_{0j} and a group-level error u_{0j}. Equation (2) explains the contextual difference of intercepts among b_0, b_{01}, b_{02}, and b_{03} in Figure 5.2. Equation (3) defines the slope in equation (1), which is measured by W_{1j} and u_{1j}. Equation (3) explains the contextual difference of slopes among b_1, b_{11}, b_{12}, and b_{13} in Figure 5.2 as well as creating an interaction term between a level-one variable (X_{ij}) and level-two variable (W_{0j}). By substituting equations (2) and (3) for equation (1), the combined model results:

$$Y_{ij} = (r_{00} + r_{01}*W_{0j} + u_{0j}) + (r_{10} + r_{11}*W_{1j} + u_{1j})*X + e_{ij}$$

$$= \underbrace{(\, r_{00} + r_{01}*W_{0j})}_{\text{intercept}} + \underbrace{(r_{10} + r_{11}*W_{1j})*X_{ij}}_{\text{slope}} + \underbrace{(u_{0j} + u_{1j}*X_{ij} + e_{ij}\,)}_{\text{error}}.$$

This equation shows the intercept variation brought about by group contextual differences ($r_{01}*W_{0j}$) in addition to the grand mean intercept (r_{00}); the slope variation brought by the group contextual differences ($r_{11}*W_{1j}$) in addition to the average slope (r_{10}); and the errors caused at the context level (u_{0j} + $u_{1j}*X_{ij}$) in addition to the error at level-one (e_{ij}).

Before discussing the specific example, it is worthwhile to elaborate on how intercepts and slopes in HLM differ from non-hierarchical linear models such as multiple regression models. In multiple regression models, the intercept indicates a general condition without effects from explanatory variables. In HLM, by contrast, the intercept indicates a general condition adjusted by group differences or unique qualities of each group. Those group differences are introduced by group-level variables as defined by equation (2) above, in which W0j brings the group uniqueness into the intercept.[11] In multiple regression models, the slope indicates a rate of change associated with a relevant explanatory variable or amount of effect associated with a relevant explanatory variable. In HLM, by contrast, the slope indicates a rate of change influenced by group differences or unique qualities of each group. Those group differences are introduced by group-level variables and defined by equation (3) above, in which W_{1j} brings the group uniqueness into the slope.[12]

In the case of this study, a model may be exemplified as below [13]:

Individual level: $Y_{ij} = b_{0j} + b_{1j}*X_{1j} + b_{2j}*X_{2j} + e_{ij}$

District level: $b_{0j} = r_{00} + r_{01}*W_{01} + r_{02}*W_{02} + r_{03}*W_{03} + r_{04}*W_{04}$
$+ r_{05}*W_{05} + r_{06}*W_{06} + u_{0j}$

$b_{1j} = r_{10} + r_{11}*W_{11} + u_{1j}$

$b_{2j} = r_{20} + r_{21}*W_{21} + u_{2j}$

Combined model:

$Y_{ij} = \underline{(r_{00} + r_{01}*W_{01} + r_{02}*W_{02} + r_{03}*W_{03} + r_{04}*W_{04} + r_{05}*W_{05} + r_{06}*W_{06})}$
  intercept

$+ (r_{10} + r_{11}*W_{11})* X_{1j} + (r_{20} + r_{21}*W_{21})* X_{2j} + (u_{0j} + u_{1j}* X_{1j} + u_{2j}* X_{2j} + e_{ij})$

  book slope   *schooling* slope   error

where,

Y_{ij}: Children's literacy (*writing*)

X_{1j}: Children's book possession (*book*)

X_{2j}: Children's schooling experience (*schooling*)

b_{0j}: Difference among districts explained by W_{01}- W_{06}

b_{1j}: Difference among districts associated with *book* explained by W_{11}

b_{2j}: Difference among districts associated with *schooling* explained by W_{21}

W_{01}: Number of dispensaries in a district (DISP)

W_{02}: Number of health staff in a district (AID)

W_{03}: Number of community bank branches in a district (BRANCH)

W_{04}: Number of teachers in a district (TCHR)

W_{05}: Number of primary schools in a district (PRIM)

W_{06}: Population with access to clean water in a district (WAT)

W_{11}: Number of teachers in a district (TCHR)

W_{21}: Number of primary schools in a district (PRIM)

e_{ij}: Uniqueness at the individual level

u_{0j}: Uniqueness at the district level for an intercept

u_{1j}: Uniqueness at the district level for a *book* slope

u_{2j}: Uniqueness at the district level for a *schooling* slope

In this model, an outcome variable *writing* (Y_{ij}) is regressed on *book possession* and *schooling experience* (X_{1j} and X_{2j}), considering the unique contributions of each district to *writing* measured by DISP, AID, BRANCH, TCHR, PRIM, and WAT for an intercept (W_{01}, W_{02}, ..., W_{06}); a district unique contribution to *writing* measured by TCHR for a *book* slope (W_{11}); and a district unique contribution to *literacy* measured by PRIM for a *schooling* slope (W_{21}).[14] TCHR for a book slope (W_{11}) and PRIM for a *schooling* slope (W_{21}) create interaction terms with the level-one variables *book* and *schooling* respectively ($r_{11}*W_{11}* X_{1j}$ and $r_{21}*W_{21}* X_{2j}$). The details and meanings of this model will be explained later in this chapter (5.2.3).

(b) Hierarchical Generalized Linear Modeling (HGLM)

As explained above, the outcome variable of this model, *writing*, is dichotomous (yes = 1, no = 0); therefore, the model assumes non-linearity. HLM with a dichotomous outcome variable is called Hierarchical Generalized Linear Modeling (HGLM). Raudenbush and Bryk (2002) consider "HLM as a special case of HGLM" (p.293) and present three problems that the standard linear model may cause when used with a dichotomous outcome variable.

1. There are no restrictions on the predicted values of the level-one outcome in the standard HLM. They can legitimately take on any real value. In contrast, the predicted value of a binary outcome Y, if viewed as the probability that Y= 1, must lie in the interval (0,1).

2. Given the predicted value of the outcome, the level-one random effect can take on only one of two values and, therefore, cannot be normally distributed.

3. The level-one random effect cannot have homogeneous variance. Instead, the variance of this random effect depends on the predicted value.

(pp.291-293)

These three problems reflect the characteristics of non-linear modeling (Hosmer & Lemeshow, 2000; Long, 1997; Pampel, 2000; Menard, 2002).

Regarding the first problem, non-linear modeling requires "a link function" to transform the predicted value to lay it in the interval between zero and one. While the estimated Y given x in a linear model is expressed as below,

$$E(Y|x) = \beta_0 + \beta_1 x, \text{ where } -\infty < E(Y|x) < \infty,$$

the estimated Y of dichotomous data must be greater than or equal to zero and less than or equal to one, which implies an S-shaped curve. The S-shaped non-linear curve is defined as:

$$E(Y|x) = \frac{e^{\beta_0 + \beta_1 x}}{1 + e^{\beta_0 + \beta_1 x}}, \text{ where } 0 \leq E(Y|x) \leq 1.$$

According to Hosmer and Lemeshow (2000), when defining:

$$E(Y|x) = \frac{e^{\beta_0 + \beta_1 x}}{1 + e^{\beta_0 + \beta_1 x}} = \pi(x) \qquad \ldots (1)$$

the logit transformation g(x) is presented:

$$g(x) = \ln\left[\frac{\pi(x)}{1-\pi(x)}\right]$$

$$= \ln[\pi(x)] - \ln[1-\pi(x)]$$

$$= \ln\left[\frac{e^{\beta_0 + \beta_1 x}}{1 + e^{\beta_0 + \beta_1 x}}\right] - \ln\left[1 - \frac{e^{\beta_0 + \beta_1 x}}{1 + e^{\beta_0 + \beta_1 x}}\right] \qquad (1)$$

$$= \ln[e^{\beta_0 + \beta_1 x}]$$

$$= \beta_0 + \beta_1 x.$$

As seen above, the function g(x) transforms the non-linear curve $\pi(x)$ into a linear equation $\beta_0 + \beta_1 x$. This function g(x) is called a link function, and the use of a link function in a non-linear model solves the first problem.

Regarding the second problem, the scatter plot of the dichotomous outcome looks like Figure 5.3, rather than Figure 5.4.

In the case of a dichotomous outcome (Figure 5.3), least square estimation does not work. Therefore, maximum likelihood estimation (ML estimation) is used instead of least square estimation. Conceptually, the ML estimate is the "value of the parameter that makes the observed data most likely" (Long, 1997, p.25); and mathematically, the likelihood function (LF) is defined as follows (Hosmer & Lemeshow, 2000, pp.8-9; Pampel, 2000, pp.40-44;

Figure 5.3 Dichotomous outcome

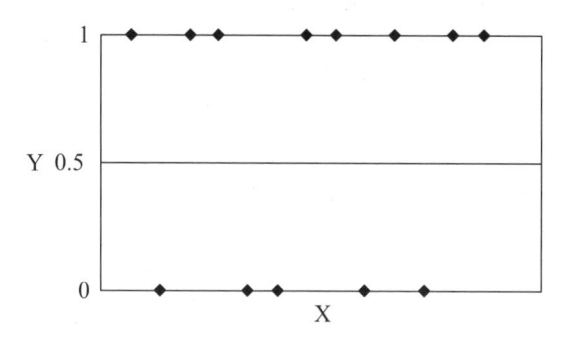

Figure 5.4 Countinuous outcome

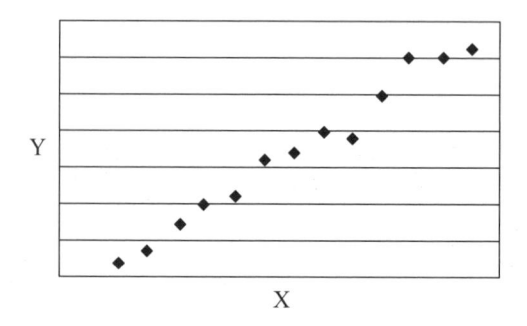

Eliason, 1993; Shiba et al., 2002, p.91):

$$LF = \prod \{p_i^{Y_i} * (1-p_i)^{1-Y_i}\},$$

where Y_i is the observed value of the dichotomous outcome variable for the case *i*, and p_i is the predicted probability for the case i. Therefore, LF includes a multiplication of products of the event probability (p_i) happening Y_i times and the non-event probability ($1-p_i$) happening ($1-Y_i$) times. In order to calculate the ML estimator, the natural log LF is defined as below for calculation convenience [15]:

$$\ln(\text{LF}) = \sum \{[Y_i * \ln p_i] + [(1-Y_i)*\ln(1-p_i)]\} \ .$$

When the likelihood value gets closer to 1, the ln likelihood value gets closer to 0; when the ln likelihood value gets closer to 0, the parameter gets closer to the observed data (Pampel, 2000, pp.43-44). Therefore, the ML estimator is a solution of the equation:

$$\ln(\text{LF}) = \sum \{[Y_i * \ln p_i] + [(1-Y_i)*\ln(1-p_i)]\} = 0.$$

This is the estimation method for a dichotomous outcome, which is not normally distributed, and this is the solution for problem two.

Regarding the last problem, the random effect in a linear model is defined as e below:

$$e = y - E(Y|x),$$

where y is an observed value and $E(Y|x)$ is an estimated Y given x.

By contrast, in the case of a dichotomous outcome variable, "we may express the value of the outcome variable given x as $y = \pi(x) + e$" (Hosmer & Lemeshow, 2000, p.7). Remembering that $\pi(x)$ is defined as:

$$\pi(x) = E(Y|x) = \frac{e^{\beta_0 + \beta_1 x}}{1 + e^{\beta_0 + \beta_1 x}} \qquad \text{see (1) above,}$$

and y is either one or zero. Therefore, when $y = 1$, then $e = 1 - \pi(x)$ with probability $\pi(x)$; when $y = 0$, then $e = -\pi(x)$ with probability $(1 - \pi(x))$. This is why Raudenbush and Bryk (2002) explained that "the variance of this random effect depends on the predicted value" (p.292). In a logistic model, the error is assumed to have a variance equal to $\frac{\pi^2}{3} \approx 3.29$ (Long, 1997, p.42).[16] Therefore, in a HGLM model, the error variance at level one (the individual level, in this study) is assumed as $\frac{\pi^2}{3} \approx 3.29$ (Snijders & Bosker, 2003, p.224).

Because of these major characteristics of non-linear modeling, HGLM will be used in this study to estimate the model since the model contains a dichotomous outcome variable, *writing*.

5.2.2 How to apply HGLM

There are many educational studies that use HLM. For example, there are studies of educational achievement (Daniels, 1995; Gamoran, Porter, Smithson & White, 1997; Sui-Chu & Willms, 1996; Pong, 1998; Raudenbush, Fotiu & Cheong, 1998; Saxe & Gearhart, 1999; Seltzer, Frank & Bryk, 1994; Wilkinson, 1998; Willms & Chen, 1989); studies on school or educational program effectiveness (Gray, Jesson & Sime, 1990; Raudenbush, Rowan & Kang, 1991; Seltzer, 1995; Tymms, 1993; Willms & Raudenbush, 1989); studies on class size (Nye, Hedges & Konstantopoulos, 1999, 2000); studies on neighborhood effects (Duncan, 1994; Garner & Raudenbush, 1991); and studies on high school organization (Bryk & Thum, 1989; Rowan, Raudenbush & Kang, 1991).

On the other hand, few educational studies employ a logistic hierarchical model.[17] Roderick and Camburn (1999) analyze patterns in the risk of course failure and recovery from failure in high school. They apply an ordered logit model for the two-level structured data (student and school levels) by using polytomous outcome variables for three classes: (a) at least one failure in major subjects in the first semester; (b) 50 percent or more failures; and (c) 75 percent or more failures (pp.313-315). They pay attention to individual students' information such as race, ethnicity, gender, age, and prior academic achievement in the level-one model; and consider school variances at the level-two. According to their study, males and Hispanic students are particularly at risk. Schiller and Muller (2000) estimate the probability of students' high school graduation by considering their individual-level information such as personal background, aspirations, and teachers' expectations, and state-level information such as testing policies. They use a dichotomous outcome variable (whether students earn a high school diploma or not) with two-level structured data (student and state levels), and construct a hierarchical model to find the effects of teachers' expectation on the likelihood of students' graduation.

In this study, I will apply a hierarchical model for the two-level structured data (individual and district levels) using a dichotomous outcome variable (whether children can write or not) to examine how individual-level variables (schooling experience and book possession) and district-level variables (educational, health, and material wealth factors) contribute to children's literacy. I use the data introduced in the previous chapter, including the rural data (n = 2985 including missing, n = 2580 after listwise deletion; 7-14 year old school-age children) and the urban data (n = 3062 including missing, n = 2941 after listwise deletion; 7-14 year old school-age children), which are created from THRDS.

Before analyzing the data, I will briefly mention some statistical issues such as missing data, selection of an estimation method, and differences between population-average and unit-specific models.

(a) Missing data

For missing data, I will use listwise deletion. Listwise deletion is the method to delete "from the sample any observations that have missing data on any variables in the model of interest" (Allison, 2002, p.6). According to Allison (2002), an advantage of listwise deletion is that it is applicable to any kind of statistical analysis including logistic modeling; and listwise deletion is even more robust than such sophisticated methods as maximum likelihood and multiple imputation to violations of the Missing-At-Random (MAR) assumption. Moreover, compared to pairwise deletion, the method to compute each of the summary statistics using all the cases that are available to estimate the missing data, listwise deletion is less problematic since pairwise deletion requires the Missing-Completely-At-Random (MCAR) condition for precise estimation of the missing data, which is a very rare condition of actual data. Many imputation methods, which substitute a "reasonable guess" for each missing value, are available, but they have an inevitable problem that "analyzing imputed data as though it were complete data produces standard errors that are underestimated and test statistics that are overestimated" (Allison, 2002, p.12). Considering the characteristics of these methods, I decided to use listwise deletion for the datasets.

In order to examine the MAR assumption, Chi-square tests are conducted for both rural and urban data as below. A variable *miss* is coded 1 for cases missing either *book* or *schooling* and 0 for cases with no missing values for these variables. The null hypothesis here is that in terms of *writing* there is no significant difference between a group which is *not* going to be analyzed due to missing and a no-missing group which is going to be analyzed after listwise deletion. The results of Chi-square tests are presented in Tables 5.13 and 5.14.

These results indicate that cases with missing data appeared to be random in the rural samples (χ^2 (1, n = 2985) = 2.67, p = 0.10), but not in the urban samples (χ^2 (1, n = 3062) =15.67, p<0.01). However, interpretation of the χ^2 may be problematic, particularly for the urban data, because the frequency tables above contain the cells with less than 5 percent.

Table 5.13 Frequency and Chi-square test: Rural

Freq(%) Row(%) Col(%)	missing 0	missing 1	total (%)
writing 0	1575 52.76 89.13 58.70	192 6.43 10.87 63.58	1767 (59.20)
writing 1	1108 37.12 90.97 41.30	110 3.69 9.03 36.42	1218 (40.80)
total (%)	2683 (38.87)	302 (61.13)	2985 (100.00)

Statistic	df	value	p
Chi-square	1	2.6688	0.1023
Likelihood ratio Chi-square	1	2.6989	0.1004
Continuity adj. Chi-square	1	2.4709	0.116

* Frequency missing = 11
* N=2996 including missing
* N=2683 after listwise deletion

(Analyzed by SAS 9.13)

Table 5.14 Frequency and Chi-square test: Urban

Freq(%) Row(%) Col(%)		missing		total
		0	1	(%)
writing	0	1370 44.74 95.54 46.19	64 2.09 4.46 66.67	1434 (46.83)
	1	1596 52.12 98.03 53.81	32 1.05 1.97 33.33	1628 (53.17)
total (%)		2966 (38.87)	96 (61.13)	3062 (100.00)

Statistic	df	value	p
Chi-square	1	15.6587	<.0001
Likelihood ratio Chi-square	1	15.8112	<.0001
Continuity adj. Chi-square	1	14.8471	0.0001

* Frequency missing = 25
* N=3087 including missing
* N=2966 after listwise deletion

(Analyzed by SAS 9.13)

The descriptive statistics for the data after applying listwise deletion and the description of variables are shown as below.

Table 5.15 Rural data

LEVEL-1 DESCRIPTIVE STATISTICS

VARIABLE NAME	VAR TYPE	N	Frequency of (yes=1, no=0) (%)
Writing	dichotomous (yes=1, no=0)	2580	(41, 59)
Book	dichotomous (yes=1, no=0)	2580	(30, 70)
Schooling	dichotomous (yes=1, no=0)	2580	(61, 39)

LEVEL-2 DESCRIPTIVE STATISTICS

VARIABLE NAME	VAR TYPE	N	MEAN	SD	MINIMUM	MAXIMUM
TCHR	continuous	57	49.54	21.62	9.82	125.39
PRIM	continuous	57	5.22	1.15	2.51	8.23
DISP	continuous	57	1.25	0.56	0.00	2.49
AID	continuous	57	1.40	0.56	0.19	3.01
WAT	continuous	57	36.32	20.98	0.08	100.00
BRANCH	continuous	57	0.07	0.06	0.00	0.36

(Analyzed by HLM 6.02)

Table 5.16 Urban data

LEVEL-1 DESCRIPTIVE STATISTICS

VARIABLE NAME	VAR TYPE	N	Frequency of (yes=1, no=0) (%)
Writing	dichotomous (yes=1, no=0)	2941	(54, 46)
Book	dichotomous (yes=1, no=0)	2941	(39, 61)
Schooling	dichotomous (yes=1, no=0)	2941	(67, 33)

LEVEL-2 DESCRIPTIVE STATISTICS

VARIABLE NAME	VAR TYPE	N	MEAN	SD	MINIMUM	MAXIMUM
TCHR	continuous	39	58.85	30.44	8.42	160.20
PRIM	continuous	39	4.37	1.75	0.24	8.96
DISP	continuous	39	1.80	1.26	0.21	6.01
AID	continuous	39	2.36	1.93	0.19	9.59
WAT	continuous	39	41.73	27.84	1.50	100.00
BRANCH	continuous	39	0.20	0.18	0.02	0.85

(Analyzed by HLM 6.02)

(b) Estimation method

Regarding the estimation method for HGLM, both maximum likelihood estimation and least square estimation are problematic because of the fact that in HGLM the individual-level model for a dichotomous outcome is a logistic model while the district-level model involves multivariate normal assumptions (Raudenbush & Bryk, 2002, pp. 332-333). According to Raudenbush and Bryk (2002), the estimation method that is frequently used to solve this problem is Penalized Quasi-Likelihood estimation (PQL). PQL is a widely used estimation method for HGLM and it is default in the statistical software HLM6.02 when using a Bernoulli model, a dichotomous outcome model (Raudenbush et al., 2004, pp.103-105, p.112).

However, Snijders and Bosker (2003) claim that "the numerical integration approach and the Laplace approximation seem to produce statistically more satisfactory estimates than the MQL [Marginal Quasi-Likelihood] and PQL approaches" (p.219). According to them, the deviance produced by using the Laplace estimation is more reliable than that produced by the MQL or PQL method. Indeed, the software HLM6.02 does not present the deviance in output when using PQL estimation since it is not sufficiently reliable for conducting the deviance test. Scientific Software International (2005a), a provider of the software HLM6.02, explains:

> A deviance statistic, such as routinely printed for linear analysis in HLM, is not provided in the output for all the HGLM models. The absence is due to the use of the Penalized Quasi-Likelihood (PQL) estimation procedure. Although the actual estimates will usually be adequate, any test of random intercepts and slopes in multilevel models for discrete outcomes based on the likelihood may be unreliable... This is also pointed out Snijders & Bosker ([2003,] p.220).

Following the indication of Snijders & Bosker (2003), Scientific Software International (2005b) made the Laplace estimation available for HGLM in April 2005.[18] Since the Laplace estimation provides the deviance, which enables model comparison by using the deviance test, I will use the Laplace estimation for HGLM.

(c) Population-average vs. unit-specific models

When interpreting an outcome probability in a unit change of predictors in logistic models, we need to hold all other variables constant; otherwise, the probability can vary depending on other variables and it cannot be defined as a single value (Long, 1997, pp.79-82). Due to its hierarchical and logistic attributes, HLM6.02 produces two types of models for HGLM analysis: one based on population-average and the other unit-specific. Generally, for both models, HGLM defines regression coefficients that can be interpreted as the expected change in the outcome associated with a one-unit increase in the relevant predictor, holding other predictors constant (Raudenbush & Bryk, 2002, p.334). The choice of either a population-average or a unit-specific model is determined by the specific purpose of the model.

In a population-average model, the predictors of fixed effects are held constant but not random effects; in a unit-specific model, all predictors and random effects are held constant. This means that a unit-specific model is more sensitive to the level-two unit (district, in this study); while a population-average model is more appropriate to determine how the outcome likelihood differs *across* the level-two units (nationwide, in this study). In this study, I am more interested in nationwide likelihood rather than some specific district cases. Therefore, I will use population-average models in the following analyses.

Raudenbush and Bryk's (2002, p.304) explanation of the statistical attributes of these two models further reinforces the appropriateness of choosing the population-average model in this study. Compared to a population-average model, a unit-specific model depends more on an assumption about the distribution of random effects. This is understandable because a unit-specific model holds all random effects constant. Therefore, a population-average model can be more robust to an erroneous assumption about random effects. Since the data used in this study do not completely satisfy statistical assumptions, it may be statistically safer to use a more robust model, that is, a population-average model. However, as a final note, there is usually no extremely large difference of estimation between these two models in terms of their estimated values.

5.2.3 Testing a theoretical model of human development

By using rural and urban datasets, containing two individual-level predictors, five district-level predictors, and one dichotomous outcome variable, I will construct models as follows.

(a) Null model

A null model (Luke, 2004) or empty model (Snijders & Bosker, 2003) or unconditional model (Raudenbush & Bryk, 2002) is defined as the simplest multilevel model with no level-one or level-two predictors. First of all, it is necessary to examine this model to make sure it is truly appropriate to analyze the data by hierarchical modeling. This is because there is no reason to analyze the data hierarchically if an outcome variable *writing* does not have enough variance at the district level. The null model with a dichotomous outcome variable *writing* is defined as below (see the equation (1) in 5.2.1 (b)). The individual-level model with no predictor:

When $E(writing = 1 \mid x) = \dfrac{e^{\beta_0}}{1+e^{\beta_0}} = \pi(x)$,

the logit transformation $g(x) = \ln\left[\dfrac{\pi(x)}{1-\pi(x)}\right] = \beta_0$.

The district-level model with no predictor: $\beta_0 = G_{00} + U_0$.
The combined model: $g(x) = G_{00} + U_0$.

This model produces the results in Table 5.17.

Table 5.17 Null model

RURAL

	Coefficient	SE	T-ratio	df	Odds Ratio	Coefficient Interval
FIXED EFFECT For Intercept B_{0j} Intercept G_{00}	-0.345	0.069	-5.033	56	0.708**	(0.617, 0.812)
	Standard Deviation	Variance Component		df	Chi-squre	
RANDOM EFFECT Intercept U_{0j}	0.417	0.174		56	159.660**	

URBAN

	Coefficient	SE	T-ratio	df	Odds Ratio	Coefficient Interval
FIXED EFFECT For Intercept B_{0j} Intercept G_{00}	0.079	0.091	0.865	38	1.082	(0.900, 1.300)
	Standard Deviation	Variance Component		df	Chi-squre	
RANDOM EFFECT Intercept U_{0j}	0.490	0.240		38	158.246**	

Note_1: ** = p<.01; * = p<.05
Note_2: Method of estimation = EM Laplace
Note_3: Distribution at level-one = Bernoulli

(Analyzed by HLM 6.02)

This model shows that variance components of the rural and urban data are both significant ($\tau^2 = 0.17$, p<0.01, in rural; $\tau^2 = 0.24$, p<0.01, in urban). The purpose of examination of the null model is to insure that multilevel modeling is truly appropriate to analyze the data; in other words, to make sure that there is sufficient variance to be explained at the district level (τ^2) in addition to the individual-level variance (σ^2). The intraclass correlation (ρ_I) is the index to examine its appropriateness (Raudenbush & Bryk, 2002, p.36; Snijders & Bosker, 2003, pp.16-17, 45-47, 224-225). It is defined as the ratio of the level-two variance (district variance, in this study) to the total variance (district variance and individual variance, in this study):

$$\rho_I = \frac{\tau^2}{\tau^2 + \sigma^2}.$$

τ^2 is the district-level variance and σ^2 is the individual-level variance. The intraclass correlation (ρ_I) reveals the impact of the district-level variance; therefore, a higher ρ_I supports the use of multilevel modeling. According to Snijders and Bosker (2003), "values [of ρ_I] between 0.05 and 0.20 are common" and values over 0.20 is considered "high" (p.46).

The variance of the logistic model is assumed to be $\frac{\pi^2}{3} \approx 3.29$ (Long, 1997, p.42; Snijders & Bosker, 2003, p.244; see 5.2.1 (b)). Since the individual-level model in this study is a logistic, the individual-level variance (σ^2) in this study is assumed to be $\frac{\pi^2}{3}$. Therefore, the intraclass correlation is defined as:

$$\rho_I = \frac{\tau^2}{\tau^2 + \pi^2/3}.$$

Since the district-level variances (τ^2) are found to be 0.17 and 0.24 for the rural and urban models respectively, the intraclass correlations for these models are computed below (Snijders & Bosker, 2003, p. 224-225)

$$\rho_{I\_RURAL} = \frac{0.174}{0.174 + 3.29} \approx 0.050 \quad \because \tau^2_{\_RURAL} = 0.174$$

$$\rho_{I\_URBAN} = \frac{0.240}{0.240 + 3.29} \approx 0.068 \quad \because \tau^2_{\_URBAN} = 0.240$$

Intraclass correlations for the two models are not very high, which indicate small variance at the district level. However, these values are both over 0.05 and are considered "common" intraclass correlations by Snijders and Bosker (2003, p.46). Therefore, multilevel modeling will be applied to these data.

(b) Level-one only model

Two level-one variables, *book* and *schooling*, are added to the null model. The individual-level model is defined as:

$$\text{when } E(writing=1|x) = \frac{e^{\beta_{0j} + \beta_{1j}*X_{book} + \beta_{2j}*X_{schooling}}}{1 + e^{\beta_{0j} + \beta_{1j}*X_{book} + \beta_{2j}*X_{schooling}}} = \pi(x),$$

the logit transformation is

$$g(x) = \ln\left[\frac{\pi(x)}{1-\pi(x)}\right] = \beta_{0j} + \beta_{1j}*X_{books} + \beta_{2j}*X_{schooling}.$$

The district-level model is defined as [19]:

$$\beta_{0j} = G_{00} + U_{0j},$$
$$\beta_{1j} = G_{10} + U_{1j},$$
$$\beta_{2j} = G_{20} + U_{2j}.$$

The combined model is defined as:

$$g(x) = G_{00} + G_{10}*X_{book} + G_{20}*X_{schooling} + U_{0j} + U_{1j} + U_{2j}.$$

This model produces the results in Table 5.18.

This model shows significant effects of *schooling* and *book* on children's literacy (*writing*). In the rural areas, children who have attended school in the past 12 months are about 22 times more likely to be literate than those who

Table 5.18 Level-one only model

RURAL

	Coefficient	SE	T-ratio	df	Odds Ratio	Coefficient Interval
FIXED EFFECT						
For Intercept B0j						
Intercept G00	-3.062	0.121	-25.266	56	0.047**	(0.037, 0.060)
For Book slope B1j						
Intercept G10	1.443	0.149	9.685	56	4.233**	(3.143, 5.703)
For Schooling slope B2j						
Intercept G20	3.090	0.121	25.450	56	21.986**	(17.245, 28.030)

	Standard Deviation	Variance Component	df	Chi-squre
RANDOM EFFECT				
Intercept U0j	0.509	0.259	54	51.299
Book slp U1j	0.856	0.733	54	96.135**
Schooling slp U2j	0.290	0.084	54	46.864

URBAN

	Coefficient	SE	T-ratio	df	Odds Ratio	Coefficient Interval
FIXED EFFECT						
For Intercept B0j						
Intercept G00	-2.884	0.125	-23.004	38	0.056**	(0.043, 0.072)
For Book slope B1j						
Intercept G10	1.422	0.117	12.145	38	4.147**	(3.273, 5.256)
For Schooling slope B2j						
Intercept G20	3.329	0.158	21.058	38	27.898**	(20.266, 38.404)

	Standard Deviation	Variance Component	df	Chi-squre
RANDOM EFFECT				
Intercept U0j	0.250	0.063	38	26.307
Book slp U1j	0.342	0.117	38	50.340
Schooling slp U2j	0.459	0.211	38	35.132

Note_1: ** = $p<.01$; * = $p<.05$
Note_2: Method of estimation = EM Laplace
Note_3: Distribution at level-one = Bernoulli

(Analyzed by HLM 6.02)

have not, holding *book possession* constant. In the urban areas, children who have attended school in the past 12 months are about 28 times more likely to be literate than other children, holding *book possession* constant. Those who own at least one book are about 4 times more likely to be literate in both rural and urban areas, holding *schooling experience* constant.

Variance components indicate variation in the intercept and slopes (Raudenbush & Bryk, 2002, pp.82-85). Only the *book* slope random effects (U_{1j}) in the rural model is significant ($\chi^2(54, n=57) = 96.135$, $p<0.01$), which means that a significant variation remains unexplained after controlling for children's book possession. All other insignificant random effects in the rural and urban models indicate no significant variations left unexplained in their intercepts and slopes.

(c) Final Model

By adding the district-level predictors to the level-one only model, the final model appears as below.

The individual-level link function is defined as:

$$g(x) = \ln\left[\frac{\pi(x)}{1-\pi(x)}\right] = \beta_{0j} + \beta_{1j}*X_{books} + \beta_{2j}*X_{schooling}.$$

The district-level model is defined as [20]:

$$\beta_{0j} = G_{00} + G_{01}*W_{DISP} + G_{02}*W_{AID} + G_{03}*W_{BRANCH} + G_{04}*W_{TCHR}$$
$$+ G_{05}*W_{PRIM} + G_{06}*W_{WAT} + U_{0j},$$
$$\beta_{1j} = G_{10} + G_{11}*W_{TCHR} + U_{1j},$$
$$\beta_{2j} = G_{20} + G_{21}*W_{PRIM} + U_{2j}.$$

The combined model is defined as:

$$g(x) = G_{00} + G_{01}*W_{DISP} + G_{02}*W_{AID} + G_{03}*W_{BRANCH} + G_{04}*W_{TCHR}$$
$$+ G_{05}*W_{PRIM} + G_{06}*W_{WAT} + G_{10}*X_{book} + G_{11}*W_{TCHR}*X_{book}$$
$$+ G_{20}*X_{schooling} + G_{21}*W_{PRIM}*X_{schooling} + U_{0j} + U_{1j}*X_{book}$$
$$+ U_{2j}*X_{schooling}$$

$$= \underbrace{\{G_{00} + G_{01}*W_{DISP} + G_{02}*W_{AID} + G_{03}*W_{BRANCH} + G_{04}*W_{TCHR} + G_{05}*W_{PRIM} + G_{06}*W_{WAT}\}}_{\text{Intercept} = \beta_{0j}}$$

$$+ \underbrace{\{G_{10} + G_{11}*W_{TCHR}\}*X_{book}}_{\text{book slope} = \beta_{1j}} + \underbrace{\{G_{20} + G_{21}*W_{PRIM}\}*X_{schooling}}_{\text{schooling slope} = \beta_{2j}}$$

178   Part II. Empirical analysis of human development

$$+ \{\underbrace{U_{0j} + U_{1j}* X_{book} + U_{2j}* X_{schooling}}_{error}\}.$$

In this model, β_0(intercept) represents the likelihood of literacy (*writing*) without controlling for individuals' conditions of *book possession* and *schooling experience*. G_{00} specifically represents the ground mean likelihood of literacy (*writing*), that is, the mean across all districts and individuals. β_{0j}(intercept) in this model assumes that this general likelihood of literacy (*writing*) may be influenced by each district's unique conditions such as educational, health, and material wealth factors (Ws). Ws in β_{0j}(intercept) are considered as direct conditions contributing to an outcome variable *writing*. In other words, all three factors are considered as direct influences on literacy because they represent general life circumstances for *all* children without reference to the individual conditions of *schooling experience* or *book possession*.

β_{0j}(*book* slope) represents an *additional* effect on the likelihood of literacy (*writing*) of those who own at least one book; in other words, the coefficient $\{G_{10} + G_{11}*W_{TCHR}\}$ will disappear if the individual does not own any book ($X_{book} = 0$). β_{0j}(*book* slope) in this model contains a predictor TCHR, assuming that teachers' encouragement to students to read the books that they possess may contribute to developing literacy, and that more teachers may provide more chances for children to receive such encouragement. However, the contribution from PRIM to β_{0j}(*book* slope) is not assumed because textbooks are usually not required in Tanzanian primary schools, and it is individual children's or their families' responsibility to decide to purchase a book.[21] I initially assumed an effect of BRANCH because it may represent an economic condition necessary to purchase a book, but a Wald test showed insignificance of BRANCH in the model ($\chi^2(4) = 6.117$, p = 0.189 in the rural model, $\chi^2(4) = 3.134$, p>.500 in the urban model; see Appendix C).

β_{2j}(*schooling* slope) represents an *additional* effect on the likelihood of literacy (*writing*) of those who have schooling experience; in other words, the coefficient {$G_{20} + G_{21}*W_{PRIM}$} will disappear if the individuals do not have schooling experience ($\because X_{school} = 0$). β_{2j}(*schooling* slope) in this model contains a district-level predictor PRIM, assuming that more schools in a district may bring children higher accessibility to education, which may contribute to literacy development. I initially assumed an effect of BRANCH because it may represent an economic condition necessary to go to school, but a Wald test shows insignificance of BRANCH in the model ($\chi^2(4) = 6.117$, p = 0.189 in the rural model, $\chi^2(4) = 3.134$, p>.500 in the urban model; see Appendix C).[22]

This model indicates two concerns: (1) how do the individual-level conditions (*book* and *schooling*) and the district-level services (six Ws) contribute to the likelihood of children's literacy (*writing*); and (2) whether there are significant interactions between children's book possession and the number of teachers ($W_{TCHR}*X_{book}$) and between children's schooling experience and the number of primary schools ($W_{PRIM}*X_{schooling}$). This model produces the result in Table 5.19.[23]

Table 5.19 contains extremely high correlations in Tau matrices ($r(U_{1j}, U_{2j})$ = -0.956 in the rural model; $r(U_{1j}, U_{2j})$ = -0.975 in the urban model). Such high correlations in Tau matrices are problematic because these random effects may measure the same thing; in other words, either of them may not be necessary in the model. In order to avoid arbitrary constraint of random effects, which may create biased estimation, the deviance test needs to be implemented to determine whether there is a significant difference between the unconstrained and constrained models.

For the rural model constraining U_{2j},[24] the deviance test comparing the constrained model to the unconstrained model resulted in being insignificant ($\chi^2(3) = 0.983$, p>0.500) and the correlation between U_{0j} and U_{1j} seems moderate ($r(U_{0j}, U_{1j})$ = -0.437). For the urban model with constraining U_{1j},[25] the

Table 5.19 Full model (Unconstrained model)

RURAL

	Coefficient	SE	T-ratio	df	OR	Coefficient Interval
FIXED EFFECT						
For Intercept B0j						
Intercept G00	-3.136	0.135	23.210	50	0.043**	(0.033, 0.057)
DISP G01	-0.172	0.138	-1.245	50	0.842	(0.639, 1.110)
AID G02	0.449	0.117	3.825	50	1.567**	(1.238, 1.984)
BRANCH G03	-1.229	1.701	-0.722	50	0.293	(0.010, 8.875)
TCHR G04	-0.005	0.004	-1.240	50	0.995	(0.987, 1.003)
PRIM G05	0.212	0.158	1.339	50	1.236	(0.900, 1.697)
WAT G06	0.004	0.003	1.261	50	1.004	(0.998, 1.010)
For Book slope B1j						
Intercept G10	1.491	0.149	9.997	55	4.443**	(3.296, 5.988)
TCHR G06	0.014	0.006	2.454	55	1.014*	(1.003, 1.026)
For Schooling slope B2j						
Intercept G20	3.157	0.139	22.758	55	23.511**	(17.812, 31.034)
PRIM G21	-0.130	0.166	-0.780	55	0.878	(0.630, 1.225)

	SD	Variance Component	df	Chi-squre
RANDOM EFFECT				
Intercept U0j	0.313	0.098	48	49.062
Book slp U1j	0.817	0.667	53	93.601**
Schooling slp U2j	0.277	0.077	53	49.374

Tau as correlations [U0j, U1j, U2j]
$$\begin{bmatrix} 1.000 & 0.339 & -0.515 \\ & 1.000 & -0.956 \\ & & 1.000 \end{bmatrix}$$

STATISTICS FOR CURRENT MODEL

	df	Deviance
For the deviance test	17	6950.161

URBAN

	Coefficient	SE	T-ratio	df	OR	Coefficient Interval
-2.999	0.148	-20.287	32	0.050**	(0.037, 0.067)
0.031	0.071	0.434	32	1.031	(0.893, 1.191)
0.026	0.042	0.612	32	1.026	(0.942, 1.118)
0.639	0.544	1.175	32	1.894	(0.627, 5.727)
0.002	0.003	0.671	32	1.002	(0.996, 1.008)
-0.111	0.061	-1.811	32	0.895	(0.790, 1.014)
-0.006	0.003	-1.674	32	0.994	(0.988, 1.001)
1.402	0.137	10.224	37	4.064**	(3.080, 5.364)
-0.002	0.002	-0.866	37	0.998	(0.993, 1.003)
3.428	0.163	21.020	37	30.801**	(22.146, 42.838)
0.062	0.070	0.887	37	1.064	(0.924, 1.224)

	SD	Variance Component	df	Chi-squre
	0.190	0.036	32	25.664
	0.252	0.063	37	49.539
	0.447	0.200	37	35.311

$$\begin{bmatrix} 1.000 & 0.690 & -0.656 \\ & 1.000 & -0.975 \\ & & 1.000 \end{bmatrix}$$

df	Deviance
17	7812.630

Note 1: ** = p<.01; * = p<.05
Note_2: Method of estimation = EM Laplace
Note_3: Distribution at level-one = Bernoulli

(Analyzed by HLM 6.02)

deviance test comparing the constrained model to the unconstrained model was insignificant ($\chi^2(3) = 1.998$, p>0.500) and the correlation between U_{0j} and U_{2j} seems moderate ($r(U_{0j}, U_{2j}) = -0.633$). Therefore, since there are no significant differences between the constrained and unconstrained models for both rural and urban samples, I will take the more parsimonious models, the constrained models, as the final models. The estimation of the final models is seen in Table 5.20.

The substantive meaning of odds ratio and the contextual interpretation of the final models for policy recommendation will be explained in the next chapter. Technical explanations of the final models are as follows.

In the rural model, both random effects (U_{0j} and U_{1j}) are significant, which means that a significant variation remains unexplained at the district level after controlling for children's book possession. In other words, there are significant unexplained factors besides the explanatory variables in the model. In the urban model, on the other hand, both random effects (U_{0j} and U_{2j}) are insignificant, which indicates that this model does not capture significant variations left unexplained at the district level although there may be unexplained factors left.

Regarding the individual-level predictors, both rural and urban final models show a similar tendency: *book possession* and *schooling experience* are positively significant in both models. Those who own at least one book are about 4 times more likely to be literate in comparison to those who do not own any book, holding other predictors constant. Schooling experience has much larger effect on children's literacy: those who have schooling experience are about 24 times in rural and 31 times in urban more likely to be literate than those who do not have schooling experience, holding other predictors constant.

Regarding the district-level predictors, the rural and urban models show different results. In the rural model, the number of maternal and child health

Table 5.20 Final model (Constrained model)

RURAL

	Coefficient	SE	T-ratio	df	OR	Coefficient Interval
FIXED EFFECT						
For Intercept B0j						
Intercept G00	-3.167	0.147	-21.523	50	0.042**	(0.031, 0.057)
DISP G01	-0.167	0.141	-1.190	50	0.846	(0.638, 1.122)
AID G02	0.459	0.120	3.828	50	1.583**	(1.244, 2.013)
BRANCH G03	-1.203	1.778	-0.677	50	0.300	(0.008, 10.617)
TCHR G04	-0.005	0.004	-1.223	50	0.995	(0.987, 1.003)
PRIM G05	0.220	0.165	1.331	50	1.246	(0.895, 1.735)
WAT G06	0.004	0.003	1.245	50	1.004	(0.998, 1.010)
For Book slope B1j						
Intercept G10	1.498	0.157	9.533	55	4.472**	(3.266, 6.125)
TCHR G06	0.015	0.006	2.401	55	1.015*	(1.002, 1.028)
For Schooling slope B2j						
Intercept G20	3.189	0.148	21.492	2569	24.261**	(18.139, 32.449)
PRIM G21	-0.146	0.174	-0.837	2569	0.864	(0.614, 1.216)

	SD	Variance Component	df	Chi-squre
RANDOM EFFECT				
Intercept U0j	0.285	0.081	48	66.959*
Book slp U1j	0.797	0.635	53	88.852**
Schooling slp U2j		Constrained		

Tau as correlations:
$$\begin{bmatrix} U0j & U1j \\ 1.000 & -0.437 \\ & 1.000 \end{bmatrix}$$

STATISTICS FOR CURRENT MODEL	df	Deviance
For the deviance test	14	6951.144

URBAN

	Coefficient	SE	T-ratio	df	OR	Coefficient Interval
	-3.009	0.160	-18.758	32	0.049**	(0.036, 0.068)
	0.027	0.067	0.405	32	1.028	(0.896, 1.179)
	0.026	0.041	0.634	32	1.027	(0.944, 1.117)
	0.687	0.541	1.269	32	1.987	(0.661, 5.974)
	0.002	0.003	0.841	32	1.002	(0.997, 1.008)
	-0.124	0.068	-1.829	32	0.883	(0.769, 1.014)
	-0.006	0.003	-1.905	32	0.994	(0.987, 1.000)
	1.407	0.144	9.771	2930	4.083**	(3.079, 5.414)
	-0.003	0.003	-1.308	2930	0.997	(0.992, 1.002)
	3.446	0.172	20.011	37	31.380**	(22.149, 44.459)
	0.068	0.079	0.856	37	1.070	(0.912, 1.255)

	SD	Variance Component	df	Chi-squre
	0.130	0.017	32	26.945
	0.336	0.113	37	30.359
		Constrained		

Tau as correlations:
$$\begin{bmatrix} U0j & U2j \\ 1.000 & 0.633 \\ & 1.000 \end{bmatrix}$$

	df	Deviance
	14	7814.628

(Analyzed by HLM 6.02)

Note_1: ** = p<.01; * = p<.05
Note_2: Method of estimation = EM Laplace
Note_3: Distribution at level-one = Bernoulli

aid staff per 10,000 people (AID: OR = 1.583, p<0.01) and the interaction between book possession and the number of teachers per 10,000 people (*book**TCHR: OR = 1.015, p<0.05) are significant. The positively significant OR of AID indicates that each additional one-unit increase of AID can improve rural children's likelihood to be literate by about 1.6 times. In other words, if a district hires one per 10,000 more health staff, it will contribute to children's literacy development. Substantive details of this finding will be discussed in the next chapter.

The positively significant odds ratio of the interaction term book*TCHR indicates that each additional teacher per 10,000 can improve the likelihood of literacy of the rural children who own at least one book 1.015 times more. In other words, if a district hires or trains one per 10,000 more teacher, it will contribute to literacy development of the children who own at least one book. Since this is an interaction term, the effect of increasing the number of teachers is applicable only for those who own at least one book. The positive effect on literacy of this interaction term can be interpreted as meaning either that teachers' encouragement motivates students to read a book that they own, or that children who own a book(s) are thereby motivated to learn from teachers. Although an interaction term does not imply causation, more substantive interpretation will be discussed in the next chapter.

The district-level predictors in the urban model do not demonstrate effects from public services on children's literacy. However, it would be hasty to conclude that public services are irrelevant to urban children. It needs to be borne in mind that there is more stratification and a greater economic gap within urban populations than rural populations. The dataset being used here does not allow me to make such distinctions at the individual or household level. We can assume that the needs of the wealthy urban population are different from those of the poor urban population. These differences cannot be distinguished in this analysis. Moreover, since it is more difficult in urban than rural areas to meet basic needs by household agricultural production, urban life can be more materially difficult for the poor than for self-sufficient rural households. The urban situations are too complicated and too stratified to be captured by one model. Ideally, the urban samples should be divided into the wealthy and the poor, but the data do not allow me to do so. I assume that the urban wealthy do not depend on public services but that the urban poor model would show a tendency similar to the rural model. However, in order to confirm this assumption, an appropriate dataset is necessary. The limitation of data availability will be discussed in the next chapter.

Notes

[1] GPI is defined that "ratio of female-to-male value of a given indicator. A GPI of 1 indicates parity between sexes; a GPI that varies between 0 and 1 means a disparity in favor of boys; a GPI greater than 1 indicates a disparity in favor of girls" (UNESCO, 2003, p.384).

[2] The definition of *writing* (if able to write a letter) seems to be problematic to represent literacy. However, this is only one variable in the dataset that may represent literacy.

[3] However, the frequency of "owning book but no schooling experience (1,0)" is less than 5 percent in both rural and urban samples, which may cause problems in interpretation.

[4] It should be noted again that the interpretation of some in χ^2 Tables 5.7 and 5.8 may be problematic because these tables contain the cells with less than 5 percent.

[5] Although more individual-level variables are introduced in Chapter four, some of them are not useful for the hierarchical analysis in this chapter, due to necessity of fair scatteration of individual samples across districts for hierarchical modeling.

[6] As introduced in Chapter four, THRDS is composed of 19 datasets, and one of them contains the district level information.

[7] The three-factor categorization of variables here is different from that in Chapter four. This is because variables introduced in Chapter four are all from the individual level and because variables such as water can be considered as both material and health factors. For example, water-related variables used in Chapter four (e.g. source of drinking water) are more directly related to health but WAT (the population with clean water) reflects the sufficient level of public goods in the district.

[8] However, Raudenbush and Bryk (2002) also note that "a failure of the normality assumption will affect the validity of the confidence intervals" (p.274). Therefore, the

validity of the confidence intervals in this analysis may be problematic.

[9] For example, square-root transformation may produce the number of teachers as $\sqrt{2} \approx 1.41$.

[10] As stated in Footnote 109, some other variables introduced in Chapter four are not useful for the hierarchical analysis in this chapter, because they are not fairly scattered across districts, which makes it difficult to secure a certain amount of samples at the district level.

[11] u_{0j} is an error associated with W_{0j}.

[12] u_{1j} is an error associated with W_{1j}.

[13] Strictly, the model analyzed in this study is not linear because an outcome variable *literacy* (*writing*) is dichotomous; therefore, the example above is not a correct expression of the model. The model above assumes a linear relation between an outcome and explanatory variables. A correct model and the meaning and justification of model building will be introduced at 5.2.3.

[14] The rationale of having TCHR and PRIM associated with *book* and *schooling* will be explained in 5.2.3.

[15] Another advantage of using the ln LF is that the distribution of $-2\ln(LF)$ is close to the Chi-square distribution, which makes a statistical test easier.

[16] For the details of the definition of the error variance in a logistic model, see pp.47-48 in Long (1997) and pp.223-224 in Snijders and Bosker (2003).

[17] Outside of educational studies, there are some studies using HGLM. Almeida, Wethington and Chandler (1999) study marital dyads and parent-child dyads. They analyze questionnaire data by considering within-family and between-families variability (DV: the occurrence of tension (yes = 1, no = 0)). Rountree and Land (1996) study the cognitive measurement of fear of crime by considering individual gender and routine-activities differences and contextual neighborhood differences (DVs: if worry at least once a week about home being burgled (yes = 1, no = 0) and if worry the neighborhood to be unsafe from crime (unsafe = 1, safe = 0)).

[18] The numerical integration method such as the Laplace estimation was not widely implemented and it has been available in the less popular statistical software MIXOR, but was unavailable in the software HLM, one of the most popular software for hierarchical modeling, until April 2005.

[19] I left random effects U_0, U_1, and U_2 in the model following Snijders and Bosker's (2003) advice: "Especially for relatively small group sizes (in the range from 2 to 50 or 100), the random coefficient model has important advantages over the analysis of covariance model [the model in which random effects are restricted to zero], provided that the assumptions about the random coefficients are reasonable" (p.43). Since the group sizes in this study are 57 for the rural model and 39 for the urban model, I decided not to con-

strain the random effects. When constraining the random effects, the deviance test needs to be implemented.

[20] Here again I left random effects U_0, U_1, and U_2 for the same reason as the level-one only model, following Snijders and Bosker (2003, p.43).

[21] Just in case, I tested PRIM by a Wald test, but it shows insignificance of PRIM in the model (see Appendix C).

[22] I tested TCHR by a Wald test too, but it shows insignificance of TCHR in the model (see Appendix C).

[23] I used the grand-mean-centered predictors at the district level, following Raudenbush and Bryk (2002), who said that "in general, the choice of location for the Ws is not as critical as for the level-1 predictors... Nevertheless, it is often convenient to center all of the level-2 predictors around their corresponding grand means" (p.35). Centering becomes a critical issue when the level-one model is linear (Raudenbush & Bryk, 2002, pp.31-35), but I did not introduce the centering issue in this chapter since the level-one model in this study is logistic.

[24] I constrained U_{2j}, rather than U_{1j}, in the rural model since the unconstrained model (the full model shown in Table 5.19) shows significant contribution of U_{1j} to the model but not that of U_{2j}.

[25] I constrained U_{1j}, rather than U_{2j}, in the urban model. Although the unconstrained model (the full model shown in Table 5.19) shows insignificance of U_{2j}, the model with constraining U_{2j} still showed a high correlation between U_{0j} and U_{1j}, which indicate that U_{1j} is the term to be constrained. In addition, U_{1j} in the unconstrained model is not significance at 5 percent level; therefore, there is no strong reason not to constrain U_{1j}.

Translating HGLM findings into policy recommendations

Chapter 6

In Chapter five, an empirical model of a modified human development theory was tested by the statistical method of Hierarchical Generalized Linear Modeling (HGLM). HGLM was selected for modeling because it can deal with the dichotomous outcome variable *literacy* or *writing* and because it is able to examine the effects of district-level public services on the literacy of individual children. However, HGLM is a sophisticated statistical technique not yet widely used for the purpose of policy analysis. The interpretation of findings is complicated, particularly because of the dichotomous outcome variable, and thus it may be unfamiliar to most policymakers. Therefore, this chapter will provide an interpretation of the models constructed in the previous chapter with an emphasis on their relevance to policy decisions. Section 6.1 will interpret the findings of the models as a form of needs assessment that can inform policy recommendation for Tanzania. The next section, 6.2, will reflect on the limitations and challenges of this form of quantitative modeling for policy purposes. The chapter concludes with a reflection on the consistency between the theoretical model and the quantitative models (6.3).

6.1 Interpretation of the models: Needs assessment and policy recommendation for literacy development

What do the rural and urban final models tell about children's literacy in Tanzania? In a comparison of the rural and urban models, the individual-level variables (*schooling experience* and *book possession*) show some similarities: children who own at least one book are about 4 times as likely to be literate as those who do not own any book, and children who have schooling experience are about 24 times (in rural) or 31 times (in urban) as likely to be literate as those who have no schooling experience. These results verify the positive effects of book possession and primary schooling for children's literacy development, supporting Elley's (2000) "Book Flood approach" and other literature that claim the significance of schooling for children's literacy development (Fuller et al., 1999; Haidara, 1990; Muller & Murtagh, 2002; Smith, 1970). Moreover, these findings endorse Samoff's (1990) statement that schooling plays a central role in Tanzanian education.

On the other hand, the district-level variables yield different results for the rural and urban models. Specifically, district-level variables make contributions to children's literacy in the rural districts but not in the urban districts. The district-level variables are defined as representing the public service conditions, including educational, health, and material wealth factors (5.1.3 (c)). This section will interpret the findings from the previous chapter to examine what public services can contribute to rural children's literacy development (6.1.2). This section also considers the urban needs (6.1.3). The findings will be summarized as policy recommendations in 6.1.4. HGLM yields statistical results in the form of an "odds ratio." Since interpretation of the statistical findings rests on an understanding of the form in which they are generated, I will first explain what "odds ratio" means in the context of this study (6.1.1).

6.1.1 What is an "odds ratio"?

(a) General definition

The reason that coefficients of HGLM are computed as odds ratios (ORs) is that the outcome variable is dichotomous.[1] The OR is also the most technically reasonable way to compute coefficients of logistic models since the outcome variable in the model takes a logged odds form in order to make the

Ch.6 Translating HGLM findings into policy recommendations *189*

model possible by using the link function (see 5.2.1 (b)).

OR, odds, and probability are all different concepts. While probability is defined as a ratio of the frequency of the event's happening divided by the total frequency of the event's happening and not happening, odds is defined as a ratio of the frequency of the event's happening divided by the frequency of the event's not happening. Therefore, while probability cannot go beyond a value of 1, odds can take on values up to infinity. Table 6.1 contrasts the characteristics of probability and odds.

The OR is a ratio of two odds: the odds of one additional unit increase of the relevant predictor over the odds of the existing condition of the relevant predictor. OR is defined as an indicator that measures "how much more likely (or unlikely) it is for the outcome to be present among those with x=1 [the event happened] than among those with x= 0 [the event did not happen]" (Hosmer & Lemeshow, 2000, p.50). OR can take the minimum value of zero to a maximum of infinity. In other words, OR indicates how many times the outcome likelihood changes to the relevant predictor changes by one unit (Hosmer & Lemeshow, 2000, pp.48-56; Long, 1997, pp.79-82; the American College of Physicians, 2000, pp.145-146). Therefore, OR=1 means no change; a value of OR greater than one indicates an increased likelihood; and a value of OR less than one implies a decreased likelihood.

The confidence interval in HGLM output indicates a possible range of OR

Table 6.1 Characteristics of probability and odds

	Probability	Odds
Ratio	$\dfrac{event}{whole}$	$\dfrac{event}{nonevent}$
Range	0 to 1	0 to ∞
Transformation	$odds = \dfrac{probability}{1 - probability}$	$probability = \dfrac{odds}{1 + odds}$

(The American College of Physicians, 2000, pp.145-146)

with a certain level of confidence.[2] When the lower value of a confidence interval of OR exceeds a value of 1, such as the OR interval of *book* in the rural model (3.266, 6.125) (see Table 5.19), the explanatory variable (in this case *book*) is predicted to have a positive effect on the likelihood of the outcome variable (in this case *literacy*). When the higher value of a confidence interval is below a value of 1, such as the intercept in the rural model (0.031, 0.057) (see Table 5.19), the intercept is predicted to have a negative effect on the likelihood of the outcome variable (*literacy*). When a 95 percent confidence interval lies across a value of 1, such as the interval of DISP in the rural model (0.639, 1.110) (see Table 5.19), the effect of DISP on *literacy* is inconclusive because the OR indicates both an increased and a decreased likelihood at that level of confidence. In such an inconclusive case, the p-value should accordingly indicate insignificance.

For comparison of odds, probability, and OR, I will provide one example. Assume that there are two groups: Group A, in which everyone has schooling experience, and Group B, in which no one has schooling experience. Also assume that 8 people of group A are literate and 2 are not, and that 3 people of group B are literate and 7 are not. Then, three indicators, odds, probability, and OR, appear as below.

As seen in Table 6.2, odds and probability are transformable to each other (cf. transformation equations in Table 6.1). However, OR is a ratio of two odds, and the transformation equations in Table 6.1 are not applicable to OR. The OR for literacy for group A (= 9.30) implies that people who have schooling experience are 9.30 times more likely to be literate than people who do not. The OR for literacy for group B (= 0.11) implies that unschooled people are 0.11 times less likely to be literate than schooled people. Similarly, the OR for *illiteracy* for group A (= 0.11) implies that schooled people are 0.11 less likely to be *illiterate* than non-schooled people, while the OR for *illiteracy* for group B (= 9.32) implies that non-schooled people are 9.32

Ch.6 Translating HGLM findings into policy recommendations   *191*

Table 6.2 Comparison of odds, probability, and odds ratio

		Group A - schooling N=10 (8 literate; 2 illiterate)	Group B - non-schooling N=10 (3 literate; 7 illiterate)
Odds	Literate	$\dfrac{8}{2} = 4$	$\dfrac{3}{7} = 0.43$
	Illiterate	$\dfrac{2}{8} = 0.25$	$\dfrac{7}{3} = 2.33$
Probability (% in literacy ratio)	Literate	$\dfrac{8}{10} = 0.8\ (80\%)$	$\dfrac{3}{10} = 0.3\ (30\%)$
	Illiterate	$\dfrac{2}{10} = 0.2\ (20\%)$	$\dfrac{7}{10} = 0.7\ (70\%)$
Odds Ratio	Literate	$\dfrac{groupA}{groupB} = \dfrac{4}{0.43} = 9.30$	$\dfrac{groupB}{groupA} = \dfrac{0.43}{4} = 0.11$
	Illiterate	$\dfrac{groupA}{groupB} = \dfrac{0.25}{2.33} = 0.11$	$\dfrac{groupB}{groupA} = \dfrac{2.33}{0.25} = 9.32$

(Created by the author)

times more likely to be *illiterate* than schooled people.

There are two possible contrasts for OR calculation: literate vs. illiterate (OR for literacy) or illiterate vs. literate (OR for illiteracy). In this study, the contrast is always literate vs. illiterate (OR for literacy), because I am interested in children's literacy, rather than their illiteracy, and I coded the outcome variable *writing* as literate= 1 and illiterate= 0.[3]

(b) Odds ratio for literacy

What does OR for literacy mean in this study? How different is the OR for literacy from a literacy ratio?

First, the OR for literacy in this study indicates how much more likely it is for a child to be literate with the presence of the condition defined by the relevant explanatory variable than other children without that condition. For example, OR of *book possession* in the rural model (OR= 4.443, p<0.01; see Table 5.20) indicates that children who have at least one book are 4.443 times more likely to be literate than those who do not have any book, when all other conditions such as *schooling experience* are the same. When the explanatory variable is continuous, for example, the OR of AID in the rural model (OR=1.583, p<0.01; see Table 5.20) indicates that children living in the district which have one more health aid staff per 10,000 people are 1.583 times more likely to be literate than those living in a district that does not. OR for literacy is always an issue of comparison between two groups of people: those who own books or who do not, those who have schooling experience or who do not, those living in a district with additional health aid staff present or those living in a district without additional staff, and so on. Also, the OR for literacy is always an issue of individuals. It represents each child's likelihood to be literate. It does not predict the aggregate possibility captured by literacy ratios.

Again, the OR for literacy is a different concept than a literacy ratio (or literacy rate). A literacy ratio represents the proportion of literate people in the total population. Thus, a literacy ratio is analogous to the probability of literacy among a group of people, since the probability of literacy is defined as the ratio of the literate divided by the whole, while literacy rate is defined as the literate divided by the whole times a value of 100 (see Table 6.2). The literacy ratio or rate is aggregative. Also, since a literacy rate has a ceiling value of 100 percent, it is easy to understand intuitively. Literacy rates can range only between 0 and 100 percent. In this sense, a literacy rate is absolute and static. By contrast, the OR for literacy is concerned with changes in the likelihood of literacy for individuals living under certain conditions, which are measured by explanatory variables. The OR for literacy is individual in the sense that it does not simply report a collective condition. The OR for literacy may be more difficult to understand intuitively because it can range from 0 to infinity. The OR for literacy can be understood only in reference to a certain condition. In this sense, the OR for literacy is relative, contextual and dynamic.

Although the literacy rate is much more widely used than OR for literacy in the policy context, the OR for literacy is more appropriate to reflect the idea of human development because it predicts the effects of changes in individual conditions. While a literacy rate is a description of the prevalence of the literate population, the OR for literacy focuses on the potential for change in literacy. Assuming that the literacy ratio is 60 percent in Tanzania, this value does not report that most of those who are literate live in conditions favorable to literacy while the 40 percent who are not literate do not. Although the literacy ratio is a useful index to understand general literacy conditions at a glance, the OR for literacy is more appropriate for formulating human development policy in the sense that it pays attention to individuals' different life circumstances and how changes in those circumstances may improve literacy.

In addition to the substantive appropriateness of using the OR for literacy in this study, technically, the OR for literacy reflects the advantage of HGLM as a form of multivariate analysis. While literacy ratios provide simple descriptive statistics, the OR for literacy, within the context of HGLM, can be discussed in relationship to other factors associated with an OR, such as AID and *book**TCHR as the rural model showed in the previous chapter.

Since the OR for literacy cannot generate aggregative information in the ways that a literacy ratio does, it may seem less convincing than a literacy ratio especially in the general policy context. However, a modified human development theory aims at providing a paradigm shift to focus more on individual humans, their life contexts, and the development of their capabilities. Therefore, human development policy also should focus on individual humans and on improvement of their life conditions for their capability building. Using the OR for literacy supports this goal.

6.1.2 Rural needs

How does the rural model speak to human development policy? In the

194   Part II. Empirical analysis of human development

rural model, the number of maternal and child health aid staff per 10,000 (AID) and the interaction of book possession and the number of teachers per 10,000 (*book**TCHR) showed significant contributions to children's literacy (see Table 5.20). Reflecting existing conditions in rural Tanzania, I will utilize the findings from the model for policy recommendation. Although there may be an uncountable number of specific issues related to human development in Tanzania, the model provides a direction for approaching them. Specifically, it verifies the important effects of health aid staff and the interactive effect of teachers and books on the likelihood that a rural Tanzanian child will be literate.

(a) Needs for maternal and child health staff

The existing conditions of public health services in Tanzania are shown in Table 6.3 below.

Based on these general descriptive statistics, I have calculated the numbers of (1) dispensaries, (2) hospitals, (3) health centers per 10 square kilome-

Table 6.3 District means: Health services

	Rural	Urban
Mean of population:	273713	315320
Mean of number of dispensaries:	30	34
Mean of number of hospitals:	2	6
Mean of number of health centers:	3	4
Mean of number of health staff:	32	50
Mean of number of doctors:	2	17
Mean of the district area (km^2):	10128	2483

(From THRDS, World Bank, 1993)

	Rural	Urban
(1) Number of dispensaries per 10km^2:	0.030	0.137
(2) Number of hospitals per 10km^2:	0.002	0.024
(3) Number of health centers per 10km^2:	0.003	0.016
(4) Number of health staff per health facility*:	0.914	1.136
(5) Number of doctors per hospital:	1.000	2.833

* Either a dispensary, hospital, or health center.

(Calculated by the author)

ters, and the number of (4) maternal and child aid staff per health facility (which may be a dispensary, hospital, or health center), and (5) the number of doctors per hospital. The number of health staff per health facility shows that less than one health aid staff member is employed for a typical health facility in a typical rural district (0.914 per health facility), while a typical urban health facility employs on average at least one health aid staff.

Although the data above are quite rough since the values are means of all rural or urban districts, it is clear that the condition of rural health services is less sufficient than it is in the urban areas. Especially because the numbers of doctors (2 in a typical rural district), hospitals (2 in rural), and health centers (3 in rural) are quite limited in rural districts, the role of dispensaries (30 in rural) and health staff (32 in rural) is crucial for children's health. Although the variable DISP resulted in being insignificant in the model, AID showed a significant contribution to children's literacy. Reflecting the insufficient condition of health services in rural districts and the statistical significance of AID, it is reasonable to consider AID as a part of literacy development policy.

The significant OR of AID (OR= 1.583, $p<0.05$) means that every additional unit of AID increases the likelihood of children being literate by 1.583 times, holding other conditions constant. In other words, if a typical rural district creates one more health aid staff per 10,000 people, it could promote children's likelihood to be literate by 1.583 times. In the context of rural Tanzania, one health aid staff per 10,000 people means 27 staff for mean population of 273,713 in a typical rural district (see Table 6.3). Although this model does not speak about budgetary issues, the model implies the need for 27 more health aid staff in a typical rural district in order to increase children's likelihood of literacy by 1.583 times.

Policymakers may need to know the anticipated effect in advance in order to decide if that policy is worth implementing. This quantitative model works as a needs assessment model by simulating the expected impact of creating more health aid staff. The model cannot assume causation; however, the OR of AID indicates a positively significant contribution to literacy. The reality is less simple than the models assume, and there are many practical issues to consider in the process of policy formulation, not least of which is the question of cost. Nonetheless, the large impact of AID on rural children's literacy strongly suggests that creating more health aid staff is worth considering as a part of literacy development policy in rural Tanzania. Issues related to budget allocation, such as cost-effectiveness analysis, will be discussed below in 6.1.4.

(b) Needs for books and teachers

Table 6.4 summarizes existing conditions of public educational services in Tanzania.

Based on the general descriptive statistics, I have calculated the numbers of primary schools per 100 square kilometers and teachers per school. The mean number of primary schools in the rural districts (=133) shows a higher value than that for the urban districts (= 82). However, adjusting for the differences in district sizes, the rural mean of the number of primary schools per 100 square kilometers becomes 1.313, while the urban mean is 3.302. Therefore, in terms of accessibility to school, rural children are under more

Table 6.4 District means: Educational services

	Rural	Urban
Mean of population:	273713	315320
Mean of number of primary schools:	133	82
Mean of number of teachers:	1191	1153
Mean of the district area (km^2):	10128	2483

(From THRDS, World Bank, 1993)

	Rural	Urban
(1) Number of of primary schools per 10km^2:	1.313	3.302
(2) Number of teachers per school:	8.955	14.061

(Calculated by the author)

difficult circumstances than the urban children. Similarly, the rural mean of the number of teachers (=1191) is slightly higher than the urban mean (=1153). However, considering the differences in numbers of primary schools, the rural mean of the number of teachers per school is 8.955, while the urban mean is 14.061. Therefore, in terms of accessibility to teachers at a school, the rural children face more difficult circumstances than the urban children. Although the data above are quite rough since they are mean values of all rural or urban districts, it is clear that the rural condition of educational services is less sufficient than the urban condition. In particular, the number of teachers is insufficient in the rural area and there is a need for more teachers in the rural districts, which is a consistent claim with the findings from the model.

The significant OR of *book**TCHR interaction (OR=1.015, $p<0.05$) means that every additional unit increase of TCHR brings 1.015 times more likelihood for children to be literate if the children own at least one book. In other words, if a typical rural district creates one more teacher per 10,000 people, it could increase the likelihood of the literacy of children who own books by 1.015 times. In the context of rural Tanzania, one teacher per 10,000 people means 27 teachers for mean population of 273,713 in a typical rural district (see Table 6.4). Although this model does not consider the cost for additional teacher positions, the model assesses the need for 27 more teachers in a typical rural district in order to increase book-owing children's likelihood of literacy by 1.05 times. The model cannot assume causation; however, the OR of *book**TCHR interaction indicates a significant contribution to literacy.

The claim that more teachers are needed in the rural districts seems to be reasonable, but it should be noted that *book**TCHR is an interaction term. Since this is an interaction term, this positive effect can be expected only for children who have at least one book (*book* = 1). For those children who do not possess any book (*book* = 0), this interaction term disappears from the model, which implies that TCHR is not a significant matter for children who have no book. Therefore, this claim is valid only for children who own at least one book. Although the model cannot assume causation, there may be two different ways of interpreting this interaction term.

(1) Teachers encourage children to own and read books. Therefore, having more teachers indicates increasing opportunity for children to be encouraged to read the books that they possess. This may be why the interaction term positively contributes to children's literacy.

(2) Children who own books are those from wealthy or educated families. Therefore, those children are amenable to education and will certainly acquire literacy if there are teachers available to them. This may be why the interaction term positively contributes to children's literacy.

In case of (1), the recommendation of creating more teachers can be justified. However, in case of (2), the significant factor is books rather than teachers, and a recommendation of free textbook distribution may be more reasonable since textbooks are not required at most Tanzanian primary schools, and the data show only 30 percent of rural children own at least one book. The model does not imply causation, but it can be said that both books and teachers are important factors for improving rural children's literacy. Further field research is necessary to determine the details of causation.

6.1.3 Urban needs

As found in the final model in the previous chapter, the urban model does not show significant effects from the district-level public services on children's literacy. This may be mainly due to data limitations: the data cannot identify the urban poor out of the general urban samples. It can be assumed that the urban poor significantly rely on public services to some extent, but because of the inability to identify socioeconomic status through the THRDS dataset, the model could not specify the public service needs of the urban poor.

Although the district level variables did not identify the urban public service needs relevant to promoting literacy, it should be noted that the individual-level variables in the urban model showed a large significant impact on children's literacy. As discussed in the previous chapter, both rural and urban models contain two individual-level variables, *book possession* and *schooling experience*, and both significantly contributed to children's literacy (OR $_{book}$ = 4.472, OR $_{school}$ = 24.261 in rural districts; OR $_{book}$ = 4.083, OR $_{school}$ = 31.380 in urban districts; all p<0.01). In particular, the variable *schooling experience* in the urban model showed a large contribution to children's literacy (OR= 31.380), which indicates that schooled children living in an urban district are 31 times more likely to be literate than non-schooled children.

The Tanzanian government (TACADIS, 2006) reports that about 300,000 pupils leave primary schools every year and that school leavers migrate to cities to become child labor. Children in urban districts are more likely to become child laborers than those in rural areas because there are more employment opportunities in urban areas. At the same time, access to schools in urban areas is more adequate than in rural areas (see Table 6.4). Reflecting the large significant effect of schooling experience on urban children's literacy, dropout reduction policies are worth considering for urban children's human development. Further field research and more robust data are necessary to generate a specific needs assessment for human development policy for urban children.

6.1.4 Needs assessment for policy recommendation

Over all, as hypothesized in 5.1.1,[4] the models show different needs in the rural and urban areas (Hypothesis 1). However, significant contributions of the district-level factors to children's literacy are seen in the rural model but not in the urban model (Hypothesis 2). In the rural model, non-educational factors demonstrably contribute to children's literacy; this is not the case in the urban model (Hypothesis 3). Although the urban results may reflect the limitations of the data and thus it may not correctly reflect the reality,[5] the rural model showed that the rural residents significantly benefit from public services. Based on the finding of the rural model, increasing the number of maternal and child health aid staff, increasing the number of teachers, and expanding book availability are recommended. It may be difficult for developing countries to prepare for necessary resources all at once, but international assistance would work for immediate needs. These findings reflect comprehensive needs of the rural children for their literacy development. Needs assessment for human development in the rural area has to maintain a comprehensive perspective that includes health factors for a substantively effective policy.

At the individual level, on the other hand, the significant effects of schooling experience and book possession on literacy are empirically confirmed across the rural and urban districts. This supports the claim made in Chapter three that "compulsory public primary education is expected to guarantee the opportunity for all children to obtain literacy for their realization of constitutive freedom" (see 3.2.1 (b) and 5.1.1), and it also fits Tanzania's post-colonial education policies as discussed in Chapter four.

While these models suggest inputs necessary for promoting a higher level of literacy among rural Tanzanian children, they do not include a salient element in policy analysis: financial data. It is difficult to move from the HGLM analysis in this study to discussion of specific financial issues for both technical and practical reasons. Regarding the former, the models take district differences into prioritized consideration. A meaningful financial analysis would require specific unit cost information from each district included. Moreover, Tanzania is one of many countries currently in the midst of administrative decentralization, a process that has been under way in this country since 1993

(Tanzania President's Office, 2005a, 2005b). It is likely that the financial capacities of local governments differ, and so the trade-offs in financing one public good over another can also vary considerably across districts. Further field research focusing on a few specific districts is necessary to determine the details of the financial feasibility of policy recommendations suggested in this chapter.

Although this study does not include a detailed discussion of specific financial issues, I would like to discuss a possible direction of financial analysis for human development policy. Cost-benefit analysis is one of the most popular methods for educational policy study (e.g. Becker, 1993; Schultz, 1971), in which the "return" from inputs is justified by economic measures such as income increases and economic growth. Philosophically, cost-benefit analysis is based on utilitarianism and as such is not consistent with the fundamental concept of human development theory. As discussed in 3.1, Nussbaum (1999b) claims that "Kantian liberalism is profoundly different from classical Utilitarian liberalism" (p.57). Sen's human development theory and the modified human development theory elaborated in this study are both rooted in Kantian liberalism, in which human beings are treated as ends, rather than means of development. Therefore, I would claim that economic effectiveness is not the fundamental criterion for determining human development policy; rather, human development policy should be determined by an outcome that is relevant to expanding human freedom, in this study, *literacy*.

The models in this study predicted odds ratios for literacy, which tells how much more likely it is for an individual living with certain conditions to be literate than those who lack those conditions. The central question addressed by the models in this study was not how much more income a person may earn, but how much more likely he or she is to be literate. The idea of likelihood for literacy presented in this study is not yet widely accepted as a policy criterion. Nonetheless, it can be observed that, instead of cost-benefit analysis (financial input vs. economic outcome), "cost-likelihood analysis" (financial input vs. literacy likelihood or freedom likelihood) is a more appropriate direction of financial analysis for human development policy. The odds ratios provided by HGLM in this study can be an important part of this financial analysis since they predict the likelihood of improvement in literacy associated with various changes in individual and district variables.

6.2 Limitations of quantitative modeling

The models developed in this chapter can support the development of policy recommendations, as discussed in the previous section. In addition, they also illuminate critical problems facing researchers who attempt to model human development theory. These specific issues related to data availability and quality are discussed in this section.

(a) Data availability

One of the most obvious difficulties raised in the model presented in Chapter five lies in the operationalization of the three factors considered relevant to literacy, this is, educational factors, health factors, and material wealth factors. The models used the number of primary schools (PRIM) and the number of teachers (TCHR) as educational factors; the number of dispensaries (DISP) and the number of maternal and child health aid staff (AID) as health factors; and the population with clean water (WAT) and the number of bank branches (BRANCH) as material wealth factors. Within the THRDS dataset, these variables represent the closest approximations of the factors under consideration, yet it is possible to imagine many other measures that might more clearly reflect the factors that they are intended to represent. The variables presented in this dataset may not in fact be the best indicators of the underlying factors. Thus, there is uncertainty about their construct validity.

One might also question the reliability of these measures over time. The THRDS data was collected in 1993. Obviously, more recent data would be highly valuable. However, this is the latest available "comprehensive" dataset for Tanzania.[6] For reasons both of timeliness and construct validity, the use of secondary data is obviously problematic, but it is equally problematic for individual researchers to collect the requisite nation-wide data all by themselves. As a result, the models developed in this study represent some compromises based on data availability and research feasibility.

The need for "comprehensive" data in this study made the data availability issue especially difficult, despite the fact that international and national bodies have recently made efforts to collect and make available more and more data. For example, the United Nations Educational, Scientific and Cultural Organization (UNESCO) Institute for Statistics provides rich databases on education, literacy, and science and technology (UNESCO Institute for Statistics, 2002). The United Nations Children's Fund (UNICEF) provides the data from the Multiple Indicator Cluster Survey on child health and nutrition (UNICEF, 2005) and also provides the Millennium Development Goals monitoring data (UNICEF, no year) in addition to general country statistics (cf. UNICEF's annual report, the State of the World's Children). The World Health Organization (WHO) Statistical Information System provides various kinds of health indicators (WHO, 2006). The World Bank provides the World Development Indicators (World Bank, 2006), in addition to the Living Standard Measurement Survey (LSMS) survey data whose Tanzanian version (THRDS) is used in this study. Macro International provides the data of the Demographic and Health Survey (DHS) (Macro International, 2006).[7] The Tanzania National Bureau of Statistics opened its website in 2003 to make available its national socio-economic database (NBST, 2004).

Most of the above datasets report data at the national level. Survey data that can illuminate contextual variations in human development and its conditions are still limited. In addition, because these surveys are independently conducted by various organizations, comprehensive databases including all three factors (education, health, and material wealth) are rare. Although it is relatively easy to merge country statistics from different sources, it is very difficult to merge survey data from different sources since their samples are usually anonymous and since their questionnaires are hardly identical. However, using survey data is inevitable for examining people's lives at the local and individual level. This is a fundamental challenge for needs assessment of human development, which has a comprehensive theoretical nature and hence requires a comprehensive database to reflect the nature of the theory.

(b) Measurement and modeling methods

Another substantive problem is that, even if ideal variables were available, it is difficult to quantify a qualitative aspect of human life. How should educational quality be quantified? How should the quality of public services be measured? The models developed in this study are not sensitive enough to measurement issues since they use secondary data. Moreover, because quality issues are often difficult to measure directly, it may be necessary to create latent variables by combining some measurable variables through factor analysis (Kim & Mueller, 1978a, 1978b). For example, a latent variable of an "educational factor" can be created from students' and parents' satisfaction level and numbers of teachers, desks, books, and other educational conditions. The method used in this study, HGLM, is not designed for latent modeling although HGLM is an appropriate method to analyze structured data (individual and district level data, in this case). The method called Structural Equation Modeling (SEM), which was briefly introduced in 5.1.2, can be an appropriate way to analyze latent variables (Anderson & Gerbing, 1988; Cheung, 2000; Kaplan, 2000; Long, 1983; Ullman, 2001). However, it requires robust and reliable data to satisfy its statistical assumptions and requires a variety of variables to create latent variables.

SEM analysis is the next challenge for the analysis of human development. It will allow considering the three factors identified in this study more precisely by using more robust and rich data that can represent these factors. The HGLM in this study analyzed contributions of three factors to children's literacy by taking level differences into consideration, and the SEM will be able to analyze how each factor is composed by what kind of measurable variables and how these latent factors are related to each other. Although the SEM will require more variety of measurement variables to create reasonable latent variables, this data analysis method will enrich the model of human development from a more qualitative perspective.

(c) Politics of data

Finally, there is a *political* problem in the data of developing countries. Nurkse (1953) uses an expression in his theory of the vicious circle of poverty: "a country is poor because it is poor." By this expression, he means that countries in need do not have enough resources to get out of poverty; therefore, poverty is continuously reproduced through its political and economic systems (see 1.1.1). This expression is applicable to the data of developing countries too. Countries in need have much poorer data than wealthy countries. This means that countries in need have much less information to explain what they really need, and hence they have a weaker voice in defining and articulating their own agendas to international agencies.

This information poverty means poverty in two senses: quality and quantity. In the sense of the poverty of *data quality*, the condition of the data in developing countries is often problematic in that too many data are missing, the data distributions are not normal, and other issues may violate statistical assumptions. These problems prevent the data from being analyzed by sophisticated methods, and hence, they make it difficult to propose plausible policy recommendations based on sophisticated models. In the models of this study, some theoretically promising district-level variables proved to be insignificant; however, it is difficult to know if this is because they are actually not contributing to child literacy or because the data are inaccurate. On the other hand, in the sense of poverty of *data quantity*, fewer datasets and fewer kinds of variables are available in developing countries than developed countries. In addition, data collection is much less frequent in developing countries, particularly in the rural areas in the least developed countries, due to difficulties of access.

In addition, there is a domestic political problem too: information about people in need is often ignored in the data collection process. For example, the models in this study could not distinguish the urban poor from their more prosperous urban compatriots. The living conditions of the urban poor are sometimes more severe than those of the self-sufficient rural poor since the urban poor have no viable alternatives to the labor market. However, it was impossible to identify such sample among the general urban sample in the THRDS data. Also, although the data used in this study shows that 47 percent of the total sample live in rural districts (rural n=2580; urban n=2941), it is said that 70 percent of the Tanzanian population live in the rural areas (Africa association, 1994, p.187). This means that the data may be contaminated by sampling bias. In other words, the data may have excluded the information from the rural population in severe need who live in the districts difficult to access for data collection. Again, here is an evidence that "the poor is poor because it is poor." The people who really need to provide the information to claim their share of resources tend to be associated with the least robust data. Since human development is a universal value for all (see Chapter three), the model for human development needs to challenge the social structure that makes the poor stay in poverty.

6.3 Conclusion of the chapter: A comprehensive perspective on human development in Tanzania

In this chapter, I interpret the findings from the models that I developed in the previous chapter. By analyzing the data from the *Tanzania Human*

Resource Development Survey (THRDS), I found that (1) schooling experience and book possession significantly contribute to literacy development at the individual level for both rural and urban children and that (2) there are significant needs for public services in the rural areas while these needs were not apparent in the urban model (6.1). This empirical analysis also raised questions about the limitations of quantitative modeling regarding data availability, measurement and modeling methods, and the politics of data (6.2).

Prior to the empirical analysis in this chapter, I characterized the theoretical model of human development as having three attributes in Chapter three: *comprehensive perspective, hierarchical structure*, and consideration of *literacy as a "promoter" of human development* (see 3.2.2 and 5.1.1). I will conclude this chapter with an overview of the consistency between these three attributes of the theoretical model and the quantitative models developed in this study.

1. Comprehensive perspective

The quantitative models developed in Chapter five and its interpretation in Chapter six maintain a comprehensive perspective on human development by taking educational, health, and material wealth factors into consideration. Although the limitation of data availability raised questions about the adequacy of the definition of factors, the quantitative models do reflect a comprehensive perspective on human development by including all three factors in the models. Considering the comprehensive nature of human development theory, human development policy needs to be formulated and implemented by using a multi-sector approach.

2. Hierarchical structure

The empirical models also reflect the characteristic of the individual-district hierarchical structure of the theoretical model. No one can live outside of the social environment, and some kinds of human capability, such as *combined capability*, require external environmental supports for their development (Nussbaum, 2000; also see 2.2.1. and 3.2.1.). Public policy can play a critical role in providing external environmental supports for capability development, which eventually contributes to developing one's constitutive freedom, a purpose of human development. Although further field research and more robust data are necessary to propose more feasible and justifiable policy recommendations, this empirical analysis demonstrated how needs assessment might improve the social conditions for individual human development.

3. Literacy as a "promoter" of human development

Finally, it is important to remember that the theoretical model assumes that the outcome variable *literacy* (*writing*, in the empirical models) is a necessary condition of capability development to improve instrumental freedoms. Literacy itself is not the goal of human development; the goal of human development is the achievement of constitutive freedom. Rather, literacy is expected to work as a "promoter" or a "central instrumental freedom" of human development (see Chapter three). This means that public policy for human development needs to have a broad perspective beyond children's literacy development since literacy is assumed as a *necessary* condition but not a *sufficient* condition of human development. Although it is too complicated for the quantitative models to capture the whole idea of human development theory, policy recommendations created from the quantitative models should not ignore this theoretical assumption. The quantitative models do not reduce the ultimate goal of human development to simply literacy development. The models may contribute to achieving the ultimate goal of human development, the realization of constitutive freedom.

Notes

[1] An outcome variable can be multinominal in HGLM, but in this study, the outcome variable *writing* is dichotomous, and thus, I used a Bernoulli model.

[2] Confidence intervals are usually computed with 95 percent confidence. The intervals in Tables 5.19 and 5.20 in Chapter five report 95 percent confidence intervals.

³ This coding method is called "reference cell coding," and a value of 1 is given to a reference group. See Hosmer and Lemeshow (2000, p.54) for the details.

⁴ I hypothesized in 5.1.1 that:
1. The environment affects individual lives: Effects of life environment at the district level may have significant impacts on children's schooling life at the individual level.
2. Individual needs differ between rural and urban areas: As shown by descriptive statistics in 4.2, there are significant differences between rural and urban districts. These differences may result in different needs in the rural and urban areas.
3. Comprehensive needs go beyond educational factors: As human development theory claims comprehensiveness of development, non-educational factors, such as health and material wealth factors, may also contribute to children's literacy, in addition to educational factors.

⁵ As shown in Tables 5.9 and 5.10 in the previous chapter, the urban data generally have larger skewness, kurtosis, and standard deviation than the rural data. This implies that there is a larger variation in the urban data.

⁶ As noted in 4.2.2., *the Tanzania Human Resource Development Survey in 1993* is one of the most comprehensive surveys, in comparison to those which contain either one or two factors out of three factors, such as: *the Household Budget Survey in 1991, the Cornell/ERB Survey in 1991, Health Financing Survey in 1991, Tanzanian National Nutrition Survey in 1991, the Sumve Survey on Adult and Childhood Mortality Tanzania in 1995, the Demographic and Health Survey in 1996, the UNICEF Multiple Indicator Cluster Survey in 1998*, and *the Reproductive and Child Health Survey in 1999*.

⁷ Macro International Inc. or Opinion Research Cooperation company <http://www.orcmacro.com> has implemented the DHS project since 1984 <http://www.measuredhs.com/>, funded by the United States Agency for International Development (USAID).

Conclusion: Toward human development Chapter 7

Summary: How much do we know about human development?

This study has aimed at answering questions about human development in the context of international development. More specifically, it has asked the questions: what does "human development" really mean? How should educational development be located in the concept of human development? How is it possible to embody the abstract concept of human development in policy processes? Each chapter of this study tries to answer these questions.

Chapter one provided a theoretical and historical overview of development economics and sociology to consider the meaning of development, westernization, and modernization. This chapter aimed at setting up a fundamental perspective on development that addresses the recently recognized need for a comprehensive and ethical perspective on development. The new perspective on development questions the classic meaning of economic development and calls for a comprehensive conception of human development. It was argued that development for "the people of that society" (Huntington, 1997) can be consistent with the process of modernization as long as the new conception of international development takes an ethical and global perspective into serious consideration.

From the perspective set up in Chapter one, Chapter two introduced the details of Sen's human development theory and analyzed its shortcomings. According to Sen (2000), human development theory considers development "a process of expanding the real freedom that people enjoy" (p.3), and developing "human capability" is assumed to contribute to the realization of human freedom. Although Sen fails to examine the universal validity of his theory, Nussbaum (1992, 2000a) defends the universal value of human capabilities, which she conceives as a list of "central human functional capabilities." Also, although Sen fails to place his theory in the context of international cooperation, Rawls (1999b) justifies the duty of "well-ordered peoples" to assist "burdened societies" in the context of global politics. However, international cooperation in globalization requires resolving the tensions between asserting universal values (such as the *Universal Declaration of Human Rights* in 1948) and accommodating cultural particularity (respect for cultural social diversity). In addition, since the concept of human development is such a comprehensive idea, human development policy in practice requires a multi-sector approach beyond distinctions between economic development and social development.

What kind of theoretical framework can overcome the tension between universality and particularity in international development? How can such a comprehensive and interdisciplinary theory of human development resolve conflicts between the goals of economic and social development to produce a practicable human development policy? To answer these questions, Chapter three defended two claims on a modified human development theory. This chapter proposed a modified version of human development theory and introduced a theoretical model of human development, which was quantitatively examined in later chapters.

In claim one, I hypothesized that a universal value of human development is consistent with cultural diversity and social particularity under Kantian liberalism. As found in Huntington's (1997) and Sen's (2000) claims introduced in Chapter one, modernization can be differentiated from westernization, and it can be considered as a dynamic process of social change driven by each society's particularity. In other words, a universal value of human development need not always ignore indigenous culture and social particularity under international development, as long as a fair decision-making process is secured for the people of that society. Therefore, claim one implies two conditions:

1. Political condition: The society has a democratic decision-making system.
2. Educational condition: The people of that society enjoy basic education that enables them to participate in the decision-making process.

Another necessary condition for resolving the tension between the universal value of human development and social particularity is Kantian liberalism. Unlike Utilitarian liberalism, Kantian liberalism is based on Kantian philosophy, which views human beings as ends, not merely as means (Kant, 1997, 2002). While Utilitarian liberalism is often understood as an individualistic philosophy, a Kantian liberalism proposes that one should "act according to the maxim which can at the same time make itself a universal law" (Kant, 1997, p.54) even if that action reduces the individual's utility. A Kantian moral order considers the individual truly autonomous only when he or she makes the right choice following a universal moral principle (the categorical imperative); otherwise his or her choice is considered as being determined by heteronymous teleological concerns (the hypothetical imperative). Human development theory is activated as an interpretation of the universal moral principle under Kantian liberalism.

In claim two, I hypothesized that the right to basic education is a central instrumental freedom to promote human capability for one's constitutive freedom. Through a reconsideration of Nussbaum's list of central human functional capabilities, I argued for three factors as components of human capability: educational, health, and material wealth factors. These factors are located in the hierarchy of human development, in which the bottom is composed of *basic capability*, the middle is composed of *internal capability*, and the top is composed of *combined capability* (Nussbaum, 2000a). Remembering Sen's concepts of two freedoms, I located *constitutive freedom* as the goal or the top of the hierarchy, and consider *instrumental freedom* as a promoter of capability building for individuals to achieve constitutive freedom (see Figure 3.3). Constitutive freedom is achieved through the exercise of combined capabilities; instrumental freedom is achieved though the exercise of internal and basic capabilities. More precisely, internal capability is developed through the exercise of capabilities generated by educational factors and the development of basic capabilities derives from basic health and material factors. I classified educational factors as relevant to internal capability following Nussbaum's definition of internal capability: the capability which is developed "with support from the surrounding environment, as when one learns to play with others, to love, to exercise political choice" (Nussbaum, 2000a, p.84).

Based on this theoretical map of human development, I focused on the role of basic education in human development as a *central* instrumental freedom because it enables young people to participate in democratic decision-making processes, and because it enables young people to acquire more advanced capabilities in the future. I specifically proposed *compulsory public primary education* as an institutionalized form of basic education for human development, because the *compulsory* and *public* nature of basic education can assure, at least to some extent, equality of educational access disregarding parents' economic backgrounds and adults' arbitrary preferences for child labor. This is also because the *primary* nature of basic education can assure a universal foundation for different kinds of subsequent education; in other words, the primary nature of basic education aims at developing children's internal capability through cultivating basic abilities. As a fundamental form of basic education, I focused on literacy since "literacy is inseparably tied to all aspects of life and livelihood" (UNESCO, 2005a) and assumed that literacy can play a significant role in promoting children's internal capability, which develops other future capabilities.

The modified human development theory introduced in Chapter three implied a theoretical model of human development. The characteristics of the model include a *comprehensive perspective* on human development (considering all three factors of education, health, and material wealth), a *hierarchical structure* of the society (considering school-age children's lives at the individual level and public services at the district level), and a perspective on *literacy as a promoter of human development* (considering literacy not as a goal but as a start toward human development). The model considers literacy as an outcome variable, and contains both individual-level and district-level explanatory variables.

Before analyzing this model empirically, Chapter four examined the case of Tanzania through historical analysis of educational and social polices and through data from the *Tanzania Human Resource Development Survey* (THRDS) (The World Bank, 1993, 1997; The World Bank & University of Dar es Salaam, 1993). This chapter described the similarity between Tanzania's original philosophy and the concept of human development at the theoretical ideal level; at the same time, this chapter clarified the dilemma in which Tanzanian society struggles to attain the *Ujamaa* (Tanzanian socialism) ideal but faces capitalist realities at the actual policy level. One possible direction for Tanzanian human development policy is to bridge this divide between ideals and actual policy implementation. Chapter four concluded with an argument for the importance of needs assessment for human development policy, specifically for reducing the rural-urban gap that was created by the externally imposed structural adjustment policy during the 1980s against the intentions of Tanzania's original policies and philosophy.

For promoting a theoretical model of human development at the actual policy level, Chapter five tested the theoretical model of human development empirically by using Tanzania's data. The modeling method called Hierarchical Generalized Linear Modeling (HGLM) was applied to the THRDS data. Rural and urban models were separately developed in this study, assuming that there are different needs in difference life circumstances. Each model posited *literacy* as an outcome variable, *book possession* and *schooling experience* as individual-level explanatory variables, and the factors of education (PRIM & TCHR), health (AID & DISP), and material wealth (WAT & BRANCH) as district-level explanatory variables.

Chapter six interpreted the technical findings of the models in the policy context and proposed policy recommendations for human development in Tanzania. The findings are summarized as follows:

1. At the individual level, the same tendency in rural and urban districts is found. In both rural and urban models, the two individual-level variables, *book possession* and *schooling experience* significantly contribute to children's literacy.

2. In the rural model, the number of maternal and child health aid staff per 10,000 people (AID) significantly contributes to children's literacy. This indicates positive effects of a health factor on literacy development. The interaction term between book possession and the number of teachers per 10,000 people (*book**TCHR) also shows a significant contribution to literacy. This indicates a positive effect of an educational factor on literacy of children who own at least one book. It is recommended for the rural districts to create more positions of health aid staff and teachers and to expand children's accessibility to books.

3. In the urban model, no district-level variable significantly contributes to children's literacy. However, it cannot simply be concluded that there is no need for public services in the urban districts.

Such insignificance may be caused by the problematic dataset, in which the urban poor sample cannot be distinguished from the urban wealthy sample. The urban poor may significantly rely on public services in reality, but the data does not precisely reflect their existence and thus the model does not capture their needs. This is an issue related to the limitation of the data. On the other hand, at the individual level, the urban model shows a much larger contribution of *schooling experience* to children's literacy than the rural model. Considering that urban children are more vulnerable to becoming child laborers than rural children, school-dropout reduction policy is recommended for the urban districts.

The models do not assume causation of the outcome variable, children's literacy, by the explanatory variables at the individual and district levels. However, the models enable us to interpret some elements of the reality surrounding school-age children in Tanzania. Further field research and more accurate data are necessary for specific policy formulation.

Recommendation for Tanzanian human development

Modeling a modified human development theory in this study suggests some policy recommendations for human development in Tanzania. Across the rural and urban districts, the models find large and significant contributions of *schooling experience* and *book possession* to children's literacy development ($OR_{schooling\_rural} = 24.261$, $p<0.01$; $OR_{schooling\_urban} = 31.380$, $p<0.01$; $OR_{book\_rural} = 4.472$, $p<0.01$; $OR_{book\_urban} = 4.083$, $p<0.01$). Considering that the Tanzanian government (TACADIS, 2006) reports that about 300,000 pupils leave primary schools every year and migrate to large cities to become child laborers, school-dropout reduction policy is imperative, particularly in the urban districts. Regarding book possession, since textbooks are not required and not free in most primary schools, free textbook distribution needs to be considered as a national educational policy. Thus, as national education policies, primary school dropout reduction and free textbook distribution need to be considered for both rural and urban children.

The rural model finds a comprehensive need for public services. In particular, the model shows the importance of developing human resources in the rural areas. The model shows significant contributions of maternal and child health aid staff per 10,000 people (AID) and of teachers-book interaction (*book**TCHR) to children's literacy. The existing conditions in the rural areas do not assure even one health aid staff member per health facility on average (average number of health staff per health facility in a rural district is 0.914; see Table 6.3). One unit increase of AID or one more health aid staff member out of 10,000 people means 27 more staff in a typical rural district. The model estimates that this change would increase children's likelihood of literacy by 1.583 times (see 6.1.2 (a)). This positive impact can justify the need for more positions of health aid staff in the rural districts.

Regarding the number of teachers in the rural districts, one unit increase of THCR or one more teacher out of 10,000 people means 27 more teachers in a typical rural district. The rural model estimates that this change would increase children's likelihood of literacy by 1.015 times (see 6.1.2 (b)). Because this increase results from an interaction between children's book possession and the number of teachers, this positive impact is applicable only for children who own at least one book. However, combined with a national policy for free textbook distribution, this positive effect could be expected for all rural children. This finding can justify the need for more teachers in the rural districts.

While the rural model implies a need for comprehensive public services, the urban model does not confirm the positive impact of public services (6.1.3). This is probably due to the inadequacy of the urban data. The urban population is generally more diverse than the rural population in terms of their social status and economic condition (e.g., the street children without primary educational access and the wealthy children with access to higher education) as well as their life circumstances (e.g., the marginal urban children without a nearby health facility and the central urban children with ample access to health services). Therefore, it is very difficult to measure their conditions with a few indicators. The data used in this study do not allow us to distinguish the marginal urban sample from the general sample. If they were identifiable, the marginal urban sample might show the results similar to those in the rural areas.

Barnett et al. (1995) insist on the importance of improving children's life and school environment especially for children's health by saying that "the problems [are] created where 'theory and practice' do not match up... The evidence from this study indicates that many of the schools visited have minimal water and sanitation facilities" (p.13). Although a limitation of data availability does not allow interpreting the urban model in this way, the district-level variables, including three factors, try to match the comprehensiveness of the theoretical model of human development and the policy recommendations for human development in Tanzania. By using the models that contain all three factors of human development, comprehensive policy recommendations become possible.

Recommendation for human development research

In addition to policy recommendations for Tanzanian human development, the importance of data improvement needs to be emphasized. I will suggest three main needs for data improvement as follows.

1. Needs for cooperative data collection

In spite of the many efforts at data collection by international and national organizations, there is very limited communication among them. Except the United Nations organizations that share data, there seems to be no exchange among private and non-profit consulting organizations. The more a comprehensive perspective on development becomes accepted, the greater the need for comprehensive data. As discussed in 6.2 (a), I had a difficult time finding a dataset containing all three factors under consideration. Collaboration among international developmental agencies may solve the difficulty and make it easier to produce comprehensive databases by taking advantage of each organization's strengths. Specifically, cooperative survey projects would be effective, and sharing some definitions and coding across different databases would help researchers to merge data to create more comprehensive databases from what currently exists.

2. Needs for structured data

For policy recommendation, the model needs to capture structural relationships in society because there are different actors and stakeholders at different levels (e.g. bureaucrats at the national government, public officers at the district government, and teachers at schools). In other words, in order to specify who should do what using whose budget, the model needs to be sensitive to differences between the levels. Therefore, structured data, data containing the information from different levels, are necessary for quantitative policy analyses. However, I had a difficult time creating structured data from the available databases. Structured data is very sensitive to missing data because only one missing data element at the district level may result in hundreds of missing elements at the individual level. When modeling three levels or more (e.g., student, school, and district levels), this problem becomes exacerbated. For example, one missing district may lead some dozens of schools to be missing, which in turn may result in thousands of students missing. Even if a database contains a large sample, it may not work for hierarchical modeling when the structure of the data is inadequate.

3. Needs for study of the data's meaning

Finally, there is a need for improving the *qualitative* aspect of the data. Many know today that school enrollment in most developing countries does not represent the actual percentage of children who attend school regularly.

In the dataset used in this study, the initial population with clean water (WAT) contained values exceeding 100 percent. Those values may reflect the industrial use of clean water and measure the level of industrialization in those districts, rather than the water access for human consumption. This issue of construct validity is a shared responsibility for both data collectors and data analysts. Moreover, this is a challenge for both quantitative researchers and qualitative researchers. Constructive and cooperative communication between them is necessary to improve the quality and reliability of the data.

The need for further research

This study has tried to establish a bridge between the theoretical consideration of human development and practical modeling for needs assessment of human development policy. It proposed a modified human development theory, in which the role of education is defined as a *central instrumental freedom*. This study also constructed needs assessment models for human development policy in Tanzania. Although this bridge may not be strong enough for policy makers to rely on in practice, this study showed at least the possibility of improving human development policies by using a modified human development theory.

1. Field research

At the same time, this study clarified what to do next. Findings from the models worked for needs assessment but were not wholly sufficient for specific policy formulation. For specifying actual policies, further field research and robust datasets are required. In particular, human resource development for health aid staff and teachers in the rural area showed significant impacts on children's literacy. In order to translate this finding into effective policy measures, it is necessary to understand how these human resources are trained on the ground and how training programs work or do not work in practice. In addition, the numbers of new health aid staff members and teachers suggested in this study (27 new staff and teachers in a typical rural district) are calculated from one-unit increase of AID and TCHR (one more staff/teachers per 10,000 people) and the mean population of the rural districts (=273,713). It is necessary to make sure of the exact numbers necessary in each district given their unique social conditions. Further field research is necessary to find the exact needs of each specific district and to specify how to create new health aid staff and teachers.

2. Financial analysis

The models did not consider financial issues either. It is obvious that the districts need more funds to create more positions for health aid staff and teachers. In particular, how to secure recurrent funding for human resources needs to be considered since recurrent funding is difficult to obtain from short-term external aid budgets. In order to propose feasible policy recommendations, it is necessary to analyze financial conditions in the districts. This study proposed a possible direction of financial analysis for human development policy, this is, "cost-likelihood analysis" (financial input vs. literacy likelihood or freedom likelihood), rather than cost-benefit analysis (financial input vs. economic outcome) (see 6.1.4). However, due to the unavailability of district-level financial data, this study did not step into financial analyses. Financial analysis based on the cost-likelihood analysis is necessary for showing the feasibility of human development policy.

3. Latent modeling

In addition to the field research and the financial analysis in Tanzania, the modeling method itself also needs to be improved. Although HGLM in this study is an appropriate method to analyze structured data for policy purposes, human development theory includes concepts that are difficult to measure directly. As introduced in 5.1.2 and 6.2 (b), Structural Equation Modeling (SEM) allows us to analyze latent variables created by combining measurable variables. By analyzing latent variables, SEM may reflect some conceptual aspects of human development better than HGLM. For creating accurate latent variables, SEM is a data hungry method, and this is a challenge for analysis of developing countries, in which very limited data are available. However, it is worth trying to model the concept of human development by using SEM in order to operationalize the conceptual aspects of this theory in the policy context.

4. Measurement of constitutive freedom

The most substantive challenge for empirical modeling of human development theory is the measurement of constitutive freedom. This study defined the outcome variable *literacy* as a central internal capability, assuming that literacy contributes to instrumental freedom development. By assuming that instrumental freedom should eventually contribute to constitutive freedom, this study focused only on instrumental freedom. However, in order to capture the whole idea of human development, it is necessary to consider how to measure the concept of constitutive freedom. Self-satisfaction surveys are not an appropriate measurement method since satisfaction or subjective happiness is a goal of utilitarianism. Following Sen's concept of freedom, the criterion of measurement should be the range of choice: how many choices the individual has to realize the life that she or he wants. Choice in this sense seems too complicated a concept to represent by one variable. It is necessary to elaborate how to represent the concept of constitutive freedom in the empirical model of human development.

5. Theoretical consideration about literacy

Finally, there is a theoretical challenge left. As described in the characteristics of the theoretical model (3.2.2 & 5.1.1), children's literacy in the quantitative models is considered as a promoter of constitutive freedom or a central instrumental freedom. Therefore, the findings from the quantitative analyses are valid for human development policy only when literacy is assumed as an appropriate internal capability for human development. In other words, this study largely relies on the potential of children's literacy for the realization of human freedoms. A theoretical justification to consider literacy as a central instrumental freedom is that "literacy is inseparably tied to all aspects of life and livelihood" (UNESCO, 2005a; also see 3.2.1 (b)). However, a conceptual model of a modified human development theory may rely too heavily on literacy, and it may create doubt that the theoretical justification is not strong enough to connect literacy directly to human freedoms. As Wagner (1990, 1992) and Bhola (1990) insist, literacy is an inevitably important ability for human life, especially in the context of international development. However, this study does not deepen the argument about literacy itself. Only being literate does not secure its function in practice (cf. functional literacy, such as: Castell, 1981; Fisher, 1981; Hammad, 1992; Kirsch, 1977; Mwansa, 1995; Ouane, 1992; Spratt, 1991; Tierney, 1986). Theoretical issues about literacy for human development need to be explored.

Contribution of this study to human development policy

Although there are still challenges left, this study can be said to contribute to the analysis of human development policy both theoretically and practically.

Theoretically, this study proposed an ethical justification of international development through establishing a modified human development theory. The issue of international development has been mainly discussed in the fields of economics and politics. The humanitarian standpoint has been one of the stances of international development, but it is considered as advocacy against dominant developmental strategies, not as a theoretical alternative comparable to other economic and political theories. This study proposed human development as another theoretical alternative that can broaden the field of international development. In addition, this study reconsidered the meaning of education in human development and clarified its role. In the dominant paradigm of economic development, the role of education has been limited to being a supplement to other developmental strategies. This study, by contrast, defined the role of education as a *central internal capability*. By doing so, this study provided a different perspective on educational development.

In practical-terms, this study proposed empirical models of human development using the existing data from Tanzania. The models developed in this study necessarily stopped with analysis of contributions to *literacy* or the realization of *instrumental freedom*. However, the ultimate meaning of instrumental freedom lies in its contribution to *constitutive freedom*. Although it is necessary to develop the models themselves by using more appropriate methods and more robust datasets, the models proposed in this study will push the focus of developmental policies towards constitutive freedom in practice. At the very least, the models may work as guidance for the advocates of human development policy. Since the concept of human development is highly abstract and complicated, concrete models for a specific country by themselves may guide those who agree with human development theory at the conceptual level but who have no clue about how to bring the idea into the policy context. I cannot insist that the models in this study are operationalized well enough to be applied to real problems, but they may provide guidance on how to formulate human development policy in reality.

Some may say that models are always far from the reality. In the sense that modeling often requires unrealistic assumptions, such as random collection and normal distribution of data, models always show not real but ideal properties, and thus, modeling is a kind of utopian approach. However, borrowing an expression from Rawls,* I will call it a "realistic utopian" approach, in which one starts with thinking of an ideal situation but does not ignore reality. When facing a difficult situation, we first need to know an ideal goal to be achieved, and then, we can measure how far we are from it. With such guidance form ideal modeling, we can think about how to get to the goal. After learning about ideal needs for human development through the models, we can start to think how to fulfill them in reality. Modeling human development theory may give us a direction for policy formulation.

In the long run, I hope, providing policy analyses with empirical models like those developed in this study will broaden perspectives among policymakers both in terms of grasping the realities of comprehensiveness or "intersectoral impacts" in policy practice and perhaps, over time, promoting a more human-focused vision of development even beyond the circle of policymakers. Continuous use of the policy model of human development may change policymakers' behaviors and minds. Before Schultz proposed his human capital theory, no one imagine that education was a matter of economic development. A half century later, now, an educational approach to economic development has become a "common sense" among policymakers. Theory, empirical modeling, and its practice may change the current common sense over time. This study may contribute to making human development theory the next common sense in international development.

* *

Despite of its complexity and abstractness, more and more people, including both practitioners and academic researchers, are interested in the idea of human development. After all, this theory more adequately represents living as humans than do the exclusively economic theories of development. Given the phenomena of globalization, it becomes apparent both how different and how similar we are as human beings. This notion can activate the idea of Kantian liberalism as I claimed that "a universal value of human development is consistent with cultural diversity and social particularity under Kantian liberalism" (see Chapter three). I assume that human development theory attracts those who recognize this substance of human life - different but the same.

Human development is a critical way of thinking for all human societies. In completing this study, however, I have often been overwhelmed by this complex concept and had to wonder whether I was up to the task. At such times, the words below have given me encouragement.

> Truth gains more even by the errors of one who, with due study and preparation, thinks for himself, than by the true opinions of those who only hold them because they do not suffer themselves to think. (Mill, 2003, p.102)

I am not quite sure if I have found the problem worth solving for human development as I intended at the beginning of this study. However, now I can believe that what I need to do is to keep thinking with due study and preparation through the rest of my life.

Notes

* According to Rawls (1999b), "Political philosophy is realistically utopian when it extends what are ordinarily thought of as the limits of practical political possibility" (p.6).

Appendices

Appendix A: Nussbaum's list of human capabilities

CENTRAL HUMAN FUNCTIONAL CAPABILITIES

1. Life: being able to live to the end of a human life of normal length.

2. Bodily health: being able to have good health (including reproductive health, adequate nutrition, and adequate shelter).

3. Bodily integrity: being able to more freely (including security against assault and opportunity for sexual satisfaction and reproduction).

4. Sense, imagination, and thought: being able to use the senses to imagine, think, and reason (including adequate education, literacy, basic mathematical and scientific training; also including experience and production of self-expressive works).

5. Emotions: being able to have attachments to things and people outside ourselves.

6. Practical reason: being able to form a conception of the good and to engage in critical reflection about the planning of one's life.

7. Affiliation:
   A. Being able to live with and toward others (including concern and compassion for other human beings and situations, various social interaction, and capability for both justice and friendship).
   B. Having the social bases of self-respect and non-humiliation (including human dignity and non-discrimination).

8. Other species: being able to live with concern for and in relation to animals, plants, and the world of nature.

9. Play: being able to laugh, play, and enjoy recreational activities.

10. Control over one's environment:
    A. Political: being able to participate in political choices that govern one's life (including political participation, freedom of speech, and freedom of association).
    B. Material: being able to hold property, not just formally but in terms of real opportunity (including equal property rights and equal employment).

(Selected from Nussbaum, 2000, p.78-80)

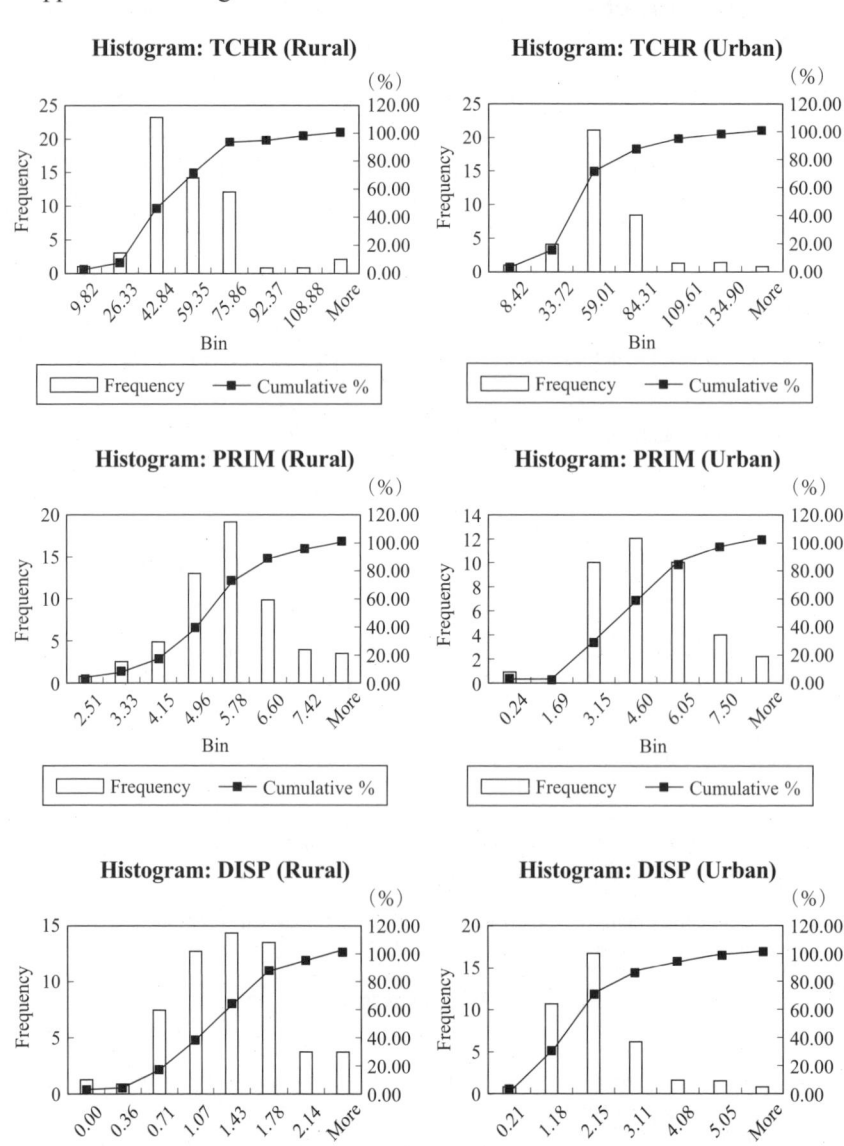

Appendix B: Histograms

Histogram: AID (Rural)

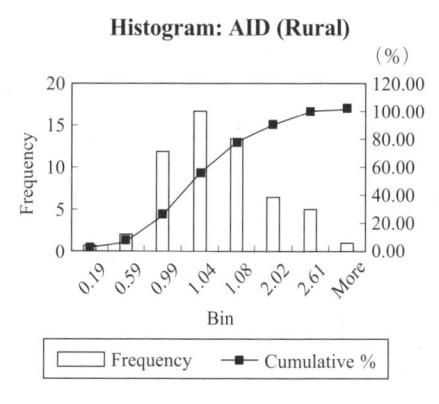

Histogram: AID (Urban)

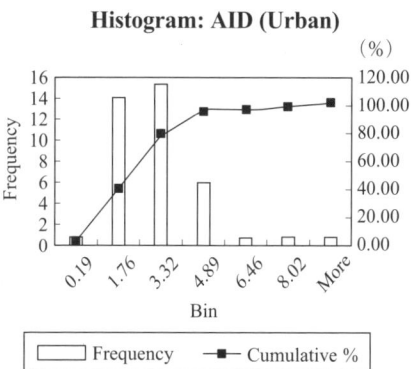

Histogram: WAT (Rural)

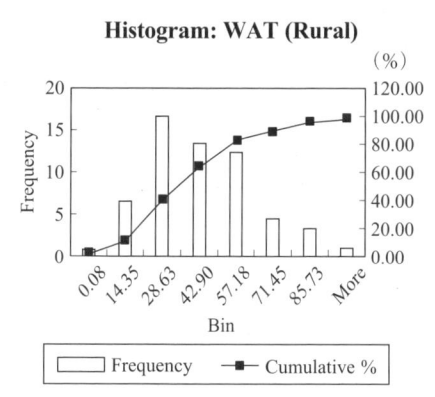

Histogram: WAT (Urban)

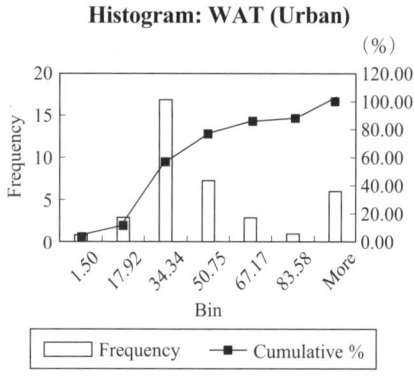

Histogram: BRANCH (Rural)

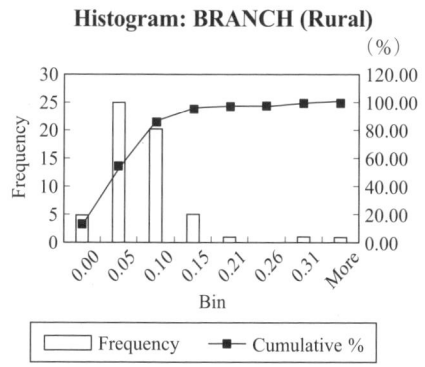

Histogram: BRANCH (Urban)

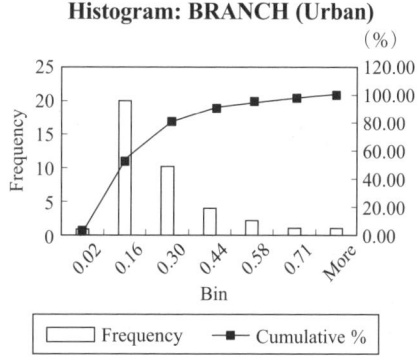

Appendix C: Wald test outputs

Results of General Linear Hypothesis Testing: Rural

	Coefficients		Contrast		
For INTRCPT1, B0					
INTRCPT2, G00	-3.191625	0.000	0.000	0.000	0.000
DISP_POP, G01	-0.156925	0.000	0.000	0.000	0.000
MCHAIDS_, G02	0.444717	0.000	0.000	0.000	0.000
BANK_POP, G03	0.239579	0.000	0.000	0.000	0.000
TCHR_POP, G04	-0.004738	0.000	0.000	0.000	0.000
PRIM_POP, G05	0.212439	0.000	0.000	0.000	0.000
CLNWAT_P, G06	0.003643	0.000	0.000	0.000	0.000
For I20 slope, B1					
INTRCPT2, G10	1.523609	0.000	0.000	0.000	0.000
BANK_POP, G11	5.513740	1.000	0.000	0.000	0.000
TCHR_POP, G12	0.003450	0.000	0.000	0.000	0.000
PRIM_POP, G13	0.262412	0.000	1.000	0.000	0.000
For I33 slope, B2					
INTRCPT2, G20	3.220520	0.000	0.000	0.000	0.000
BANK_POP, G21	-2.621860	0.000	0.000	1.000	0.000
TCHR_POP, G22	0.002089	0.000	0.000	0.000	1.000
PRIM_POP, G23	-0.177454	0.000	0.000	0.000	0.000

Chi-square statistic = 6.116963
Degrees of freedom = 4
P-value   = 0.189312

Note_1: H_0: Gij=0
Note_2: Contrast=1.000 means constraint.

(Analyzed by HLM6.02)

Results of General Linear Hypothesis Testing: Urban

	Coefficients		Contrast		
For INTRCPT1, B0					
INTRCPT2, G00	-2.928250	0.000	0.000	0.000	0.000
DISP_POP, G01	0.017106	0.000	0.000	0.000	0.000
MCHAIDS_, G02	0.038862	0.000	0.000	0.000	0.000
BANK_POP, G03	0.118862	0.000	0.000	0.000	0.000
TCHR_POP, G04	0.000796	0.000	0.000	0.000	0.000
PRIM_POP, G05	-0.091114	0.000	0.000	0.000	0.000
CLNWAT_P, G06	-0.005038	0.000	0.000	0.000	0.000
For I20 slope, B1					
INTRCPT2, G10	1.466095	0.000	0.000	0.000	0.000
BANK_POP, G11	0.268648	1.000	0.000	0.000	0.000
TCHR_POP, G12	-0.005543	0.000	0.000	0.000	0.000
PRIM_POP, G13	0.061894	0.000	1.000	0.000	0.000
For I33 slope, B2					
INTRCPT2, G20	3.322627	0.000	0.000	0.000	0.000
BANK_POP, G21	0.854835	0.000	0.000	1.000	0.000
TCHR_POP, G22	0.002344	0.000	0.000	0.000	1.000
PRIM_POP, G23	0.046533	0.000	0.000	0.000	0.000

Chi-square statistic = 3.133552
Degrees of freedom = 4
P-value   = >.500

Note_1: H_0: Gij=0
Note_2: Contrast=1.000 means constraint.

(Analyzed by HLM6.02)

Reference

Abrokwaa, C. (1999). Africa 2000: What development strategy? *Journal of black studies, 29*(5), 646-668.

Ackoff, R. L. (1974). *Redesigning the future: a systems approach to societal problems.* NY: Wiley.

Adelman, I. (2000). Fallacies in development theory and their implications for policy. In G. M. Meier & J. E. Stiglitz (Eds.), *Frontiers of devleopment economics: The future in perspective.* Washington DC: The World Bank.

Afurika kyokai [Africa association]. (1994). *Afurika Nennkan 1993-94 [Africa year book 1993-94].* Tokyo: Afurika kyokai [Africa association].

Ahsan, M. (2004). Human development in the Muslim world: From theory to practice. *The Muslim World, 94*, 181-200.

Almeida, D., Wethington, E., & Chandler, A. (1999). Daily transmission of tensions between marital dyads and parent-child dyads. *Journal of marriage and the family, 61*(1), 49-61.

Amin, S. (1974). *Accumulation on a world scale: Acritique of the theory of underdevelopment* (B. Pearce, Trans.). London: Monthly Review Press.

Amin, S. (1996). On devleopment: For Gunder Frank. In S. Chew & R. Denemark (Eds.), *The underdevelopment of development.* CA: Sage Publications.

Anderson, J., & Gerbing, D. (1988). Structural equation modeling in practice. *Psychological bulletin, 103*(3), 411-423.

Asou, K. (1995). "Sai" to "kyozon" ["Difference" and "coexistence"]. In S. Hasumi & M. Yamauchi (Eds.), *Bunmei no shototsu ka kyozon ka [Clash or coexistence of civilization].* Tokyo: Tokyo University Press.

Baldwin, R. (1993). *A domino theory of regionalism.* MA: National Bureau of Economic Research.

Banks, J. A. (Ed.). (2004). *Diversity and citizenship education.* CA: Jossey-Bass.

Barnett, E., Koning, K., and Francis, V. (1995). *Health and HIV/AIDS education in primary and secondary schools in Africa and Asia* (Vol. 14). London: Department For International Development.

Basu, K. (2000). On the goals of development. In G. M. Meier & J. E. Stiglitz (Eds.), *Frontiers of development economics: The future in perspective.* Washington DC: The World Bank.

Bauer, P. (1971). *Dissent on development.* London: Widenfeld and Nicolson.

Becker, G. (1967). *Human capital and the personal distribution of income: an analytical approach.* MI: The University of Michigan.

Becker, G. (1993). *Human Capital: A theoretical and empirical analysis, with special reference to education* (3rd ed.). IL: The University of Chicago Press.

Becker, G., Murphy, K., & Tamura, R. (1990). *Human capital, fertility, and economic growth*. MA: National Bureau of Economic Research.

Bhola, H. (1990). An overview of literacy in Sub-Sahara Africa-Images in the making. *African Studies Review, 33*(3), 5-20.

Bicego, G., Curtis, S., Raggers, H., Kapiga, S., & Ngallaba, S. (1997). *Sumve survey on adult and childhood mortality, Tanzania 1995: In-depth study on estimating adult and childhood mortality in settings of high adult mortality*. MD: Macro Internaitonal Inc.

Black, C. (1966). *The dynamics of modernization*. NY: Harper and Row.

Block, L. S. (1984). National development policy and outcomes at the University of Dar es Salaam. *African studies review, 27*(1), 87-115.

Bryk, A., & Thum, Y. M. (1989). The effects of high school organization on dropping out: An exploratory investigation. *American educational research journal, 26*(3), 353-383.

Buchert, L. (1994). *Education in the development of Tanzania 1919-90*. London: James Currey.

Bull, B., Fruehling, R., & Chattergy, V. (1992). *The ethics of multicultural and bilingual education*. NY: Teachers College Press.

Cameron, J. (1980). Education, idividuality and community: Education for Self-Reliance in Tanzania. *British Journal of Educational Studies, 28*(2), 100-111.

Castell, S. d., Luke, A., & MacLennan, D. (1981). On defining literacy. *Canadian Journal of Education, 6*(3), 7-18.

Chenery, H. B. (1979). *Structural change and development policy*. NY: Oxford University Press.

Cheung, D. (2000). Evidence of a single second-order factor in student ratings of teaching effectiveness. *Structural equation modeling, 7*(3), 442-460.

Chew, S., & Denmark, R. (Eds.). (1996). *The underdevelopment of development*. CA: Sage Publications.

Cliffe, L. (1969). From independence to self-reliance. In I. N. Kimambo & A. J. Temu (Eds.), *A history of Tanzania* (pp. 239-257). Nairobi: East African Publishing House.

Cooksey, B., & Riedmiller, S. (1997). Tanzanian education in the nineteis: beyond the diploma disease. *Assessment in Education, 4*(1), 121-136.

Cummings, R. (1986). Africa between the ages. *African studies review, 29*(3), 1-26.

Cunningham, G. L. (1968). Education for rural development. In I. N. Resnick (Ed.), *Tanzania: Revolution by education* (pp. 181-190). Arusha: Longmans of Tanzania.

Daniels, S. (1995). Can pre-school education affect children's achievement in primary schools? *Oxford review of education, 21*(2), 163-178.

Duncan, G. (1994). Families and neighbors as source of disadvantage in the schooling decisions of white and black adolescents. *American journal of education, 103*(1), 20-53.

Eliason, S. R. (1993). *Maximum likelihood estimation: Logic and practice.* CA: Sage Publications.

Elley, W. (2000). The potential of book floods for raising literacy levels. *International review of education, 46*(3/4), 233-255.

Esho, H. (1997). Keizaikaihatu to hinkonmondai [Economic development and poverty problems]. *Kokusai kyoryoku kenkyu [Journal of international cooperation], 13*(2), 1-7.

Esho, H. (1999). *Kaihatu no seiji-keizai-gaku [Political economics of development].* Tokyo: Nihon hyoron sha.

Ferreira, M. L., & Griffin, C. C. (1996). *Tanzania human resource development survey: Final report.* Washington DC: The World Bank.

Fisher, D. L. (1981). Functional literacy tests: A model of question-answering and an analysis of errors. *Reading research quarterly, 16*(3), 418-448.

Frank, A. (1981). *Crisis: In the third world.* NY: Holmes & Meier Publishers.

Frank, A. (1996). The underdevelopment of development. In S. Chew & R. Denemark (Eds.), *The underdevelopment of development.* CA: Sage Publications.

Fuller, B., Dellagnelo, L., Strath, A., Bastos, E. S. B., Maia, M. H., Matos, K. S. L. d., et al. (1999). How to raise children's early literacy?: The influence of family, teacher, and classroom in northeast Brazil. *Comparative Education Review, 43*(1), 1-35.

Gamoran, A., Porter, A., Smithson, J., & White, P. (1997). Upgrading high school mathematics instruction: Improving learning opportunities for low-achieving, low-income youth. *Educational evaluation and policy analysis, 19*(4), 325-228.

Garner, C., & Raudenbush, S. (1991). Neighborhood effects on educational attainment: A multilevel analysis. *Sociology of education, 64,* 251-262.

Gereffi, G., & Fonda, S. (1992). Reginal paths of development. *Annual review of sociology, 18,* 419-448.

Gershenkron, A. (1966). *Economic backwardness in historical perspective.* MA: Belknap.

Goodin, R., & Klingemann, H.-D. (Eds.). (1996). *A new handbook of political science.* MA: Oxfort University Press.

Grant, C. A., & Lei, J. L. (Eds.). (2001). *Global constructions of multicultural education.* NJ: Lawrence Erlbaum Associates.

Gray, J., Jesson, D., & Sime, N. (1990). Estimating differences in the examination performances of secondary schools in six LEAs: A multi-level approach to school effectiveness. *Oxford review of education, 16*(2), 137-158.

Grosh, M., & Glewwe, P. A. (1995). *A guide to living standards surveys and their data sets* (No. 120). Washington DC: The World Bank.

Gutmann, A. (1999). *Democratic education*. NJ: Princeton University Press.

Haidara, B. (1990). *Regional programme for the eradication of illiteracy in Africa: Literacy Lessons*. Switzerland: International Bureau of Education.

Hammad, A. E. B., & Mulholland, C. (1992). Functional literacy, health, and quality of life. *Annals of the American Academy of Political and Social Science, 520*, 103-120.

Haq, K. (2000). Human development challenges in South Asia. *Journal of Human Development, 1*(1), 71-82.

Haq, M. (1995). *Reflections on human development*. NY: Oxford University Press.

Hara, S. (1999). *Kokusai-kankei-gaku kougi [Study on international relations]*. Tokyo: Yuhikaku.

Hasegawa, K., & Takasugi, T. (1998). *Gendai no kokusai-seiji [International politics]*. Kyoto: Minerva publishing.

Hirschman, A. (1958). *The strategy of economic development*. CT: Yale University Press.

Hosmer, D., & Lemeshow, S. (2000). *Applied logistic regression*. NY: John Wiley & Sons.

Huntington, S. (1997). *The clash of civilizations and the remarking of world order*. NY: Touchstone.

Ie, M. (2000). *Kokusai kankei [International relations]*. Kyoto: Sekai shiso sha.

Ishida, Y. (1995). Shibirian pawa no seiji-gaku [Political science of civilian power]. In S. Hasumi & M. Yamauchi (Eds.), *Bunmei no shototsu ka kyozon ka [Clash or coexistence of civilization]*. Tokyo: Tokyo University Press.

Ishikawa, F. (1995). *Kanto Nyumon [Introduction to Kant]*. Tokyo: Chikuma Shobo.

Johnson, P. (2002). New technology tools for human development? towards policy and practice for knowledge societies in southern Africa. *Compare, 32*(3), 381-389.

Jolly, R. (2002). Statisticians of the world unite: the human development challenge awaits. *Journal of Human Development, 3*(2), 263-272.

July, R. (1983). Toward cultural independence in Africa: Some illustratons from Nigeria and Ghana. *African studies review, 26*(3/4), 119-131.

Kageyama, S. (1997). Kaihatu-enjo no kako no tenkai to kongo no houkou [The past and future of development assistance]. *Kaihatu-enjo kenkyu [The journal of development assistance], 4*(1), 4-6.

Kant, I. (1997). *Foundation of the metaphysics of morals* (L. Beck, Trans. 2nd ed.). NJ: Prentice-Hall.

Kant, I. (2002). *Critique of practical reason* (W. Pluhar, Trans.). IN: Hackett Publishing Company.

Kaplan, D. (2000). *Structural equation modeling*. CA: Sage publications.
Kawamoto, T. (2002). *Rawls: Seigi no genri [Rawls: The principles of justice]* (5th ed.). Tokyo: Kodansha.
Kerr, D. (1976). *Educational policy: Analysis, structure, and justification*. NY: David McKay.
Khoi, L. T. (1991). *L'education comparee [Japanese]* (Y. Maehira, Trans.). Tokyo: Kojisha.
Kim, J.-O., & Mueller, C. W. (1978a). *Introduction to factor analysis*. CA: Sage Publications.
Kim, J.-O., & Mueller, C. W. (1978b). *Factor analysis: Statistical methods and practical issues*. CA: Sage Publications.
Kirk, R. E. (1999). *Statistics* (4th ed.). FL: Harcourt Brace.
Kirsch, I., & Guthrie, J. T. (1977). The concept and measurement of functional literacy. *Reading research quarterly, 13*(4), 485-507.
Kitajima, Y. (1997). Dochaku bunka to jinrui no mirai [The future of indigenous culture and humanity]. In Y. Kataoka (Ed.), *Jinrui - kaihatu - NGO [Humanity - development - NGO]*. Tokyo: Shinhyoron.
Kusano, A. (1997). *ODA no tadashii mikata [The perspective to ODA]*. Tokyo: Chikumashobo.
Lambert, S., & Sahn, D. (2002). Incidence of public spending in the health and education sectors in Tanzania. In C. Morrisson (Ed.), *Education and health expenditure and poverty reduction in East Africa: Madagascar and Tanzania* (pp. 115-172). Paris: OECD.
Lindblom, C. E. (1959). The science of "Muddling Through". *American society for public administration, xix*(2).
Lindblom, C. E. (1979). Still muddling through. *Public Administration Review*, 517-526.
Long, S. (1983). *Covariance structure models*. CA: Sage Publications.
Long, S. (1997). *Regression models for categorical and limited dependent variables*. CA: Sage publications.
Luke, D. (2004). *Multilevel modeling*. CA: Sage publications.
Macro International Inc. (2006). *Demographic and health surveys*. Retrieved Mar. 10, 2006, from http://www.measuredhs.com/start.cfm
Mason, A. D., & Khandker, S. R. (1996). *Measuring the opportunity costs of children's time in a developing country: Implications for education analysis and interventions* (No. HCDWP72). Washington D.C.: the World Bank.
Mazrui, A. A. (1990). *Cultural forces in world politics*. London: James Currey.
Mbilinyi, M. L. (1982). History of formal schooling in Tanzania. In H. Hinzen & V. H.

Hundsdorfer (Eds.), *Education for liberation and development: The Tanzanian experience* (pp. 76-87). Hamburg: Unesco Institute for Education.

Mbunda, F. L. (1982). Primary education since 1961. In H. Hinzen & V. H. Hundsdorfer (Eds.), *Education for liberation and development: The Tanzanian experience* (pp. 88-96). Hamburg: Unesco Institute for Education.

McKinnon, R. I. (1964). Foreign exchange constraints in economic development and efficient aid allocation. *Economic Journal, 7*, 388-409.

Meier, G. M., & Stiglitz, J. E. (Eds.). (2000). *Frontiers of development economics: The future in perspective*. Washington DC: The World Bank.

Menard, S. (2002). *Applied logistic regression analysis* (2nd ed.). CA: Sage publications.

Mill, J. S. (2003). *On liberty*. CT: Yale University Press.

Mine, Y. (1999). *Gendai afurika to kaihatsu keizai-gaku [The economics for an African rebirth]*. Tokyo: Nihon shoron sha.

Ministry of Health Tanzania. (2000). *National package of essential health interventions in Tanzania*. Dar es Salaam: Ministry of Health.

Morrison, D. R. (1976). *Education and politics in Africa: The Tanzanian case*. Montreal: McGill-Queen's University Press.

Muller, A., & Murtagh, T. (2002). Literacy: The 877 million left behind. *Education Today, 2*, 4-7.

Murakami, A. (2002). School hygiene in primary schools in Tanzania: Imperative need for the trans-sector cooperation. *Asian educational study monographs, 3*, 27-46.

Mwansa, D. M. (1995). Perspectives on literacy, gender and change: A case for Zambia. *British Journal of Sociology of Education, 16*(4), 495-516.

Nagao, R. (1995). Shisou no kyoten toshite no gurobarizumu [Globalism as the basis of thinking]. In S. Hasumi & M. Yamauchi (Eds.), *Bunmei no shototsu ka kyozon ka [Clash or coexistence of civilization]*. Tokyo: Tokyo University Press.

Nakamura, Y., Hamano, T., Nagata, Y., Yokozeki, Y., & Kurashimo, J. (1998). Sabu-sahara-afurika no kisokyoiku ni taisuru nihon no enjo-kanousei [On the possibility of Japanese assistance for basic education in Sub Saharan Africa]. *Kokusai kyoryoku kenkyu [The Journal of international cooperation], 14*(1), 9-18.

Ngallaba, S., Kapiga, S. H., Ruyobya, I., & Boerma, J. T. (1993). *Tanzania demographic and health survey 1991/1992*. MD: Bureau of Statistics and Macro International Inc.

Nishigaki, A., & Shimomura, Y. (1993). *Kaihatu-enjo no keizai-gaku [Economics of developmental assistance]*. Tokyo: Yuhikaku.

Nurkse, R. (1953). *Problems of capital formation in underdeveloped countries*. Oxford: Basil Blackwell.

Nussbaum, M. C. (1992). Human functioning and social justice: in defense of Aristotelian essentialism. *Political theory, 20*(2), 202-246.

Nussbaum, M. C. (1999b). *Sex and social justice*. NY: Oxford University Press.

Nussbaum, M. C. (2000a). *Women and human development*. NY: Cambridge University Press.

Nussbaum, M. C. (2000b). Women's capabilities and social justice. *Journal of human development, 1*(2), 219-247.

Nye, B., Hedges, L., & Konstantopoulos, S. (1999). The long-term effects of small classes: A five-year follow-up of the Tennessee class size experiment. *Educational evaluation and policy analysis, 21*(2), 127-142.

Nye, B., Hedges, L., & Konstantopoulos, S. (2000). Do the disadvantaged benefit more from small classes? Evidence from the Tennessee class size experiment. *American journal of education, 109*(1), 1-26.

Nyerere, J. K. (1969a). Ujamaa: The basis of African socialism. In K. E. Svensen & M. Teisen (Eds.), *Self-reliant Tanzania* (pp. 158-166). Dar es Salaam: Tanzania Publishing House.

Nyerere, J. K. (1969b). The Arusha declaration and TANU's policy. In K. E. Svendsen & M. Teisen (Eds.), *Self-reliant Tanzania* (pp. 184-208). Dar es Salaam: Tanzania Publishing House.

Nyerere, J. K. (1969c). Education for self-reliance. In K. E. Svendsen & M. Teisen (Eds.), *Self-reliant Tanzania* (pp. 219-239). Dar es Salaam: Tanzania Pulishing House.

Nyerere, J. K. (1969d). Socialism and rural development. In K. E. Svendsen & M. Teisen (Eds.), *Self-reliant Tanzania* (pp. 246-271). Dar es Salaam: Tanzania Publishing House.

Nyerere, J. K. (1982a). Education in Tanzania. In B. Fafunwa & J. U. Aisiku (Eds.), *Education in Africa: A comparative survey* (pp. 235-253). London: George Allen & Unwin.

Nyerere, J. K. (1982b). The overall educational conception. In H. Hinzen & V. H. Hundsdorfer (Eds.), *Education for liberation and development: The Tanzanian experience* (pp. 17-55). Hamburg: Unesco Institute for Education.

Ogura, M. (1982). *Kihatsu to hatten no shakai-gaku [sociology of development and evolution]*. Tokyo: Tokyo University Press.

Omari, I. M., Mbise, A. S., Mahenge, S. T., Malekela, G. A., & Besha, M. P. (1983). *Universal primary education in Tanzania*. Dar es Salaam: University of Dar es Salaam.

Ouane, A. (1992). Functional literacy: North-south perspectives. *Annals of the American Academy of Political and Social Science, 520*, 66-75.

Pampel, F. (2000). *Logistic regression: A primer*. CA: Sage publications.

Panigrahi, R., & Sivramkrishna, S. (2002). An adjusted human development index: Robust contry rankings with respect to the choice of fixed maximum and minimum indicator values. *Journal of Human Development, 3*(2), 301-311.

Paul, A. D. (2002). *Missing data* (Vol. 136). CA: Sage publications.

Pisani, M., & Pagan, J. (2004). Self-employment in the era of the new economic model in Latin America: A case study from Nicaragua. *Entrepreneurship & regional development, 16*, 335-350.

Pong, S.-l. (1998). The school compositional effect of single parenthood on 10th-grade achievement. *Sociology of education, 71*, 24-43.

Raphael, D. D., & Macfie, A. L. (Eds.). (1982). *Adam Smith: The theory of moral sentiments*. IN: Liberty Classics.

Raudenbush, S., & Bryk, A. (2002). *Hierarchical linear models: Applications and data analysis methods* (2nd ed.). CA: Sage publications.

Raudenbush, S., Bryk, A., Cheong, Y. F., Congdon, R., & Toit, M. d. (2004). *HLM6: Hierarchical linear & nonlinear modeling*. IL: Scientific software international.

Raudenbush, S., Fotiu, R., & Cheong, Y. F. (1998). Inequality of access to educational resources: A national report card for eighth-grade math. *Educational evaluation and policy analysis, 20*(4), 253-267.

Raudenbush, S., Rowan, B., & Kang, S. J. (1991). A multilevel, multivariate model for studying school climate with estimation via the EM algorithm and application to U.S. high-school data. *Journal of educational statistics, 16*(4), 295-330.

Rawls, J. (1993). The law of peoples. In S. Shute & S. Hurley (Eds.), *On Human Rights: The Oxford Amnesty Lecture 1993*. NY: Harper Collins Publishers.

Rawls, J. (1999a). *A theory of justice* (Revised ed.). MA: Harvard University Press.

Rawls, J. (1999b). *The law of peoples*. MA: Harvard University Press.

Roberts, G. (1981). *Questioning development: Notes for volunteers and others concerned with the theory and practice of change*. Hampshire: Alver Press.

Roderick, M., & Camburn, E. (1999). Risk and recovery from course failure in the early years of high school. *American educational research journal, 36*(2), 303-343.

Rostow, W. W. (1960). *The stages of economic growth*. NY: Cambridge University Press.

Rountree, P., & Land, K. (1996). Perceived risk versus fear of crime: Evidence of conceptually distinct reactions in survey data. *Social forces, 74*(4), 1353-1376.

Rowan, B., Raudenbush, S., & Kang, S. J. (1991). Organizational design in high schools: A multilevel analysis. *American journal of education, 99*(2), 238-266.

Saito, M. (2003). Amartya Sen's capability approach to education: A critical exploration. *Journal of Philosophy of Education, 37*(1), 17-33.

Samoff, J. (1990). "Modernizing" a socialist vision: Education in Tanzania. In M. Carnoy

& J. Samoff (Eds.), *Education and social transition in the third world* (pp. 209-273). NJ: Princeton University Press.

Sangmpam, S. N. (1995). Sociology of "primitive societies," evolutionalism, and Africa. *Sociological forum, 10*(4), 609-632.

Saxe, G., & Gearhart, M. (1999). Relations between classroom practices and student learning in the domain of fractions. *Cognition and instruction, 17*(1), 1-24.

Schiller, K., & Muller, C. (2000). External examinations and accountability, educational expectations, and high school graduation. *American journal of education, 108*(2), 73-102.

Schultz, T. (1971). *Investment in human capital*. NY: The Free Press.

Scientific Software International. (2005a). *Comparing non-linear models in HLM*. Retrieved Feb. 20, 2006, from http://www.ssicentral.com/hlm/faqs6.html

Scientific Software International. (2005b). *FAQs for HLM 6*. Retrieved Feb. 20, 2006, from http://www.ssicentral.com/hlm/faqs.html

Seers, D. (1983). *The political economy of nationalization*. Oxford: Oxford University Press.

Seltzer, M. (1995). Furthering our understanding of the effects of educational pragrams via a slopes-as-outcomes framework. *Educational evaluation and policy analysis, 17*(3), 295-304.

Seltzer, M., Frank, K., & Bryk, A. (1994). The metric matters: The sensitivity of conclusions about growth in student achievement to choice of metric. *Educational evaluation and policy analysis, 16*(1), 41-49.

Sen, A. (1981). *Poverty and famines: an essay on entitlement and deprivation*. Oxford: Clarendon Press.

Sen, A. (1987). *On ethics and economics*. Oxford: Basil Blackwell.

Sen, A. (1992). *Inequality reexamined*. MA: Harvard University Press.

Sen, A. (1994). Growth economics: What and why? In L. Pasinetti & R. Solow (Eds.), *Economic growth and the structure of long-term development*. London: Macmillan.

Sen, A. (1997a). *On economic inequality*. Oxford: Clarendon Press.

Sen, A. (1997b). Editorial: Human capital and human capability. *World Development, 25*(12), 1959-1961.

Sen, A. (1999a). *Reason before identity*. NY: Oxford University Press.

Sen, A. (1999b). *Commodities and capabilities* (Oxford India Paperbacks ed.). New Delhi: Oxford University Press.

Sen, A. (1999c). Assessing human development. In *Human development report 1999: Globalization with a human face*. NY: Oxford University Press.

Sen, A. (2000). *Development as freedom*. NY: Anchor books.

Sen, A. (2002a). *Rationality and freedom*. MA: The belknap press of harvard university press.

Sen, A. (2002b). Capability and well-being. In M. Nussbaum & A. Sen (Eds.), *The quality of life*. Oxford: Oxford University Press.

Sherman, M. (1990). The university in modern Africa: Toward the twenty-first century. *The journal of higher education, 61*(4), 363-385.

Shiba, Y., Watanabe, H., & Ishizuka, T. (2002). *Toukei yogo jiten [Statistics dictionary]*. Tokyo: Shinyo-sha.

Silagan, M. (1986). The genealogy of mukama: The methodology of oral tradition. *Dialectical Anthropology, 10*(3-4), 229-247.

Smith, A. (2004a). *Dotoku kanjo ron [The theory of moral sentiments]* (Vol. 1). Tokyo: Iwanami shoten.

Smith, A. (2004b). *Dotoku kanjo ron [The theory of moral sentiments]* (Vol. 2). Tokyo: Iwanami shoten.

Smith, G. A. (1970). *A preliminary report on literacy training, savings clubs and development in Seki Tribal Trust Land*: Canadian School Library Association.

Snijders, T., & Bosker, R. (2003). *Multilevel analysis: An introduction to basic and advanced multilevel modeling*. CA: Sage publications.

Snyder, F. (1980). Law and development in the light of dependency theory. *Law & society review, 14*(3), 723-804.

Spratt, J. E., Seckinger, B., & Wagner, D. A. (1991). Functional literacy in Moroccan school children. *Reading research quarterly, 26*(2), 178-195.

Stambach, A. (1998). "Too much studying makes me crazy": School-related illness on Mount Kilimanjaro. *Comparative Education Review, 42*(4), 497-512.

Stewart, F., & Deneulin, S. (2002). Amartya Sen's contribution to development thinking. *Studies in Comparative International Development, 37*(2), 61-70.

Streeten, P., & al., e. (1981). *First things first: Basic human needs in developing countries*. Washington DC: World Bank Publication.

Sui-Chu, E. H., & Willms, D. (1996). Effects of parental involvement on eighth-grade achievement. *Sociology of education, 69*, 126-141.

Sunkel, O. (1979). The development of development thinking. In J. Villamil (Ed.), *Transnational capitalism and national development: New perspectives on dependence*. NJ: Humanities Press.

Sutton, M., & Levinson, B. (Eds.). (2001). *Policy as practice: Toward a comparative sociocultural analysis of education policy*. CT: Ablex Publishing.

Svendsen, K. E. (1969). Problems after the Arusha declaration. In K. E. Svendsen & M. Teisen (Eds.), Self-reliant Tanzania (pp. 209-218). Dar es Salaam: Tanzania

Publishing House.

Taasisi ya Elimu Tanzania. (1999). *Sayansi 5: Kitabu cha mwanafunze: Darasa la tano [Science 5: The book for children: Lesson grade fifth].* Dar es Salaam: Mture Educational Publishers.

Tabachnick, B., & Fidell, L. (2001). *Using multivariate statistics* (4th ed.). MA: Allyn & Bacon.

Takagi, Y. (1996). *Kaihatsu keizai-gaku [Development economics].* Tokyo: Yuhikaku.

Tanzania Commission for HIV/AIDS (TACAIDS). (2006). *HIV/AIDS in Tanzania.* Retrieved Feb. 25, 2006, from http://www.tanzania.go.tz/hiv_aids.html

Tanzania National Bureau of Statistics (TNBS). (2004). *2000 population and housing census,* from http://www.nbs.go.tz/indicators.htm

Tanzania National Bureau of Statistics (TNBS), & Macro International Inc. (1997). *Tanzania demographic and health survey 1996.* MD: Bureau of Statistics and Macro International Inc.

Tanzania National Bureau of Statistics (TNBS), & Macro International Inc. (2000). *Tanzania reproductive and child health survey 1999.* MD: National Bureau of Statistics and Macro International Inc.

Tanzania President's Office, Public Service Management. (2005a, 2005). *Public Service Reform Programme (PSRP) background.* Retrieved Mar. 8, 2006, from http://www.estabs.go.tz/background.php

Tanzania President's Office, Public Service Management. (2005b, 2005). *Public Service Reform Programme (PSRP) overview.* Retrieved Mar. 8, 2006, from http://www.estabs.go.tz/psrp_overview.php

Thang, N. M., & Popkin, B. (2003). Child malnutrition in Vietnam and its transition in an era of economic growth. J Hum *Nutr Dietet, 16,* 233-244.

The American College of Physicians. (2000). Primer on probability and odds and interpreting their ratios. *Effective clinical practice, 3*(3), 145-146.

The World Bank. (1988). *Adjustment lending: An evolution of ten years of experience.* Washington D.C.: World Bank.

The World Bank. (1993). *Human resource development survey: Individual/household questionnaire*: The Wold Bank.

The World Bank. (1997). *Tanzania human resource development survey.* Retrieved November 1, 2004, from http://www.worldbank.org/lsms/country/tza/tanzhome. html

The World Bank. (2006). *Data & statistics.* Retrieved Mar. 10, 2006, from http://web.worldbank.org/WBSITE/EXTERNAL/DATASTATISTICS/0,,contentMDK:20398986~menuPK:64133163~pagePK:64133150~piPK:64133175~theSitePK:239419,00.html

The World Bank, & University of Dar es Salaam. (1993). *Human resource development survey: Interviewer's manual*: The World Bank.

Thomas, S. (2004). Reconfiguring the public sphere: Implications for analysis of education policy. *British Journal of Educational Studies, 52*(3), 228-248.

Thompson, A. R. (1968). Ideas underlying British colonial education policy in Tanganyika. In I. N. Resnick (Ed.), *Tanzania: Revolution by education* (pp. 15-32). Arusha: Longmans of Tanzania.

Tierney, R. J., & Rogers, T. (1986). Functional literacy in school settings. *Theory into Practice, 25*(2), 124-127.

Tilak, J. (2002). Education and poverty. *Journal of human development, 3*(2), 191-207.

Tymms, P. (1993). Accountabiity: Can it be fair? *Oxford review of education, 19*(3), 291-299.

Ullman, J. (2001). Structural equation modeling. In B. Tabachnick & L. Fidell (Eds.), *Using multivariate statistics* (4th ed., pp. 653-771). MA: Allyn & Bacon.

UNDP. (1990). *Human development report 1990: Concept and measurement of human development*. NY: Oxford University Press.

UNDP. (1991). *Human development report 1991: Financing human development* NY: Oxford University Press.

UNDP. (1992). *Human development report 1992: Global dimensions of human development* NY: Oxford University Press.

UNDP. (1993). *Human development report 1993: People's participation*. NY: Oxford University Press.

UNDP. (1994). *Human development report 1994: New dimensions of human security*. NY: Oxford University Press.

UNDP. (1995). *Human development report 1995: Gender and human development*. NY: Oxford University Press.

UNDP. (1996). *Human development report 1996: Economic growth and human development*. NY: Oxford University Press.

UNDP. (1997). *Human development report 1997: Human development to eradicate poverty*. NY: Oxford University Press.

UNDP. (1998). *Human development report 1998: Consumption for human development* NY: Oxford University Press.

UNDP. (1999). *Human development report 1999: Globalization with a human face*. NY: Oxford University Press.

UNDP. (2000). *Human development report 2000: Human rights and human development*. NY: Oxford University Press.

UNDP. (2001). *Human development report 2001: Making new technologies work for human development.* NY: Oxford University Press.

UNDP. (2002). *Human development report 2002: Deepening democracy in a fragmented world* NY: Oxford University Press.

UNDP. (2003). *Human development report 2003: Millennium Development Goals: A compact among nations to end human poverty* NY: Oxford University Press.

UNDP. (2003). *What is human development?* Tokyo, JPN: UNDP Tokyo.

UNDP. (2004). *Human development report 2004: Cultural liberty in today's diverse world* NY: Oxford University Press.

UNDP. (2004, March 29, 2004). *Human development reports: glossary*, from http://hdr.undp.org/hd/glossary.cfm

UNDP. (2005). *Human development report 2005: International cooperation at a crossroads: Aid, trade and security in an unequal world*. NY: Oxford University Press.

UNESCO. (2003). *The leap to equality: gender and education for all*. Paris: UNESCO.

UNESCO. (2005). *International literacy day 2005 to focus on sustainable development.* Retrieved September 10, 2005, from http://portal.unesco.org/education/en /ev.php-URL_ID=41537&URL_DO=DO_ TOPIC&URL_SECTION=201.html

UNESCO Institute for Statistics. (2002, Feb. 23, 2006). *Database access*. Retrieved Mar. 10, 2006, from http://www.uis.unesco.org/

UNICEF. *Millennium Development Goals (MDG) monitoring*. Retrieved Mar. 10, 2006, from http://www.unicef.org/statistics/index_24304.html

UNICEF. (1996). *The state of the world's children 1997*. NY: UNICEF.

UNICEF. (1998a). *The state of the world's children 1999*. NY: UNICEF.

UNICEF. (1998b). *Multiple indicator cluster survey*. Retrieved Dec. 4, 2004, from http://www.childinfo.org/index2.htm

UNICEF. (2002). *The Convention on the Rights of the Child*, from http://www.unicef. org/crc/crc.htm

UNICEF. (2003). *The state of the world's children 2004*. NY: UNICEF.

UNICEF. (2004). *The state of the world's children 2005*. NY: UNICEF.

UNICEF. (2005). *Monitoring the situation of children and women*. Retrieved Mar. 10, 2006, from http://www.childinfo.org/

United Nations. (2005). *UN Millennium Development Goals*. Retrieved Jan. 25, 2006, from http://www.un.org/millenniumgoals/

Valenzuela, S., & Valenzuela, A. (1979). Modernization and dependence: Alternative perspectives in the study of Latin American underdevelopment. In J. Villamil (Ed.), *Transnational capitalism and national development*. NJ: Humanities Press.

Wagner, D. A. (1990). Literacy assessment in the third world: An overview and proposed schema for survey use. *Comparative Education Review, 34*(1), 112-138.

Wagner, D. A. (1992). World literacy: Research and policy in the EFA decade. *Annals of the American Academy of Political and Social Science, 520* (World Literacy in the Year 2000), 12-26.

Wildavsky, A. (1979). *Speaking truth to power*. Boston: Little Brown.

Wilkinson, I. (1998). Dealing with diversity: Achievement gaps in reading literacy among New Zealand students. *Reading research quarterly, 33*(2), 144-167.

Willms, D., & Chen, M. (1989). The effects of ability grouping on the ethnic achievement gap in Israeli elementary schools. *American journal of education, 97*(3), 237-257.

Willms, D., & Raudenbush, S. (1989). A longitudinal hierarchical linear model for estimating school effects and their stability. *Journal of educational measurement, 26*(3), 209-232.

World Health Organization. (2006). *WHO statistical information system*. Retrieved Mar. 10, 2006, from http://www3.who.int/whosis/menu.cfm

Yamamoto, K. (1994). Kaihatu-enjo no kokusaiteki-choryu to wareware no tachiba [The international trend of developmental assistance and the standing point of Japan]. *Kaihatu-enjo kenkyu [The journal of development assistance], 1*(1), 4-6.

Index

Number
3Rs 147
95 percent confidence interval 190

A
adult literacy 53, 55
advocacy 15, 223
agency achievement 44
agency freedom 44, 45
aid fatigue 13
Amin 18
Aristotelian essentialism 56
Aristotelian essentialist 55, 78
Arusha Declaration 112, 116, 121
average slope 160

B
basic capabilities 58, 90, 91, 213
basic capability 90, 91, 92, 94, 213
basic needs 14, 15
Bernoulli model 170
bi-lateral aid 87
binary 162
binary data 145
Book Flood approach 149, 188
British administration 106, 108
British colonial period 106, 109
British government 106, 107
budget allocation 196
burdened societies 59, 61, 87, 211

C
capabilities 42
capability 42
capitalism 20, 105, 114, 134

categorical imperative 85, 212
causation 183, 196, 197, 198, 216
central human functional capabilities
.... 55, 56, 57, 59, 89, 211, 212
central human functional capability 57, 63
central instrumental freedom
... 71, 88, 93, 212, 213, 220, 222, 223
Chenery 12
Chi-square test 151, 152, 168, 169
child labor 199, 213, 216
Christian missionaries 107
civil rights 17, 26
class size 166
colonial education 110, 116
colonial government 107, 108, 109
Colonial Office 106
Colonial Office Advisory Committee 108
combined capabilities
.... 58, 89, 90, 91, 92, 207, 213
combined model   159, 160, 173, 175, 177
communitarianism 80, 81, 83, 86
comprehensive data ... 124, 203, 204, 219
constitutive role of freedom 46, 62
Convention of the Rights of the Child 95
compulsory education 95
conceptual model
.... 64, 88, 89, 140, 141, 223
conceptual variables 145
confidence interval 189, 190
confirmatory factor model 144
conscious social reproduction 93, 94
constitutive freedom 51
constrained model 179, 181
Cornell/ERB survey 125
correlation coefficients 148, 155, 156

cosmopolitanism ·················· 114
cost-benefit analysis ········ 14, 201, 221
cost-effectiveness analysis ············ 196
cost-likelihood analysis ········ 202, 221
count data ························· 145
cultural confidence ················· 76
cultural diversity ············ 55, 71, 86
cultural particularity················ 35, 71
cultural revival ················ 28, 74, 76
cultural subversion ················ 74, 75
cultural tradition ··· 61, 83, 84, 85, 86, 97

D

data analysis······················· 104, 205
data availability
       ······ 99, 155, 184, 202, 203, 207, 218
data quality ························ 205
data quantity ······················ 206
decent people ···················· 60, 61
decision-making process
       ············ 74, 75, 77, 78, 85, 93, 212
decision-making system············ 85, 212
deliberation······ 76, 77, 78, 81, 82, 86, 94
deliberative consensus ················ 77
democracy ······ 58, 76, 77, 80, 81, 82, 85
democratic citizens ·················· 93
democratic deliberation ············ 76, 82
democratic deliberation system ·········· 86
democratic principle ················· 76
democratic procedure················· 84
democratic regime ··················· 76
democratic society ············ 76, 81, 93
Demographic and Health Survey 125, 203
dependency theory   18, 19, 21, 27, 38, 72
deprivation of entitlement ····· 36, 37, 62
descriptive statistics
       ··· 124, 134, 144, 169, 193, 194, 196

developed countries ············ 13, 18, 206
development as freedom
       ··················· 24, 36, 43, 48, 51, 62
development economics
       ··············· 12, 14, 15, 16, 25, 26, 27
deviance test············· 171, 179, 180, 181
DHS ································ 203
dichotomous outcome variable··· 146, 162,
       164, 165, 166, 167, 172, 173, 187
direct effects ······················· 145
disadvantageous choices ············ 45, 46
district-level model
       ··············· 142, 170, 173, 175, 177
district-level predictors 172, 177, 181, 183
district-level public services 146, 187, 198
district-level variables
       ··············· 157, 167, 188, 205, 218
district-level variance ················ 174
domestic equality··················· 128, 135
donor governments ···················· 88
drinking water ·············· 52, 130, 132
dropout······················· 199, 216, 217

E

Economic and Social Action Program 122
economic entitlements ··············· 47, 79
economic freedoms ················· 47, 79
economic productivity ··············· 49, 50
Economic Recovery Program ········ 122
economic sector····················· 16, 122
Education Act ······················ 118
Education for Adaptation ··· 108, 110, 111
Education for All ················· 97, 135
Education for Citizenship in Africa ··· 109
Education for Self-Reliance ··· 105, 110,
       112, 116, 117, 118, 119, 121, 122
Education Policy in British Tropical

Africa ························ 108
educational access ······ 94, 144, 213, 218
educational expenditure ················ 123
educational ladder ················ 93, 94, 96
efficiency ···························· 49, 50
empirical model ········· 72, 142, 143, 189,
   207, 208, 222, 225
empirical research ····················· 140
empty model ··························· 172
entitlement approach ····················· 35
equality of opportunity ··················· 95
error term ························· 158, 159
estimation method ·········· 165, 167, 170
ethical justification ············ 59, 63, 223
event probability ······················· 164
exchange entitlement ····················· 36
exchange entitlement mapping ·········· 37

F

factor analysis ························· 204
feasibility ················ 140, 201, 203, 221
field research
   ··· 198, 199, 201, 208, 216, 220, 221,
final model ············· 177, 181, 187, 198
financial analysis ······· 200, 201, 202, 221
financial dependency ··················· 123
financial feasibility ····················· 201
financial issues ················ 200, 201, 221
First Five-Year Plan (FFYP) for
   Economic and Social Development
   ······································· 111
first generation ······ 11, 12, 13, 14, 15, 25
five stages of development ··············· 12
fixed effects ······················· 146, 171
Food Availability Decline (FAD)
   approach ····························· 36
foreign aid ······················· 122, 123

Frank ··································· 18
freedom of speech ····················· 114
functional literacy ····················· 223
functioning ····························· 39

G

GDP per capita ················· 53, 55, 86
Gender Parity Index ···················· 144
generalization ························· 140
Gini coefficients ······················· 127
girls' education ························ 144
global age ·························· 64, 71
global cooperation
   ················ 64, 71, 72, 73, 86, 87, 88
global politics ················· 22, 59, 211
global society ···················· 57, 61, 83
government failure ······················ 13
GPI ···································· 144
grand mean ···························· 160
group-level error ······················· 159
group-level variables ············· 159, 160

H

happiness function ······················· 41
HDI ···································· 52
Health Financing Survey ················ 125
Hierarchical Generalized Linear
   Modeling (HGLM) ················ 144
hierarchical model
   ··· 143, 158, 159, 166, 167, 173, 219
hierarchical structure
   ···················· 98, 143, 146, 207, 214
Hirschuman ····························· 13
Household Budget Survey ············· 125
household economies ··················· 154
human capability approach ·············· 35
human capital theory ······ 14, 98, 49, 50

Human Development and Capability
    Association 88
Human Development Index 52
human freedoms 17, 223
human investment 48, 49, 50
human right
    ... 16, 50, 53, 60, 61, 63, 95, 114, 211
human-focused visio 225
humanitarian 223
hypotheses 141
hypothetical imperatives 85, 212

I

IMF 15, 121
imputation methods 167
indigenous culture
    .... 23, 24, 28, 73, 74, 75, 76, 212
indirect effects 145
individual-level model
    .... 99, 142, 170, 173, 174, 175
individual-level predictors 172, 181
individual-level variables
    .... 157, 167, 187, 199
individual-level variance 174
industrialization 74
infant mortality 15
instrumental freedom 46
instrumental role of freedom 46, 62
interactions 145, 179
intercepts 159, 160, 171, 177
internal capabilities
    .... 58, 90, 91, 92, 96, 97, 98
international aid 86
international assistance
    .... 12, 26, 28, 55, 56, 59, 86, 200
international cooperation
    .... 55, 59, 61, 63, 64, 211

International Labor Organization 15
international literacy day 97
International Monetary Fund 121
international organizations 15, 63, 88
intersectoral impacts 225
intraclass correlation 174, 175

K

Kantian liberalism 64, 71, 72, 73, 80,
    83, 84, 85, 86, 201, 211, 212, 225
Kantian moral order 212
Kantian morality 84
Kantian philosophy 84, 85, 212
Kantian priority order 84
Kemalism 23, 74
kurtosis 155

L

Laplace approximation 170
Latent modeling 204, 221
latent variables
    .... 144, 145, 204, 205, 221, 222
Law of Peoples 56, 60, 61, 75
least square estimation 163, 170
level-one only model 175, 177
level-two variance 174
LF 163, 164, 165
likelihood function 163
likelihood of literacy
    .... 178, 183, 192, 195, 197, 217
linear model 145, 162, 163, 165
link function 162, 163, 177, 189
listwise deletion 167, 169,
Living Standard Measurement Survey 203
logged odds 188
logistic model 165, 170, 174
logit transformation 163, 173, 175

Index 249

Lorenz curves 127
lost decade 16, 122
LSMS 203

M

macroeconomic approach 11
manpower development 111, 124
MAR 167, 168
Marginal Quasi-Likelihood 170
market failure 13
mass education ... 112, 122, 123, 124, 135
Mass Education in African Society
.... 108, 109
maximum likelihood estimation 163, 170
MCAR 167
measurable variables 204, 205, 221
measurement model 144
microeconomic approach 11
Millennium Development Goals ... 88, 97
Millennium Development Goals
    monitoring data 203
missing data 146, 167, 168, 219
missing values 168
Missing-At-Random 167
Missing-Completely-At-Random 167
missionaries 107
ML estimation 163
model specification 146
modeling method 134, 141, 144, 146,
    204, 207, 215, 221
modernization 18
modernization theory 18
modified human development theory ... 71
moral principle 85, 212
MQL 170
multi-lateral aid 87
multi-sector approach 207, 211

multicollinearity 150, 157
multiculturalism 64, 72
multilevel modeling 174, 175
multilevel-structured data 157, 158
multinominal data 145
Multiple Indicator Cluster Survey
.... 125, 203
multiple realizability ... 58, 59, 60, 78, 86
multiple regression 160
multiple regression models 160
multivariate analysis 193
multivariate normality 146
Musoma Resolution 119, 121

N

National Educational Conference 119
national-level policies 133
natural log 164
needs assessment model ... 139, 195, 220
negative effect 190
neoclassical economics 14
nested 145, 157, 158
non-event probability 164
non-hierarchical models 158
non-linear modeling 146, 162, 165
non-linearity 162
nongovernmental organizations 88
North-South gap 13
null hypothesis 168
null model 172, 173, 174, 175
numeracy 121, 130, 147
Nurkse 11
Nyerere 105
Nyerere administration 113, 115, 122

O

observed variables 144, 145

odds ratio (OR)
.... 181, 183, 188, 191, 201, 202
opportunity cost 126, 127
ordered logit model 166

P

p-value 190
pairwise deletion 167
parsimonious model 151, 181
Pearson correlation coefficients
.... 148, 155, 156
Penalized Quasi-Likelihood estimation
.... 170
Phelps-Stokes Commission 107
Phelps-Stokes report 108
Phi coefficient 151, 152
pluralism 60, 61, 78, 82, 83, 86
plurality 59, 82
policy analysis 134, 140, 187, 200
policy formulation
.... 140, 196, 216, 220, 225
policy makers 127, 220
policy studies 140
political deliberation 94
political entitlements 47
political freedom 47, 62, 79, 109
political justice 59
political morality 83, 84, 85
political participation 58, 85, 114
political sphere 60, 61, 75
politics of data 205, 207
polytomous 166
population-average 167, 171, 172
positive effect
.... 183, 188, 190, 197, 215, 217
post-primary 122, 123
post-secondary 119, 124, 133, 135

PQL 170, 171
primary health care 52
primary school enrollment 15, 119
principle of adaptation 108
priority order 80, 81, 82, 84, 134
problem finding 6
problem solving 6
production function 14
protective security 47, 79
public education 94, 118, 196

Q

qualitative 140, 204, 205, 219, 220
quality issues 204
quantification 140
quantitative analysis 89, 222
quantitative model 98, 139, 140, 189,
195, 202, 207, 20,8 222
quantitative studies 140

R

random effect
.... 162, 165, 172, 177, 179, 181
realistic utopian 224
reasonable peoples 60
reasonable pluralism 60, 61, 78, 86
recipient nations 15
reformism 23, 74
regression coefficients 158, 171
rejectionism 23, 74
reliability 202, 220
Reproductive and Child Health Survey
.... 125
research feasibility 203
respect for law 114
role of education 220, 223, 224
Rostow 12

Index *251*

rural data 154, 155, 156, 167
rural-urban gap 123, 124, 127, 133, 134, 135, 136, 214

S

S-shaped curve 163
Sabot's test 129
SAL 15
sample size 146
sampling bias 206
sanitation 15, 121, 218
school education system 93
school enrollment 15, 16, 53, 55, 109, 119, 219
school-age 98, 107, 124, 125, 129, 147, 167, 214, 216
Schultz 14
Scientific Software International 171
second generation 11, 13, 14, 26
secondary education 93, 96, 108, 119, 124, 127, 133, 135
Self-satisfaction 222
self-sufficiency 154
SEM 144, 145, 146, 204, 205, 221, 222
Sen 17
sense of participation 77, 78
simultaneous equations 145
skewness 155
slope variation 160
slopes 159, 160, 171, 177
social change 18, 25, 34, 73, 74, 75, 78, 110, 111, 211
social class 54, 108, 110, 139
social complexity 78
social conditions 43, 121, 208, 221
social development 13, 16, 64, 82, 104, 111, 112, 211

social equality 113, 123, 135
social justice 7
social modernization 74
social opportunities 47, 62, 79
social particularity 71, 72, 73, 78, 79, 86, 211, 212, 225
social service sector 16
social stratification 123
social transformation 122, 123
Society of Peoples 59, 60, 61
socio-economic database 203
standpipe 132
statistical assumptions 146, 158, 172, 204, 205
statistical data 104, 134
statistical description 128, 133
statistical methodology 100
statistical modeling 55
structural adjustment 15, 16, 104, 121, 124
Structural Adjustment Loans 15
structural adjustment policy 104, 134, 214
structural adjustment program 121, 122
Structural Equation Modeling 144, 204, 221
structural model 144
structured data 145, 157, 158, 166, 167, 204, 219, 221
substantive freedom 43, 46, 47, 52, 79
Sumve Survey on Adult and Childhood Mortality Tanzania 125
survey data 125, 203, 204
Swahili 107, 113, 118, 150

T

takeoff 12
Tanganyika 105, 106, 111, 113

Tanganyika African National Union (TANU) 111, 113
Tanzania 100
Tanzania Human Resource Development Survey (THRDS)
 ...... 124, 133, 141, 146, 147, 214
Tanzania National Bureau of Statistics
 203
Tanzanian government ... 111, 121, 122, 124, 134, 135, 144, 199, 216
Tanzanian National Nutrition Survey 125
Tanzanian socialism 112, 113, 121, 123, 135, 149, 214
Tanzanian socialist policy 105
Tanzanian society
 ... 104, 118, 123, 124, 134, 136, 214
Tau matrices 179
teaching medium language 150
technological progress 74
teleological concerns 85, 212
tertiary education 93
two gap approach 12
theoretical alternative 223
theoretical assumptions 20, 145
theoretical framework 26, 64, 71, 72, 73, 80, 82, 83, 84, 86, 88, 211
theoretical model 140, 141, 142, 146, 157
third generation 17
total variance 174
transformation equations 190
transparency guarantees 47, 79
trickle down 13

U

Ujamaa 105
Ujamaa philosophy 115, 122
Ujamaa socialist nation 121, 133
unconditional model 172
unconstrained model 179, 181
underdevelopment 17, 18, 19, 27
UNESCO 97, 147, 203
UNESCO Institute for Statistics 203
UNICEF 125, 203
unit-specific 167, 171, 172
United Nations 13, 218
United Nations Children's Fund 203
United Nations Educational, Scientific and Cultural Organization 203
universal consensus 71, 72
Universal Declaration of Human Rights 63, 211
universal framework 59
universal law 212
Universal Primary Education (UPE)
 ...... 120, 135
universal priority order 80
United Republic of Tanzania ... 105, 106
universal threshold 56, 58
universality ... 28, 35, 56, 58, 59, 63, 64, 72, 73, 86, 211
unobserved variables 144
urban data 150, 155, 156, 167, 168, 172, 174, 217
urban poor 184, 198, 199, 206, 216
utilitarian liberalism 84, 201, 212
utility 40, 41, 62, 84, 212
utilization function 41, 42
utopian approach 224

V

validity 202, 203, 211, 220
variable selection 55
variance component 174, 177

vicious circle of poverty 11, 205

W
Wald test 178, 179
well-being 39
well-being freedom 44
well-ordered peoples 59, 61, 87, 211
women's needs 144
World Development Indicators 203

World Health Organization (WHO)
    Statistical Information System ... 203
world system 18, 27
World War 10, 16, 25, 86, 105
WWII 11

Z
Zanzibar 105, 106

■著者略歴

米原　あき（Aki Yonehara）
2002年　京都大学大学院教育学研究科　比較教育政策学修士
2006年　米国インディアナ大学教育学部　教育政策学PhD
　　　　国際開発コンサルタント等を経て、
2007年より東京工業大学大学院社会理工学研究科にて（独）日本学術振興会特別研究員

専門著書

『開発途上国の教育』（田中圭治郎編「比較教育学の基礎」第11章、ナカニシヤ出版、2004年）
『初学者のためのブック・ガイド』（山内乾史、杉本均編「現代アジアの教育計画　上」第3章、学文社、2006年）
"Quantitative approaches as a bridge from the invisible to the visible: The case of basic education policy in a disadvantaged nation" (Wagner, R. W., et al. eds. "Bridging the gap between theory and practice in educational research: Methods at the margins." Chapter 14, New York: Palgrave MacMillan, 2009)

HUMAN DEVELOPMENT POLICY IN THE GLOBAL ERA:
A PROPOSAL FROM AN EDUCATIONAL VIEW

2009年11月30日　初版第1刷発行

■著　者──米原あき
■発行者──佐藤　守
■発行所──株式会社 大学教育出版
　　　　　〒700-0953　岡山市南区西市855-4
　　　　　電話（086）244-1268(代)　FAX（086）246-0294
■印刷製本──モリモト印刷(株)
■装　丁──原　美穂

© Aki Yonehara 2009, Printed in Japan
検印省略　　落丁・乱丁本はお取り替えいたします。
無断で本書の一部または全部を複写・複製することは禁じられています。

ISBN978-4-88730-951-7